The Politics of Water in Africa

The Politics of Water in Africa

Norms, Environmental Regions and Transboundary Cooperation in the Orange-Senqu and Nile Rivers

Inga M. Jacobs

continuum

Continuum International Publishing Group
A Bloomsbury Company

50 Bedford Square   80 Maiden Lane
London   New York
WC18 3DP   NY 10038

www.continuumbooks.com

ISBN: 978-1-4411-4982-4 (Hardback)

Library of Congress Cataloging-in-Publication Data
A catalog record for this book is available from the Library of Congress

Typeset by Newgen Imaging Systems Pvt Ltd, Chennai, India
Printed in the United States of America

Contents

List of Illustrations

List of Tables

Foreword

Is water a technical or a political issue? Certainly the water sector is totally dominated by technical people, mostly engineers, but also natural scientists of various persuasion. Political scientists are a rare breed in the water sector, certainly in South Africa, but also globally. Personally I believe that water is not purely a technical issue. In fact, I have gone so far as to say that our national economy is a wholly owned subsidiary of our national hydrology. This is so because economic development is predicated on the one flawed assumption of continued growth. Indeed, financial analysts value shares traded on the various stock exchanges of the world, by taking the net asset value and multiplying it by the future growth potential. Without future growth potential that multiplier equals zero, and so the share is deemed to have insufficient value to trigger a buy option. Our economy is thus predicated on the flawed assumption that growth is inevitable and continuous, and this probably lies at the heart of the current global economic crisis.

This makes water political, because our economies are nested within ecosystems and these are sustained by the flow of water across landscapes and through countries. These environmental systems provide the source and sink relationship to the economy that is starting to become relevant. A fundamental assumption underpinning ecology is that of dynamic equilibrium. This is not a stable state, but rather an equilibrium that sees a series of processes balancing each other to the point where those ecosystems function within a range of parameters that are 'useful' to mankind. Economies can grow while ecosystems are capable of providing the source/sink services needed, because we know it is simply illogical to assume that something which is assumed to be driven only by constant growth can be nested within, and sustained by, something that is known to be in dynamic equilibrium. In short there are finite limits to ecosystems, and by implication there are finite limits to the economic growth potential, and thus capacity to create jobs, of the various national economies.

After the global economic meltdown in 2008, the investment community suddenly became aware of undisclosed risk. This triggered a new drive to understand risk inherent to stocks being traded on global markets, and from this came an interest in water as an element of economic growth and development. One such analyst – Susan Chang – published a piece in The Investment Professional, the official journal of the New York Society of Security Analysts, entitled *A Watershed Moment: Calculating the Risks of Impending Water Shortages*. Chang noted that 'by 2025 it is estimated that 1.8 billion people will be living in conditions of absolute water scarcity (defined as annual per capita freshwater availability below 1,000 cubic metres a year), and two-thirds of the world's population could be living under water-stressed conditions (with annual freshwater availability below 1,700 cubic metres per capita)'. This has major implications for governments, security forces, investors and decision-makers in both the public and private sectors, because in effect, many of the problems currently plaguing the developing world will start to manifest in the developed countries as well. The financial and investment community is smart and they have got it right the first time. Water is indeed the foundation to our global economy, so with population growth trends being what they are, and water availability being finite, it is inevitable that increased competition over water resources will drive politics globally.

That is why this book is so important, because it seeks to offer a systematic understanding of how sovereign states engage over the emerging issue of water as a limiting factor to future economic development potential. The big question is, will sovereign states seek to cooperate or compete for dwindling resources? Will they find new optima at levels of analysis and management above the river basin or sovereign nation state? If so, what will that unit of management be? If it is at the supranational level, then what norms, environmental regions and instruments of transboundary cooperation will emerge? Will sovereignty cease to be relevant in a new world redefined by water availability, as opposed to boundaries arbitrarily determined by former colonial powers and past military conflict?

Africa has the lowest conversion ratio of rainfall to run-off in the world. This has caused the World Bank to suggest that Africa is hostage to hydrology, with many national economies being directly coupled to the vagaries of the weather. The more developed countries in Africa have managed to decouple their national economies by building hydraulic infrastructure. But is this enough to sustain economic growth and job creation in the face of finite limits to water resources, and variable flow regimes driven by climate change? Will these countries' comparative advantage be slowly eroded away as population growth drives water stress, or will they be able to renegotiate themselves into an advantaged future in the various transboundary river basins of the continent? Will endemic water scarcity provide currently disadvantaged states with new leverage to negotiate better equity in the allocation of natural resources? Will the various governments manage to incentivize the creation of the type of ingenuity needed to solve these increasingly complex problems?

All of these are political questions and all of these are based on water. Indeed, Africa has 64 known transboundary rivers that collectively contain around 93% of the total water available, covering 61% of the surface area of the continent, in which a staggering 77% of the population lives. If water is important, then transboundary water is a very big deal indeed, and this is why the book is relevant. It represents the state of the art with respect to Political Science and international relations (IR) theory as it pertains to the management of rivers that cross international borders. Drawing heavily on the work of various Political Science and IR scholars active in the global water sector, the author has systematically pieced together a body of knowledge that exceeds the value of the sum of its constituent parts. In short, this is an authoritative presentation of theory and practice in the management of water resources that is of use to managers, technicians, decision-makers in government and the corporate world, journalists and scholars.

Dr. Anthony Turton
Professor: Centre for Environmental Management,
University of Free State, South Africa
Founding Trustee: Water Stewardship Council Trust

Preface

My journey with water, and specifically, transboundary rivers started seven years ago. As a scholar of international relations (IR), I started out intrigued by the popular dinner table topic at the time that the wars of the twenty-first century could be about a resource as 'unassuming' as water. Water has and always will be a vital resource essential to human survival and for which there is no substitute. While water is still seen as a 'renewable resource', reality dictates that there is only a finite quantity of water available, a limitation acutely felt in water-scarce regions. It therefore necessitates sharing but is rather desired to be controlled and confined.

The late 1990s saw a surge of literature investigating the links between water and war, labelling water disputes as one of the 'New Wars' in Africa, and comparing it to the likes of other resource wars such as those over oil and diamonds. In response, a slew of research from a diverse range of disciplines found evidence to the contrary and the debate over 'water wars' was won in favour of *cooperation*. However, despite numerous pro-peace academic accounts, fear perceptions forecasting conflict scenarios still rear their heads from time to time in the public mind. The most recent contributions (Warner, 2012) attribute this to frames and narratives created by individuals who convincingly promote conflict threat perceptions that others believe, and so giving life to perceptions of water conflict in the global discursive community.

With a shifted focus on cooperative management of transboundary waters, I delved a little deeper to further my understanding of how and why nation states and other actors cooperate over internationally shared water resources. The application of a constructivist approach to African international politics focusing on the role of norms and norm adaptation was particularly helpful in depicting the complexity of transboundary water governance. Norms literature on international river basin management within the field of hydropolitics has undergone major development in recent years, however, there have been few attempts to conceptualize a multi-level normative framework for transboundary water governance. Specifically, particular norms created at specific levels of scale have been researched in isolation of those existing at other levels. I believe that this exclusionary approach endangers the harmonized and integrated development of international water law and governance, producing sub-optimal cooperative strategies.

I then set out to understand and conceptualize how particular norms of water cooperation constructed at different levels of scale are developed, transformed and are interconnected in two African regions. Several research ideas were based on my doctoral thesis entitled *Norms and Transboundary Cooperation in Africa: The Cases of the Orange-Senqu and Nile Rivers*, from the School of International Relations, St. Andrews University, Scotland. This book therefore owes its comprehensive analysis to extensive PhD fieldwork and project work conducted in all four Orange-Senqu riparian states – South Africa, Botswana, Namibia and Lesotho; and Uganda and Rwanda in the Nile Equatorial Lakes-Sub-Basin. I am indebted to the hundreds of policymakers, academics, researchers, activists, students and community members who shared their experiences and insights in the form of semi-structured interviews, informal discussions, email correspondence, and participatory methods such as workshops, focus groups, closed meetings and participant observation, to determine the relationships between global, regional and domestic norms; the degree to which individuals identify with particular norms.

This book builds on dominant models of norm development such as the 'norm life cycle' model (Finnemore and Sikkink, 1998; Finnemore and Sikkink, 2001), the 'spiral model' (Risse, Ropp and Sikkink, 1999), and the 'ideational life-cycle model' (Marcussen, 2000). All of these models share the premise that norms tend to be stable structures acting as constraints on agents' behaviour and as constitutive of identity and interests, and furthermore provide a cognitive framework with which agents are able to make sense of a complicated world (Marcussen, 2000). In contrast, this book's point of departure is that norms are not stable structures, but rather dynamic entities that affect and are affected by interactions with other norms and levels of scale. Flockhart's (2006) model of 'complex socialization' as well as Acharya's (2004) model on norm localization is also particularly useful in this investigation since it draws on factors that create variance in socialization processes.

Finally, in its objectives to illustrate the ways in which water is embedded within other natural resources, and to emphasize that effective water management should reflect this embeddedness, the book draws attention to the traditional over-emphasis by the water epistemic community of water as the integral and strategic resource for economic development. The danger in this outlook is the tendency to develop strategies and research agendas in isolation from other resource-, sector- or issue-based strategies. There is now a shift in the global trend of the water discourse, that is from insufficient focus on water and environmental issues in development studies, to environmental and water as the most important drivers to cooperation. Now, the shift should move towards viewing water and other resources such as land, oil, human capital etc. in an integrated and interconnected manner beyond theoretical conceptualizations such as integrated water resource management (IWRM). This entails a paradigm shift in how water is managed, but also how water professionals see themselves.

Acknowledgements

Family, the most basic social unit in the human context signifies affiliation by consanguinity, affinity or co-residence, but may also refer to the socially constructed kind based on region, nationhood, culture, tradition, honour, friendship, geographic or virtual sense of place and even profession. Seeing as this book is about collectively shared understandings, it is only appropriate that I thank the various families that have shaped my understanding and who have walked this journey investigating norms on the Orange-Senqu and the Nile.

First, I am indebted to my professional extended family. This includes my study supervisors: Professors Ian Taylor, Scarlett Cornelissen and Willie Breytenbach for their encouragement and guidance from the very beginning of my interest in water politics and beyond. I am also indebted to the School of International Relations at the University of St. Andrews in Scotland; the Political Science Department at the University of Stellenbosch in South Africa; Grinnell College in the United States; and Li Po Chun United World College in Hong Kong, for contributing to my understanding of international relations (IR).

I would also like to thank my 'Community of Elders', true greats if you will, for patiently giving up their time to share their wisdom on water governance in Africa. These include: Dr Anthony Turton, Dr Marius Claassen, Mr Piet Heyns, Dr Pete Ashton, Mr Dudley Biggs, Mr Peter Pyke, Dr David Phillips, Mr Peter Pyke, Mr Lenka Thamae, Adv. Lucy Sekoboto, Mr Jakob Granit, Mr Peter Nthathakane, Mr Audace Ndzayeye, Mr Washington Mutayoba and Professor Afunaduula. Few people outside of the water sector may know them, but these men and women, driven by their concern for sustainable knowledge transfer have helped to address this challenge by advising me and so many other scholars that have sought their guidance. They are our primary scarce resource. Additionally, to the countless interview participants, informal discussants and email responders, who shared their experiences and insights – you provided me with an insurmountable knowledge base from which I was able to draw, and for that I thank you. I am eternally grateful to the Council for Scientific and Industrial Research (CSIR) in South Africa, and specifically, the Water Governance Research group, led by Dr Marius Claassen, who have helped me articulate many of the ideas represented in this book, and who epitomize the essence of family in colleague form.

Finally, I am blessed to have the 'love' family I have. I am indebted to my mother, Lydia Jacobs, and my father, Johnny Jacobs, in so many ways, but primarily for arming their children with a good education, and instilling in us a sense of 'Yes, I can.' You have instilled in me a sense of hard work, smart work and perseverance . . . this book's finishing factors. I also express my very sincere gratitude to Jodi, Kurt, Jonathan, Nikki, Howard, Bronwyn, Connor, Cassidy, Amber and Micah for helping me maintain my sanity throughout the research and writing process. Lastly, I would like to thank my dear Luis for your love and patience, reading drafts, making coffee and being a supportive critique. I celebrate this achievement with you.

> *The spirit of Ubuntu – that profound African sense that we are human only through the humanity of other human beings – is not a parochial phenomenon, but has added globally to our common search for a better world.*
>
> *Nelson Mandela*

List of Abbreviations

AEC	Assessment and Evaluation Commission
AfDB	African Development Bank
AMCOW	African Ministerial Council on Water
ANC	African National Congress
ATP	Applied Training Project
AU	African Union
AUC	African Union Commission
BBC	British Broadcasting Corporation
CBO	community-based organization
CBSI	Confidence Building and Stakeholder Involvement Project
CCP	Cities for Climate Protection Programme
CEMAC	Community of Central African States
CEN-SAD	Community of Sahel-Saharan States
CEPGL	Economic Community of Great Lakes Countries
CFA	Cooperative Framework Agreement
CMA	Catchment Management Agency
CNDD-FDD	National Council for the Defence of Democracy-Forces for the Defence of Democracy
COMESA	Common Market for Eastern and Southern Africa
CPA	Comprehensive Peace Agreement
DRC	Democratic Republic of Congo
DWA	(South African) Department of Water Affairs
EAC	East African Community
ECCAS	Economic Community of Central African States
ECGLC	Economic Community of the Great Lakes Countries
ECOWAS	Economic Community of West African States
EN-COM	Eastern Nile Council of Ministers
ENSAP	Eastern Nile Subsidiary Action Programme
ENSAPT	Eastern Nile Subsidiary Action Programme Technical Team
EPA	Economic Partnership Agreement
EU	European Union
FAO	Food and Agriculture Organization
FTA	Free Trade Agreement
GDP	gross domestic product
GEF	Global Environmental Facility
GHG	greenhouse gas
GNU	(Sudanese) Government of National Unity
GoSS	Government of South Sudan
GWP	Global Water Partnership
HDI	Human Development Index
HPC	Hydropolitical Complex

HSCT	Hydrosocial Contract Theory
IBT	Inter-basin transfer
ICJ	International Court of Justice
ICLEI	International Council for Local Environmental Initiatives
ICOLD	International Committee on Large Dams
ICT	information and communication technology
IGAD	Inter-Governmental Authority for Development
IGO	Intergovernmental Organization
ILC	International Law Commission
INGO	International Non-governmental Organization
IOC	Indian Ocean Commission
IR	international relations
IWA	International Water Association
IWRM	integrated water resource management
JIA	Joint Irrigation Authority
JPTC	Joint Permanent Technical Commission
JTC	Joint Technical Committee
KBO	Kagera Basin Organization
LHDA	Lesotho Highlands Development Authority
LHWC	Lesotho Highlands Water Commission
LHWP	Lesotho Highlands Water Project
LVBC	Lake Victoria Basin Commission
LVEMP	Lake Victoria Environmental Management Project
LVFO	Lake Victoria Fisheries Organization
MAP	mean annual precipitation
MAR	mean annual run-off
MDG	Millennium Development Goal
MENA	Middle East and North African region
MRU	Mano River Union
MW	megawatt
NBD	Nile Basin Discourse
NBDF	Nile Basin Discourse Forum
NBI	Nile Basin Initiative
NEL-COM	Nile Equatorial Lakes Council of Ministers
NELSAP	Nile Equatorial Lakes Subsidiary Action Program
NELTAC	Nile Equatorial Lakes Technical Advisory Committee
NEP	National Environmental Policy of Lesotho
NEPAD	New Partnership for Africa's Development
NGO	non-governmental organization
NILE-COM	Council of Ministers of Water Affairs of the Nile Basin States
NILE-SEC	Nile Basin Initiative Secretariat
NILE-TAC	Nile Technical Advisory Committee
NRA	National Resistance Army
NTEAP	Nile Transboundary Environment Action Project
NWA	National Water Act (South Africa, 1998)
OAU	Organisation of African Unity
OKACOM	Okavango River Basin Commission
ORASECOM	Orange-Senqu River Commission

POE	panel of experts
PPP	Purchasing Power Parity
PWC	Permanent Water Commission
RBO	River Basin Organization
REC	regional economic community
REDD+	Reducing Emissions from Deforestation and Forest Degradation
REO	regional environmental organization
RIA	Regional Integration Agreement
RISDP	Regional Indicative Strategic Development Plan (SADC)
RPF	Rwandese Patriotic Front
RSAP	Regional Strategic Action Plan (SADC)
RSCT	Regional Security Complex Theory
RWP	Regional Water Policy (SADC)
RWS	Regional Water Strategy (SADC)
SACU	Southern African Customs Union
SADC	Southern African Development Community
SADCC	Southern African Development Co-ordination Conference
SADC PF	SADC Parliamentary Forum
SADC WD	SADC Water Division
SAHPC	Southern African Hydropolitical Complex
SANCOLD	South African National Committee on Large Dams
SAP	Strategic Action Programme
SIRWA	Structurally Induced Relative Water Abundance
SOLD	Survivors of the Lesotho Dams
SPLM/A	Sudan People's Liberation Movement/Army
SVP	Shared Vision Program
SWI	Shared Watercourse Institution
TCTA	Trans-Caledon Tunnel Authority
TECCONILE	Technical Cooperation Committee for the Promotion of Development and Environmental Protection on the Nile
TFDD	Transboundary Freshwater Dispute Database
TRC	Transformation Resource Centre
UEMOA	West African Economic and Monetary Union
UMA	Arab Maghreb Union
UN	United Nations
UN Convention	UN Convention 1997 United Nations Convention on the Law of the Non-Navigational Uses of International Watercourses
UNDP	United Nations Development Programme
UNECA	Economic Commission for Africa
UNEP	United Nations Environment Programme
UNESCO-IHP	United Nations Educational, Scientific and Cultural Organization – International Hydrological Programme
UNFCCCC	United Nations Framework Convention on Climate Change
VNJIS	Vioolsdrift and Noordoewer Joint Irrigation Scheme
WB	World Bank
WMA	Water Management Area
WRMP	Water Resource Management Programme

WUA	Water user association
WWC	World Water Council
WWF	World Water Forum
ZACPLAN	Zambezi River Basin System Action Plan
ZACPRO	Zambezi River Basin System Action Project
ZAMCOM	Zambezi River Commission

Introduction

The politics of water, as is the case with all other forms of politics, is as much about the distribution of resources as it is about the search for conflict resolution and not necessarily about its achievement of the latter. It involves inherently social activities of decision-making involving power, persuasion, compromise and consensus. This very basic characteristic of hydropolitics is where we begin because it alludes to the disparity between the activity of water governance and its study. Throughout the world water has been governed on the basis of competing demands, which has implied an inextricable link between diversity and conflict on the one hand, and a willingness to cooperate and act collectively on the other. These processes are largely based on subjective and normative understandings. However, the ways in which we have *studied* the governance of water have been based on notions of objectivity, quantification, accuracy, linearity and rationality.

Added to the dichotomy of the study of water governance and its practice, the governance of any river basin, but particularly international or *transboundary*[1] river basins that are shared between two or more states, implies the management of competing demands on the resource (Postel, 1999). These demands will continue to intensify as a result of increasing water scarcity, degrading water quality, rapid population growth, urbanization and uneven levels of economic development (Giordano and Wolf, 2002). Along with growing urban challenges, the twenty-first century has come to be characterized by widespread environmental changes, with rising demands for resources, higher levels of pollution and the ever-increasing effects of climate change. Among these, achieving and maintaining water security is one of the greatest challenges that modern-day states will have to overcome.

This makes it imperative that demands on the resource are governed carefully to ensure its availability, at an affordable price and of a good quality, to existing and future generations. The 2006 United Nations (UN) Development Report convincingly states that 'governance issues form the central obstruction to sound and equitable water sharing and management' (UN, 2006: 12).

Based on the myriad demands on our water resources by many stakeholders, humankind has developed a complex system of normative codes of conduct that prescribe how we ought to act when managing such resources. Over time, we have developed global, regional and domestic laws, policies, principles of best practice and norms, that dictate appropriate behaviour in the governance of transboundary rivers in an attempt to eradicate or minimize real, perceived or predicted conflicts over water. Here, I adopt Katzenstein's widely used definition of norms as 'collective expectations for the proper behaviour of actors with a given identity' (Katzenstein, 1996: 5). Norms therefore provide standards of appropriate conduct and prescribe social practices (Dimitrov, 2005).

Despite our awareness of its existence, very rarely have we tried to grapple with the interconnected complexity of this normative sphere governing our transboundary waters. In so doing, we have failed to move water governance beyond rational, linear, quantifiable and objective understandings. It is only in delving into this normative complexity that we begin to see how truly political and social the governance of water can be. Indeed, multi-level analyses further our understanding of the ways in which the multiplicity of norms, actors, power, knowledge and capacity influence each other at different levels of scale from the international to the sub-national. Additionally, even fewer analyses have made the causal linkages between forms of soft power or normative governance, and how they can promote the development of *communities of interest*[2] or environmental regions. This logic is closely associated with the need to advance the short-term, and territorially bound notion of water as an economic good for national security and immediate demand, to the utilization of water resources as a long-term tool for regional integration and the development of regional communities of interest beyond political boundaries. For this, a multi-level governance framework is necessary.

Moreover, multi-level analyses have not only received less attention in the water governance discourse to date, but mainstream analyses have tended to prioritize a *particular* level of scale – the hydrological basin – as the primary unit of analysis (Jacobs, 2010a). In this book, I use a definition of international river basins that encompasses 'lived in' social spaces, that is the sum of social practices and discourses that exist within a biophysical space. This space is given direction by regionalizing state and non-state actors including riparian states, as well as external actors that may physically originate outside of the river basin and/or region, but which form part of its social space of normative influence all the same. China's role as the new hydraulic infrastructure financier in East Africa has had a major impact on how African states have forged out a new set of normative principles in realizing their dam-building imperatives. The expanded definition of the unit of analysis allows transboundary governance to free itself from the constraints of a bounded and territorialized nature of water and state, and move into a fluid transnational space that is largely social, normative and subjective, and where norms provide impetus for political will and action. This logic sheds light on where water *is* and *should be* managed – the river basin versus the river community, and the national versus the transnational level.

Similar to the isolation of scale, particular norms (e.g. equitable utilization) created at specific levels of scale (e.g. international norms) have also been researched in isolation of those existing at other levels of scale (Jacobs, 2010a). The degree to which principles contained within the 1997 United Nations Convention of the Non-navigational Uses of International Watercourses (referred to as the 1997 UN Convention from hereon) have diffused to lower levels of scale has been studied at length. Much less emphasis has been placed on the degree to which locally based norms and principles have filtered up into the global policy landscape. This exclusionary ('silo') approach endangers the harmonized and integrated development of international water law producing sub-optimal cooperative strategies (De Chazournes, 2009). More specifically, the isolation of one norm ignores the manner in which the norm affects another norm's development trajectory, its acceptance, the resistance to it, the manner in which it is localized and morphed into something new (Jacobs, 2010a). Surely norms and principles related to a country's political democratization process will have an impact on how water management norms develop in that particular context?

The isolation of norms also mars the opportunity that water presents for regional integration as an *entry point* to integration processes and not only as an *outcome* of successful regional integration efforts. This thinking perpetuates the development of sectoral 'silos' as each sector strives to maximize development opportunities from within, with limited coordination with other sectors.

I address these critical knowledge gaps through a re-conceptualization of how particular norms of water cooperation constructed at different levels of scale (international, regional, basin, national, sub-national) are developed, transformed and are interconnected in two African regions. The relationships between norms constructed at different levels of scale in Africa's Orange-Senqu and Nile River basins will be investigated, as well as the ways in which both norm and context are transformed as a result of the other. Also, the process of norm diffusion from different levels of scale is particularly relevant, following three main processes of norm development (1) Top-down norm diffusion from the global level (2) Regional norm convergence (state-to-state, and basin-to-basin-to-region) and (3) Bottom-up (sub-national to national) convergence. In essence, the interface between these international, regional and domestic norms will be explored in an attempt to understand which norms gain acceptance and why. And through this process, a multi-level normative framework for water governance is advocated based on the premise of norm, as well as context-specific dynamism, and non-linear norm development in the case-study areas. Finally, the linkages between multi-level norm convergence processes and multi-level governance institutions will allow scholars of international relations (IR), development studies, and African studies to review the broad policy implications that these two transboundary river basins have for environmental regions in Africa, connected by virtue of their riparian status to water resources and resultant economic ties.

I therefore advocate for a more systemic and integrated interpretation of normative transboundary water governance because each level of scale, from the international to the local, forms part of an international normative framework that governs transboundary waters, and various norms interact and function in the context of the system as a whole (De Chazournes, 2009). Each level of scale gives meaning to how norms are translated and socialized, and how they in turn, transform contexts. Also, I examine the non-linear process of norm diffusion from one level of scale to another. The discovery made is that almost all interests are redefined, although to varying degrees, when norms are socialized. Power relations between actors and also between norms therefore form a critical piece in the puzzle of norm development in cooperative water management.

This means that norm diffusion from the global level is taking place, although some norms are highly contested, and local resistance to them is evident, while others display a legitimating effect and are congruent with pre-existing local norms. At the basin level, I focus on the sociopolitical, legal and institutional processes that symbolize a movement towards norm convergence in the case-study areas. Regional norm convergence is possible, and is occurring in both case studies analysed, although to varying degrees as a result of different causal factors and different historical, sociopolitical and cultural contexts. Convergence towards a cooperative agenda is facilitated by several drivers but is also hampered by barriers to regional convergence. The way in which these are managed ultimately determines the degree of convergence experienced.

Drivers to norm convergence act as catalysts to the development of a 'community of interests' by explicitly steering state and/or basin behaviour towards a multilateral cooperative agenda into which the majority of agents buy. They may also actively facilitate this process by becoming enabling agents (through technical cooperation, capacity building, sustainable knowledge transfer policies); or alternatively, implicitly shaping the normative context (e.g. congruent norm sets and norm localization). These drivers facilitate norm convergence in different ways due to the various ways in which norms are diffused. Barriers to achieving norm convergence include but are not limited to: skills flight and a lack of sustainable knowledge transfer, a lack of trust, a lack of (or varied) capacity (human resources) and weak, unsustainable institutions.

It is also important to note that the basket of drivers and barriers will be unique to each transboundary basin. The Orange-Senqu and Nile River riparian states present very different political identities and local contexts, each containing existing constellations of norms, which have affected the ways in which they have responded to the influence of external norms, how the norm has been translated at the local level, and the degree to which it has been incorporated into state policy.

In this regard, the book aims to achieve several key research objectives. First, it will describe and examine processes of emergence and socialization of the global norm set of transboundary cooperation of water resources, or lack thereof, as well as its influence on the domestic structures of riparian water policy in the Orange-Senqu River and Nile River basins. Secondly, it will examine the domestic political milieu of riparian states. Notwithstanding their varying degrees of water demand, Orange-Senqu and Nile riparians present fairly different political identities, each containing existing constellations of norms, which have affected the ways in which they have responded to the influence of these norms, how the norm is translated at the local level and to what extent it is incorporated into state policy. In so doing, we will explore the interface between these international norms and regional/domestic norms in an attempt to understand which norms gain acceptance and why. Thirdly, it will examine lateral norm convergence at the regional level from state to state as well as from the national to basin to regional levels. Fourthly, it aims to review policy harmonization as an indicator of norm convergence but also explore sociopolitical processes as drivers and barriers to this convergence. And finally, it aims to conceptualize multi-level norm convergence as it exists in the Orange-Senqu and Nile River basins using examples of norm sets at various levels of scale.

Approach and methodology

This study employs a qualitative approach based on a comparative case-study descriptive-analysis of the Orange-Senqu River basin and the Nile River basin. The methodological approach comprises of two stages: (1) theoretical research based on a textual analysis conducted through a mixed-method conceptual lens and (2) field research in the two case-study basins. A mixed-method data collection strategy was adopted, consisting of semi-structured interviews, informal discussions, email correspondence and participatory methods such as workshops, focus groups, closed meetings and participant observation, to determine the relationships between global, regional and domestic norms, and the degree to which individuals identify with particular norms.

Several of these norms have been codified in international law. For constructivists, adherence to international law is an important indicator of the socialization of international norms. A crucial indicator of international norm effects used in this investigation is the 1997 UN Convention, to mitigate the impending water crisis by using legal means to resolve transboundary watercourse disputes. However, the 1997 UN Convention is not yet in force, and therefore, no legally binding mechanism exists at the international level to ensure compliance with global norms. As such, using international water law as a sole indicator of norm effects would not explain acceptance, compliance or resistance to norms at the local level. Additional research was therefore needed to ascertain the extent of socialization of normative principles in terms of implementation and compliance, as well as its effectiveness. This translates into the exploration of sociopolitical processes as drivers and barriers to this convergence. A second category of important indicators used in this study are legal acts, policies and other multilateral agreements of international and regional organizations/institutions. International and regional organizations teach states new norms of behaviour as well as help disseminate them (Finnemore and Sikkink, 2001).

Finally, the respective river basins will be examined in detail within their real-life contexts. As case studies are usually multidimensional analyses a number of actors, mechanisms, institutional procedures and causes were identified within the study's domain. Therefore, a single unit of analysis does not confine this study. For instance, the role of non-state interest groups exist on the sub-national, basin, regional and international levels; states on international, national and basin levels; while transnational bodies blur the lines between national, regional and global levels of analysis. This multilayered approach to the levels of analysis is challenging and presents a complex but more holistic and integrated picture of the impact of norms. Their interplay may be cohesive and harmonious, but may also be disjointed and conflicting. In short, not only do variations in norm effects exist due to variations in domestic and regional structural contexts (political, cultural, ethnic, historical cooperation or lack thereof), but also norm effects differ as a result of the variations in the interplay of norm diffusion and/or contestation.

A focus on Africa

This book's focus on Africa, and the hydropolitical and normative frameworks governing its transboundary rivers, is significant in that all major rivers and freshwater lakes and aquifers on the continent are shared by two or more countries. Each country on the continent shares at least one freshwater body with its neighbours, which has at times resulted in hostile relations among riparian states (Toepfer, 2005). There are 263 international lake and river basins in the world today, 64 of which are in Africa as is evident in Map I.1.

Additionally, the hydropolitical climate in Africa is characterized by a diversity of local configurations, including a multitude of biophysical, sociocultural and political

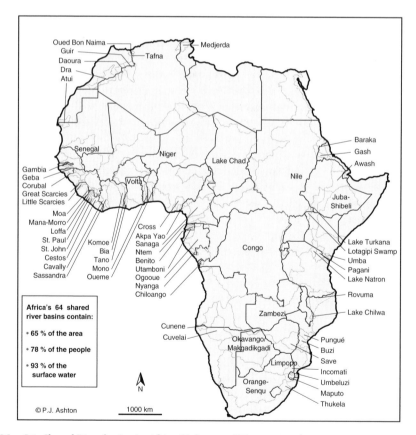

Map I.1 Shared River basins in Africa (Ashton and Turton, 2009)

contexts which contribute to Africa's hydropolitical fragility. These include, but are not limited to, a range of domestic policy variance between riparian states. There is also a great deal of variability in economic development between states and a broad spectrum of social, economic and cultural institutions, as well as the highly varied spatial and temporal precipitation and the (mal)-distribution of water. The multi-level interaction of norms is implicitly recognized in African hydropolitics due to the shared nature of freshwater on the continent however, there is still a schism between this interconnected reality and how norms are researched in isolation.

The choice of the Orange-Senqu River basin in Southern Africa and the Nile River basin in East and North Africa rests first, on the need to analyse and compare regional norm convergence in two African regions; East Africa and the Greater Nile region, and the Southern African Development Community (SADC), as a means to compare and contrast any similarities and/or differences that may exist as a result of regional dynamics. The preponderance of an Anglophone legacy in southern Africa and in the Nile Equatorial Lakes Sub-Basin (NELSB) (which is the area of the Nile that will be most extensively covered in this book because of the new and emerging sociopolitical dynamics affecting transboundary water governance there) also allows for a comparative analysis in terms of colonial legacies as well as the wave of independence in both regions and its impact on hydropolitics. Secondly, while the definition of each case-study area is based on the biophysical resource, that is the river, and therefore includes the geographical grouping of states surrounding the resource, these particular cases were also chosen for the unique sociopolitical communities they have formed. Both case studies are examples of lived-in social spaces, our definition for an international river basin.

The use of two vastly different river basins as case studies is also significant for several other practical reasons. First, norms follow different development trajectories in the Orange-Senqu River basin than they do in the Nile. This is as a result of biophysical, sociopolitical and historical differences. Biophysically, the Nile River is longer and the river basin is therefore larger. Secondly, Nile River basin management involves many more state actors than does the Orange-Senqu River, flowing through eleven riparian states including: Egypt, Sudan, South Sudan, Ethiopia, Kenya, Eritrea, Democratic Republic of Congo (DRC), Tanzania, Burundi, Rwanda and Uganda (Abraham, 2004; NBI, 2007; Waterbury, 2002; Wolf, 1998). This has resulted in a multitude of local cultures and ethnic groups with a wide range of local norms and customs. The range of historical, sociopolitical and legal variance; as well as the varying levels of stakeholder participation, have also determined the level of institutional development and cooperation in these basins. Context-specific factors have also affected the level of trust shown for external norms and as such, the degree to which they have been successfully institutionalized.

In the Orange-Senqu River basin, for instance, there is a comparatively high level of collaboration not only between states, but also between sovereign states and non-state entities (Meissner, 2000a). Technical cooperation is particularly dominant in the basin (ibid.). Additionally, in parallel with technical collaboration, political institutions and agreements have also been enacted (ibid.). Yet, while collaboration in the

Orange-Senqu River basin has been predominantly of a technical nature (as opposed to political), multilateral collaboration makes for easier socialization of environmental norms of transboundary cooperation since the mechanisms and organizational platforms which foster and facilitate norm diffusion are already in place.

In contrast, Nile River basin governance has been embroiled in bilateral agreements/treaties and unilateral action for longer than its southern African counterpart. Political instability, tense co-riparian relations and a general lack of trust as a result of cleavages brought about by colonial treaties, have led to greater resistance to the transboundary cooperation norm set in the Nile River basin than it has in the Orange-Senqu River, with some scholars going so far as to argue that a community of riparians does not exist in the Nile Basin (Waterbury, 2002). This is largely as a result of the contestation between the global norms of equitable and reasonable utilization and historic rights.

These case studies will be analysed individually for the value they add to a study of norm convergence due to the unique ways in which norms have influenced contexts and vice versa. They will then be reviewed together in a comparative summation of case-specific norm convergence, which eventually constructs the multi-level normative framework.

It should also be noted that when norm development is analysed in an African context, it is usually approached from the point of analysing international/external norms and tracking the ways in which they have been accepted in the African context. As Amitav Acharya argues 'Constructivist scholarship on norms tends to focus on "hard" cases of moral transformation in which "good" global norms prevail over the "bad" local beliefs and practices' (Acharya, 2004: 239). While these types of analyses are useful in understanding global norm dynamics, they uncover little about the local response to such norms, the interface between these and regionally or locally constructed norms, and the dynamics between the coexistence and/or contestation between these norms operating at different levels of scale. Through a multi-level lens, we are able to capture the dynamism and interplay of norms, and we begin to see where the most powerful normative influences lie and why they dominate.

Bridging the theoretical gap between science and policy

The theoretical significance of this investigation stems from the need for more nuanced theorization in transboundary water governance analyses, including more water literature explicitly conceptualized in non-realist or critical theory approaches of IR. Since Du Plessis made this claim in 2000, little progress has been made that goes beyond realist theoretical frameworks or implicit adoptions of this, with few exceptions (Furlong, 2006, 2008). Even Warner and Zeitoun who provide a compelling argument for the significance of IR frameworks to understanding transboundary water issues, concede that '. . . the number of serious studies applying IR frameworks to transboundary water issues remains limited' (Warner and Zeitoun, 2008: 803).

Allan refers to the evolution of almost identical concepts in different academic disciplines, all of which are relevant to hydropolitics, but none of which have been integrated or harmonized in any useful way (Allan, 2001). Scholars of hydropolitics have, however, used the two rival theoretical traditions, that is the dominant school of rationalism versus the marginal school of reflectivism to argue for or against the existence of water conflict (Du Plessis, 2000; Meissner, 2000a, 2004; Turton, 2000a), albeit concealed under policy analysis and issues of security. Moreover, the hydropolitical discourse has been reactionary and has therefore, developed in parallel lineage with the great debates in IR (Du Plessis, 2000).

Contemporary hydropolitical discourse is therefore subliminally situated within the mainstream (and particularly realist), rationalism of IR theory. Since these theories demarcate the discursive parameters, many scholars, writing from a mainstream perspective, have thereby subconsciously defined what can and cannot be talked about in the hydropolitical discourse. Thus, a discursive elite advocating for hegemonic theories has been produced. While competing theoretical conceptions are on the increase, there is still 'a need and an opportunity for conciliatory, theorising and bridge-building' (Du Plessis, 2000: 12). It is because of this need that I apply various constructivist approaches on norms of water cooperation to investigate the degree to which they influence behaviour.

Despite the growing popularity of non-mainstream discourse and the turn that science has taken in exploring alternative approaches to conceptualizing water governance, there is still a lag between science and policy. Policymaking and implementation still exist within a positivist paradigm, which encourages the development of solutions based on well-defined policy problems. Scientific inputs are then solicited to fill an identified knowledge gap, thereby solving the problem. There appears to be very little alternative ways of developing and implementing policy and, as such, very little consideration is given to the idea of the social construction of policy problems and the inherent subjectivity of moral judgements involved in these problems and related decision-making (Strydom et al., 2010). An analysis of global, regional, basin-wide and local norms is therefore useful and has implications for the rest of Africa, because it illustrates the significance of their interconnectedness in terms of the interaction at play as well as how their content is affected whether by moral judgements, or subjective preferences or alignment with pre-existing principles.

The global norm set of transboundary water cooperation

The water conflict and cooperation discourse will be approached from a constructivist perspective to include an analysis of the effect of norms and norm development on regional approaches to water governance. This approach highlights the applicability of a normative conceptual framework to understanding multi-level water governance. Indeed, as Conca (2006) argues, an uneven landscape exists comprising of multiple normative orientations and institutional developments. The global norm set of transboundary cooperation can be defined as the basket of principles as articulated in the 1997 UN Convention listed below:

1. **Participation of riparian states**
   Article 4 (UN, 1997a) stipulates that every riparian state is entitled to participate in negotiations surrounding an international watercourse, and to consult on any lesser agreements affecting that state.
2. **Equitable (and reasonable) utilization**
   This is an ambiguous rule referring to equal sharing, although a review of the standards for equitable utilization demonstrates that while equal access is guaranteed, equal shares are not (ibid.: Article 5).
3. **No harm doctrine**
   This principle stipulates that watercourse nations, in using an international watercourse, should take all 'appropriate measures' to prevent the causing of significant harm to other watercourse nations (ibid.: Article 7).
4. **Inter-riparian cooperation and information exchange**
   Article 8 obliges states to cooperate, on the basis of 'sovereign equality, territorial integrity, mutual benefit and good faith' while Article 9 calls for regular exchanges of information and data between riparians. Similarly, information exchange and consultation with the other parties on the effects of any 'planned measures' is also stipulated (ibid.: Article 11).
5. **Prior notification**
   This principle is defined as the requirement to make other riparian states aware that a planned measure 'might change the course or volume' of water resources, 'so that if they might threaten the rights of riparian owners of the adjoining sovereignty a claim may be lodged . . . and thus the interests on both sides will be safeguarded" (ibid.: Article 12), and
6. **Ecosystem protection**
   Ecosystem as defined in the 1997 UN Convention imposes on states an obligation to 'protect and preserve the ecosystems' (ibid.: Article 20) of international watercourses and to 'prevent, reduce and control the pollution of an international watercourse that may cause significant harm to other watercourse states or to their environment, including harm to human health or safety, to the use of the waters for any beneficial purpose or to the living resources of the watercourse' (ibid.: Article 21). Articles 22 and 23 elaborate further on environmental concerns, obliging governments to prevent the introduction of alien species or new species and protect and preserve the marine environment.
7. **Dispute resolution**
   Guidelines are outlined for dispute resolution procedures that include an obligation to resolve disputes peacefully, an endorsement of arbitration and mediation, and procedures for the creation and workings of fact-finding commissions (ibid.: Article 33).

Scholars disagree on whether these above-mentioned guidelines are in fact principles (Conca, 2006; Wolf, 1999) or the codification of existing norms (McCaffrey and Sinjela, 1998). According to McCaffrey and Sinjela (1998), the important elements of the UN Convention such as equitable utilization, no harm and prior notification are codifications of existing norms; whereas Wolf (1999) argues that these principles have only been explicitly invoked in a handful of water negotiations or treaties. Similarly, Conca et al. (2006) avoid the use of the term 'norm' because it connotes a logic of appropriateness, characterized by norm convergence, that is whether governments are converging on common principles for governing shared river basins in the form of a global regime. Conca et al. (2006) argue that unidirectional progression towards a global regime for international rivers is not occurring because the rate at which international agreements are being reached has not increased. Instead, a more complex pattern of principled evolution is at play (ibid.). The authors produce evidence of convergence on two different normative frameworks (one stressing shared river protection, the other stressing the state's rights to water). Some key principles appear to be subject to a global normative pull and take on deeper meaning over time, but simultaneously, many others do not. Normative dynamism exists, but is not at all unidirectional. This will be elaborated in greater detail in the book, but it is noteworthy for conceptualization purposes to note the classification debate between norms and principles. This investigation found that external norms do get diffused and socialized in ways that are unique to particular contexts. These context-specific processes allow for norm localization and translation, and norms may *look different* to what they were initially. Norms also may follow different development tracks while evidence of their influence may be quite different to preconceived perceptions that spring from restrictive theoretical frameworks. Other externally produced norms will also be referred to in this study such as the subsidiarity principle and historic rights.

Even though these principles of transboundary cooperation were articulated in the 1997 UN Convention and therefore act as an 'emerging' global norm set, they date back to the 1960s and 1970s when the UN responded to the need for clearer rules governing transboundary waters by requesting the International Law Commission (ILC) to codify and progressively develop the rules applicable to the development and management of international watercourses. These rules (referred to today as the 1966 Helsinki Rules) formed the foundation for the 1997 UN Convention. A broader global environmental agenda, propelled by the North (particularly Scandinavian states) therefore, emerged in the 1970s, appearing most significantly at the 1972 UN Stockholm Conference (UN, 1972). The UN then pursued transboundary water issues again at the 1977 Mar del Plata Conference, where the Action Plan adopted by the participants contained 11 resolutions and 102 recommendations (UN, 1977). From then on, water became enveloped in a general concern for the environment, losing its relatively distinctive status as a separate area of global concern. Yet, in recent years, water has regained its importance on the international agenda.

The 1997 UN Convention offers much value as a water governance framework as well as an indicator of norm diffusion since it shows which countries have committed themselves in principle to abiding by the principles of transboundary cooperation such as equitable utilization and the no harm doctrine. However, while the 1997 UN Convention is codified international water law, since it is not yet in force, it acts only as a framework agreement.

Chapter outline

This introductory chapter has outlined the rationale, central thesis, objectives, theoretical approach and research methodology of this study. Chapter 1 then builds on this foundation and provides the conceptual framework. It situates the book within the domain of environmental and water politics and the conflict-cooperation problematique, and also introduces the influence of 'soft power' in transboundary water governance in Africa. Chapter 1 also aims to develop a theoretical framework on which the analyses of the case studies may be built. This entails a brief description of the hydropolitical discourse, its linkages to IR theory and an analysis of several dominant IR theories as well as their applicability or inapplicability to the impact of norms on regional water governance. Specifically, Chapter 1 describes the importance and utility of a constructivist approach as opposed to realist and liberal interpretations of IR. Additionally, it provides greater theoretical elaboration on norms and norm development with a focus on the socialization of norms at the international, regional and local levels.

Chapter 2 sketches the method used to analyse norm convergence in the case-study chapters, using four main tracks: global norm convergence from the top-down, regional norm convergence (involving lateral processes of state-to-state and state-to-basin-to-region) and bottom-up (local to national) norm convergence. The fourth track is more an outcome of the coexistence of these three tracks, that is, norm dynamism or contestation.

Chapters 3 and 4 introduce the two case studies. Drivers and barriers to norm convergence will be unpacked in more detail and compared in the ensuing comparative analysis chapter. Chapter 3 will apply the central thesis of multi-level governance in the analysis of the Orange-Senqu River basin. At the basin level, this chapter focuses on legal and institutional processes that symbolize a movement towards norm convergence in the Orange-Senqu River basin. Also, qualitative research in the basin revealed significant drivers and barriers to the development of a community of interest in the Orange-Senqu River basin around water resources. Sustainable knowledge transfer policies or the lack thereof is of paramount importance to the sustainability of competence and to the ability of a river basin organization to absorb institutional shocks such as skills flight. The maintenance of institutional memory in this regard, also helps to facilitate norm convergence through social learning. These are some of the drivers and barriers investigated in the Orange-Senqu River basin that not only affect regional norm convergence at a basin level, but are particularly relevant to sub-national normative influences.

Similarly, Chapter 4 will apply the central thesis of multi-level governance in the analysis of the Nile River basin. It incorporates results of a textual analysis as well as qualitative interviews, to argue for regional norm convergence around specific issue clusters of cooperative management norms through processes of institutional strengthening and benefit-sharing. This chapter will provide evidence that non-linear norm diffusion from the global level is taking place, although some norms are highly contested, and local resistance to them is evident. Moreover, in the case of the Nile, global principles found in the global norm set, such as the no harm doctrine and equitable utilization have clashed as a result of upstream-downstream differences. At the sub-basin level, there has been a movement towards norm convergence with NELSB states starting to articulate a joint development agenda for its resources as a result of political stability and economic growth as well as the support of new infrastructure financiers such as China. This is a tremendous achievement given the history of institutional incapacity, lack of trust and varied levels of capacity.

Chapters 5 and 6 focus on the causal linkages between drivers and barriers of norm convergence, and the creation of a community of interest, as well as the policy implications for using water as a tool for regional integration. Chapter 5 conceptualizes the development tracks of norms in the two case-study areas. It analyses the relationships between cooperative management norms constructed at different levels of scale in the Orange-Senqu and Nile Rivers, and the ways in which both norm and context are transformed as a result of the other. Also, it examines the non-linear process of norm diffusion from one level of scale to another. The discovery made is that almost all interests are redefined, although to varying degrees, when norms are socialized. Power relations are therefore imperative; between actors and also between norms. This chapter therefore constructs a normative framework based on the premise of norm, as well as context-specific dynamism.

What then is the link between norm convergence and practical policy interventions? How can an understanding of the complexity of multi-level norm development improve decision-making in the management of transboundary waters? Chapter 6 links the conceptualization of 'soft power' to how it is implemented, enforced and institutionalized in policy.

This chapter also links the process of norm convergence to increased integration efforts between sectors. International river basins are part of an increasingly complex landscape of policies, trading relations and sectoral demands. This institutional complexity presents challenges but also opportunities for the water sector to increasingly integrate with other sectors in terms of decision-making in agriculture, energy, industry and urban development in particular. Chapter 6 examines natural resources and water in particular, as tools to facilitate regional integration efforts because of the need to address important resource questions in an integrated manner. It grapples with the ever-looming challenge of moving from science to policy, and from policy to implementation.

Chapter 6 also highlights regional economic communities as key multi-level institutions through which cooperative water governance can take place, particularly as these communities become part of bilateral or multilateral trade agreements with other trading blocs and given their inherent links to river basin organizations.

In addressing governance challenges facing the water sector today, and advancing the understanding of the multi-level governance approach, the concluding chapter examines the applicability of multi-level governance and water norms to governance in other natural resource issue areas. In reflection, environmental governance mechanisms are found on a multiplicity of levels, from the global to the local. Norms and other regulatory/constitutive mechanisms are therefore closely linked, and make up a complex normative architecture that shape how we behave.

Notes

1   The term *transboundary river* is used to refer to rivers which cross or flow along international state (and therefore political) boundaries. The term *international river* is also used in this book and refers to a freshwater source (surface and groundwater) whose basin is situated within the borders of more than one sovereign state as well as the lakes and wetlands through which some of these flows may pass. International rivers can therefore either be successive (crossing) or contiguous (flowing along the boundary, which is then normally the 'Thalweg' or deepest part of the watercourse) rivers. ('Thalweg' is the German word for the 'deepest valley' under the water).

2   A community of interest is defined as a group of people that shares a common bond or interest. Its members take part in the community to exchange information, to improve their understanding of a subject, to share common passions or to play. In contrast to a spatial community, a community of interest is defined not by space, but by some common bond (e.g. a feeling of attachment) or entity (e.g. farming, church group). As such, the definition is broad, leaving communities a lot of discretion in determining which issues are important to them.

1

Soft Power in Transboundary Water Governance

The management of international rivers has become increasingly problematic due to the state of freshwater water today – the only scarce natural resource for which there is no substitute (Wolf, 1998), and one which fluctuates in both time and space (Giordano and Wolf, 2003). As a result, 'water' and 'war' are two topics that have been assessed together at great lengths. Water disputes have indeed been labelled as one of the 'New Wars' in Africa, comparing it to the likes of other 'resource wars' such as those over oil and diamonds (Jacobs, 2006). Thus, there is a great fascination with the notion of a 'water war', and while there is evidence to the contrary and the debate over 'water wars' won in favour of cooperation (Jacobs, 2006; Turton, 2000a, 2000b) this argument still rears its head time and again.

Norms and trends in the water conflict discourse

The perception of water as a source of international warfare is pervasive not only in the public mind but also in political circles. In 1985, former Secretary General of the UN, Dr Boutros Ghali, uttered the now (in)famous words: 'The next war in the Middle East will be fought over water, not politics.' Academic literature on water resources as well as popular press are filled with similar sentiments, particularly as a result of the real or perceived impact that increased scarcity may have on socio-economic development and the lives of people all over the world. Furthermore, the scarcity of water in an arid and semi-arid environment may lead to intense political pressures, or to what Falkenmark (1989) refers to as 'water stress'. The Middle East is considered to be the ideal example of this, where armies have been mobilized and water has been cited as the primary motivator for military strategy and territorial conquest. However, this territorial argument, based on a state's desire to obtain water beyond its borders, is limited when one considers the nature of water-sharing agreements, particularly over the use of the Jordan River between Israel and its neighbours. As part of the 1994 Treaty of Peace, Jordan is able to store water in an Israeli lake while Israel leases Jordanian land and wells (Giordano and Wolf, 2002). This example reflects the ability of states to cooperate without the desire to conquer territory, particularly in a politically contentious region.

Since the allocation of water has often been closely linked with conflict situations, there has been a tendency to rely on history (by reinterpreting history in a way which justifies a conflict potential) as proof of water's ability to cause interstate war (Church, 2000). Arguments such as these, however, isolate specific cases in which water becomes embedded in sociopolitical, economic, cultural or religious tensions, and are therefore used as (falsely) justifiable reasons for going to war. For example, Church refers to the early 1950's dispute between Syria and Israel, where sporadic fire was exchanged due to the Israeli water development in the Huleh Basin (ibid.). But the author questions the degree to which this dispute can be classified as a water war, since the causal relationship between water and war is greatly obstructed by ethnic, cultural and religious tensions that existed between these states (ibid.). This leads one to ask the question, what really was the cause of the war? The unsuccessful military expedition by Egypt into disputed territory between itself and Sudan in the late 1950s is another (mis)-cited example, and again, begs the question, what really was the cause of the conflict – water or a disputed territorial boundary? According to Church, this suggests that history does not provide the clear-cut lesson upon which contemporary literature relies (ibid.).

Some scholars have also argued that the problems of water management are compounded in the international arena by the fact that the international law regime that governs it is poorly developed, contradictory and unenforceable (Giordano and Wolf, 2002). Analyses based on this argumentation, however, ignore the fact that there are more water agreements in the world than there are, or have been, water-related conflicts (ibid.).[1] Despite the obstacles riparian states face in the management of shared water resources, these very states have demonstrated a remarkable ability to cooperate over their shared water supplies.[2] However, analyses cautiously point out that despite the lack of interstate warfare, water has acted as both an irritant and a unifier. As an irritant, water can make good relations bad, but is also able to unify riparians with relatively strong institutions (Ashton, 2000a, 2000b; Wolf, 2005).

Water's ability to increase interstate tensions is most prevalent in the debate between sovereignty and equitable distribution of shared water resources. Underlying this is the contradiction between the compartmentalization of states who claim sovereignty rights over resources in their territory versus the indivisible and uninterrupted continuum of water (Westcoat, 1992). The question here is simple: can a country use its water as it pleases? This results in a clash of two global norms, that is sovereign ownership and exclusive rights over one's resources versus the principle of shared ownership and equitable utilization of an international river. Depending on which side of the debate states sit, either the *securitization* of water as an issue of high politics and national security is prioritized, or the *desecuritization* of water as an issue to be debated in the public domain wins out.

In current debates, there are those who focus on the regional (and global) conflict potential of accelerating environmental problems such as drought and sea-level rise. Here, the Malthusian discourse is noteworthy. It hypothesizes a linear relationship between population growth and scarcity. Malin Falkenmark is instrumental in this regard, for developing the 'water scarcity indicators', based on the central notion of a 'water barrier' (Falkenmark, 1989: 112). Her thesis postulates that as populations increase, so too does water scarcity, which leads to competition and potential conflict. This type of theorization then led other authors to conclude that the inherent linkages between water scarcity and violent conflict predicted the inevitable occurrence of water wars in the twenty-first century.

Homer-Dixon, the most prominent author on the subject of scarcity and conflict, outlines three major sources of environmental scarcity and their interaction (Homer-Dixon, 1994). First, supply-side scarcity describes how the depletion and pollution of resources reduce the total available volume. Secondly, demand-side scarcity explains how changes in consumptive behaviour and a rapidly growing population can cause demand to exceed supply. And thirdly, structural scarcity occurs when some groups receive disproportionably large slices of the resource pie, leaving others with progressively smaller slices (Turton, 2000a). Homer-Dixon does, however, acknowledge that environmental scarcity is never a conflict determining factor on its own, and is usually found in conjunction with other more detrimental causes (Homer-Dixon, 1994). As such, environmental scarcity can aggravate existing conflict and make it acute. In southern Africa, this plays out when marginalized communities are forced to migrate and settle on contested land, thereby bringing these incoming communities into conflict with people who are already struggling to survive. Migrations away from the Kalahari towards the panhandle of the Okavango Delta, and urban migration towards Windhoek in Namibia, are two such examples.

Then, there are those who see environmental degradation as an opportunity for social ingenuity, conflict prevention and management. Leif Ohlsson argues that as water scarcity increases, so too does the need for social adaptation to the consequences of this scarcity (ibid.). With increased desertification or the greater frequency of droughts, lifestyles have been forced to adapt and social patterns have been forced to shift. Ohlsson also distinguishes between first-order resources, and social or second-order resources. Adaptive capacity is therefore determined by the degree to which some states that are confronted by an increasing level of first-order resource scarcity (scarcity regarding the resource, that is water) can adapt to these conditions provided that a high level of second-order resources (social adaptive capacity or what Homer-Dixon refers to as 'ingenuity') are available.

Still, other scholars oppose any causal linkages between scarcity and war (as opposed to conflict). Anthony Turton defines a water war simply as a war caused by the desire for access to water. 'In this case, water scarcity is both a necessary and sufficient condition for going to war' (ibid.: 36). Turton therefore identifies 'pseudo' wars as those conflict events that take place when hydraulic installations such as dams and water treatment plants become targets of war. A war in this category is thus caused by something quite unrelated to water scarcity, and is therefore, not considered to be a true water war, but rather a conventional war, with water as a tactical component.

Furthermore, when rivers form part of contested international boundaries, they may also be the focal point of war as water issues become politicized. In this case again, water scarcity is neither a necessary nor a sufficient condition for going to war (ibid.). One example is that of the military confrontation that broke out between Botswana and Namibia over the control of an island (important for grazing) situated in the contested boundary area of the Chobe River (Breytenbach, 2003). As such, water as the cause of war is a very narrowly defined condition, with limited empirical evidence of its existence over time. Most authors, arguing for the increasing threat of water wars, are often misled when labelling conventional wars as water wars, or exaggerating the threat of a dispute escalating into military aggression.

Norms and trends in the water cooperation discourse

Norms and trends in water therefore originated largely in an attempt to eradicate or minimize real, perceived or predicted conflicts (Jacobs, 2010a). The global norm set of transboundary cooperation is arguably the most prominent, comprising of principles such as equitable and reasonable utilization, the no harm doctrine, information exchange, consultation with other riparian states and ecosystem protection. This norm set has evolved over time into its current form because of the need to reconcile the tension between shared river protection and the rights of states to utilize their water resources as they see fit.

Criteria for normatively assessing 'good' and 'bad' practice in transboundary water management

Global fatigue

It can certainly be argued that the need to accommodate the multiplicity of demands on water, has led to an 'institutionalized' way of knowing and dealing with water (Lach et al., 2005) that is considered to be normatively 'good', driven largely by influential state and non-state actors of the North. Research conducted on the degree to which global norms have diffused to lower levels of scale raise the question of the appropriateness of these global norms to different contexts, which are often accepted rather uncritically as a goal for which to strive. Described by Acharya (2004) as the first wave of normative change, these analyses tend to give causal primacy to 'international prescriptions' and in so doing, often undermine the important agential role of 'norms that are deeply rooted in other types of social entities – regional, national, and sub-national groups' (Legro, 1997: 32). As Checkel observes, this focus on the global scale, creates an implicit dichotomy between what is considered to be 'good' global norms, seen as more desirable and 'bad' regional or local norms (Acharya, 2004; Checkel, 1999; Finnemore, 1996; Finnemore and Sikkink, 1998). Analyses that take this stance often perpetuate a biased moral superiority of the 'global', by regarding global norm diffusion as a process of 'teaching by transnational agents', which downplays the agency role of local actors (Acharya, 2004).

If the global norm set was in fact the most appropriate standard to be emulated in water agreements at lower levels of scale, and applicable to all contexts, then there would be evidence of easy and exact diffusion of the entire norm set at regional, basin, sub-basin and national levels. The fact that several norms found in the global norm set of transboundary cooperation are at times inappropriate or inapplicable to particular (and specifically developing country) contexts is reflected in the ineffectiveness of many international environmental agreements, as a result of powerful actors who impose foreign norms onto local contexts, for instance, as lip service rhetoric to external donors or other international institutions. At best, these norms are manipulated and transformed into a context-specific code of conduct, but may also become institutionalised in their globally relevant but locally inapplicable form. In essence, "bad" (or inapplicable) norms become institutionalized too. Similarly, that which is considered to be best practice is in most cases, context specific. There is therefore, not one set of criteria for normatively assessing 'good' and 'bad' practice in transboundary water governance.

Cooperation versus environmental multilateralism

It is also important to emphasize that cooperation and environmental multilateralism are not one and the same. Additionally, they are often regarded as the ideal despite producing sub-optimal outcomes that is vacuous institutions. Indeed, policymakers have used these terms interchangeably as if referring to one concept. It should be emphasized at the onset that multilateral institutions have increased in the past three decades (Meyer et al., 1997) but this has not necessarily led to ideal cooperation between states or effective regimes that are intended to provide governance (Dimitrov, 2005). Riparian cooperation is celebrated for its potential to produce benefits to the river, *from* the river, *because* of the river and *beyond* the river (Sadoff and Grey, 2002, 2005). However, the extent to which riparian interactions actually produce such benefits has been widely overlooked by the international water community. The persistence of such oversights contributes to a growing stream of well-intentioned but misinformed policy. Moreover, norms, institutions and governance are not conterminous despite being treated as such in existing scholarship (Dimitrov, 2005). This neo-institutionalist assumption stems from the premise that institutions are instruments for providing governance, and norms serve as the basis for both (ibid.).

The conflict-cooperation problematique

Research and evidence has proven that while there is an unlikely probability of interstate water wars (conventional warfare) erupting in the future, the lack of cooperation *does* carry security implications and sub-optimal water management

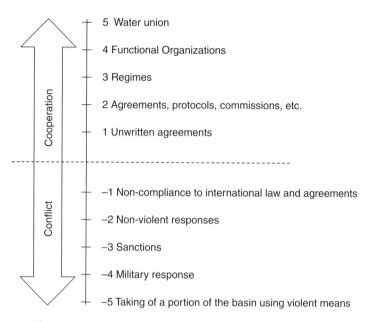

Figure 1.1 The conventional cooperation-conflict continuum of cater (adapted from Meissner, 2000a)

strategies. Yet even this focus is misleading, for there is a danger in interpreting it to imply a normative *appropriateness* towards unprecedented cooperation and the sharing of international freshwater supplies. Framing the debate in this way places the concepts of cooperation and conflict on a continuum, as an all-or-nothing outcome, with *cooperation* existing as an extreme in direct opposition to *war* as depicted in Figure 1.1 (Sadoff and Grey, 2005).

Although not explicitly indicated in most analyses, most literary contributions to the hydropolitical discourse subscribe to the neo-realist notion of an anarchical or 'governless' international system, in which state behaviour is not only the product of state attributes themselves, but also of the structure of the international system within which these interactions take place (Du Plessis, 2000). But it is also believed, under a neo-liberal institutionalist perspective, that cooperation and collaboration are possible (and necessary or even inevitable) under conditions of anarchy through the establishment of formal cooperative regimes/institutions. This problematique between peace, stability and progress is a fragile and very important one, because the emphasis is on the potential for 'water wars' based on the threat water-related contingencies pose to security (Du Plessis, 2000). These approaches prioritize the inevitability of either water conflict or water cooperation (in the form of ideal multilateral collaborations).

As such, a linear continuum between conflict and cooperation is often conceptualized and the formation of institutions and regimes ranging from informal to formal are the rungs by which to measure success, that is cooperation (see

Figure 1.1). Similarly, a linear transition from 'water wars' to 'water peace' is implied in several scholarly works (Allan, 2001; Ohlsson and Turton, 1999). In this regard, scholars have argued that Africa's transboundary rivers could become *either* drivers of peace and economic integration *or* sources of endemic conflict (Turton, 2003a). Cooperative management of shared watercourses has therefore been trumpeted as the ideal, since it can optimize regional benefits, mitigate water-related disasters and minimize tensions.

But as Warner (2012) argues, the water wars thesis painted too gloomy a picture, but in parallel, the water cooperation thesis was overly optimistic to resonate with context-specific realities. In practice, cooperation and conflict coexist. Or as Brouma (2003) explains, water issues are highly politicized and securitized, but also simultaneously constitute an element of cooperation. Indeed, the logic argued here is that the conflict-cooperation problematique is one in which degrees of conflict and cooperation regarding transboundary waters can occur simultaneously. The type of cooperative strategy negotiated should therefore be unique to a particular context.

Best practice from the North?

Additionally, current studies focus on the need to develop appropriate scientific/economic methodologies that can explain and predict future patterns of conflict and cooperation (Turton, 2003a, 2003b, 2003c, 2003d). Technocratic templates from Europe and North America, such as the concept of integrated water resources management (IWRM),[3] have also been suggested as best practice. However, not enough attention has been placed on factoring in local configurations, domestic policy, political identities and social and cultural institutions, particularly in the African context.

Developing a community of interest

What is lacking in hydropolitics literature is *how* we get to this state of cooperative management (the practicalities thereof), and which types of cooperative strategies are best for each region and river basin. Indeed, transboundary river basins and the management thereof occur within coexisting conflictive and cooperative dimensions, with actors cooperating on a particular aspect (e.g. information exchange for instance) and not cooperating or 'fighting' over another (e.g. the volumetric allocation of water).

The normative frameworks within which regions and transboundary river basin management exist are therefore critical to understanding the conflict-cooperation problematique. A central question in this regard relates to the convergence and/or resistance of norms and values around issues of governance, and particularly cooperative management in these shared ecosystems (Conca, 2006). Recently too, cooperation has begun to be viewed more broadly than just an outcome of the sharing of volumetric allocations of water. Policymakers have now begun to see transboundary cooperation as the way to jointly identify *development options* and *socioeconomic benefits* that can be achieved in a transboundary and multilateral context.

This benefit-sharing[4] paradigm instigated by cooperative management strategies has implications for normative frameworks and vice versa. Can norms on water-sharing[5] evolve into a benefit-sharing normative framework[6] where actors begin to believe that the benefits of cooperating transcend merely sharing volumetric allocation of water but include benefits of regional integration, such as economic development and sociopolitical benefits? To what degree does norm resistance affect this dynamic? One way of addressing these questions is through an analysis of the way in which states perceive themselves. Sadoff and Grey (2005) refer to this as the movement away from national agendas that are unilateral, to national agendas that incorporate significant cooperation and that converge on a shared cooperative agenda. Essentially, this refers to notions of sovereignty, and the evolution in the perception of sovereign interests.

Indeed, the degree to which riparians share a common 'water ethos' or a regional culture of managing shared rivers is a major determinant of the level, types and effectiveness of cooperative strategies (Hogan, 2005). But given the multiplicity of meanings that water has for various stakeholders, how possible is it to create a shared water 'ethos' at the international level that is able to cascade down successfully to the regional and local levels? Alternatively still, can a shared water 'ethos' be constructed at the regional level within a hydropolitical complex, where similar interests converge on a normative trajectory in ways that are unique to specific basins?

An overview of the hydropolitical discourse and its theoretical foci

Also, conceptions of security after the Cold War have acquired wider meanings than protection from a military threat and have broadened to include a greater focus on natural resources. Hydropolitics has therefore emerged as an issue of practical and scholarly concern that extends beyond issues of water use, to economics, development, security, human rights and joint cooperation. Thus the hydropolitical discourse covers a diverse spectrum of issues. It is therefore important to review past discourse and its theoretical foci and examine how this relates to the broader realm of IR theory before attempting to demarcate this study along more specific lines. Anton Du Plessis describes several theoretical foci, which are relevant in this study (Du Plessis, 2000).

The first theoretical tenet is a focus on the environment, ecology and related ideas that humanity is fast depleting its natural resources, and this premise dates back to the nineteenth century (ibid.). In more recent times, however, there has been a resurgence of ecocentrism and ecocentric issues. As a result, green politics, environmentalism and environmental multilateralism have emerged as three very important political forces internationally (ibid.). The second focus includes the emphasis on global ecology as it relates to development. This theoretical focus rests on the claim that development is inherently anti-ecological since it undermines sustainable practices (ibid.). Furthermore, the main argument here involves the danger of development and specifically, entrenching the power of the powerful (ibid.).

The third theoretical focus exists within the realm of security studies, that is the concern of security (ibid.). This concern extends more broadly to environmental security, and more specifically, to water security (ibid.). This focus, and its theoretical conceptualizations, is inextricably linked to the war-peace and conflict-cooperation problematique if one considers water to be a potential source or cause of (violent) conflict. The underlying logic, although not new, has become more prevalent since the Cold War, resulting in the emergence of a new strategic imperative labelled as 'environmental security' (ibid.: 13). This concept addresses the environmental factors that underlie potentially violent conflicts, and the impact of global environmental degradation on the well-being of societies and economies (Porter, 1998). Additionally, this development is in part borne from the 'new' security paradigm that has expanded the security agenda to include non-military ('low politics') threats, and also non-state, security stakeholders at all levels of society (Du Plessis, 2000). It is therefore also linked to common security or a shared interest in survival (Butfoy, 1997). It is with this theoretical foundation in mind that this study attempts to elevate water resource management out of a strict water conflict versus water cooperation analysis overly consumed with whether or not water conflict will erupt, but rather how behaviour and policy is determined, that is how it is that agents (both state and non-state actors) get to be positioned, which normative frameworks are created and how.

Arguments about global dangers are however understood very differently by the South and particularly Africa, which is often regarded as a main source of these 'new threats' (Dalby, 1998: 183). In part, this concern originates from the environmental security debate, which also involves sustainable development as a formulation that can allow injustice and environmental degradation to continue as part of the ideologically renewed process of development (Du Plessis, 2000). Thus, from the South's perspective, the 'discourses of danger' that define the environmental security discourse are often perceived as hegemonic or imperialist attempts to reassert domination of the South by northern superpowers, albeit in the name of protecting the planet (Dalby, 1998).

As a logical extension of (in)security, the fourth theoretical focus rests on the relationship between environmental change, scarce natural resources and conflict (Du Plessis, 2000). Relevant here is the notion that scarcities of critical environmental resources such as water are powerfully contributing to widespread violence in certain areas of the world (ibid.). More specifically, Homer-Dixon (1994) who is regarded as the intellectual founding father of this theoretical focus, argues that resource depletion, resource degradation and resource scarcity (induced by issues of supply and demand, as well as structural scarcity) contribute to mass violence. Additionally however, the focus here is not solely on a preoccupation with conflict but also includes the preconditions for peace. Therefore, as Du Plessis (2000) argues, it involves conflict termination, containment, management and resolution, as well as strategic approaches to peace. Scholars have therefore debated whether growing water stresses create cooperative or conflictual incentives (Homer-Dixon, 1991, 1994; Postel and Wolf, 2001) and whether existing agreements are effective mechanisms of shared governance (Bernauer, 1997, 2002).

The fifth theoretical focus in the discourse comprises of normative dimensions and it involves value-based issues such as settled norms (e.g. sovereignty); nascent norms (e.g. intervention and political space); ethical concerns (e.g. the distribution of and access to scarce resources); as well as human rights (Du Plessis, 2000). According to Conca, Wu and Mei (2006), no systematic analysis has been undertaken of the principles underpinning shared river cooperation. Moreover, scholars have paid less attention to the *principled* content of cooperation or the direction in which principles are trending (Conca et al., 2006). In other words, not enough attention has been placed on the influence of norms in influencing behaviour; socialization processes of global, regional and domestic norms; norm contestation; describing and analysing whether socialization processes are top-down or bottom-up, or whether they even exist at all. Conca et al. (2006) posit that shared rivers provide a useful domain in which to examine precisely this: the evolution of principled cooperation. 'Theoretically, the often-asymmetric bargaining context between upstream and downstream states offers strong tests of claims about norm diffusion and progressive legalisation. Empirically, shared river governance provides an unusual opportunity to link previously separate levels of analysis: the effort to cultivate a body of global principles and the many basin-specific cooperative agreements among smaller groups of countries' (ibid.: 264).

The sixth theoretical focus, international and domestic water law, also forms part of the 'principled' discourse as a basis for order, justice, cooperation and governance (Du Plessis, 2000). Scholarship on the law of international rivers, however, has treated global, basin-specific and local levels as conceptually disconnected and analytically distinct (Conca et al., 2006). IR scholars are on the one end of the spectrum, concentrating on the basin-specific level, and producing a large body of research on cooperation and conflict among co-riparian states (Beach et al., 2000). The central focus for IR scholars is therefore to predict the possibility or the inevitability of international cooperation or conflict rather than the principled content of cooperation (Conca et al., 2006). In terms of the variables shaping cooperation-conflict, Conca et al. (2006) ascertain that IR research could easily be divided into two main categories: the basin-level distribution of power (Bernauer, 1997; Frey, 1993; Turton, 2001a, 2008b; Turton and Ashton, 2008; Wolf, 1997); and the effects of specific state characteristics, for example, regime type (Hamner, 2002), the level of international economic interdependence (Durth, 1996) or the level of domestic water scarcity (Frey, 1993; Gleditsch and Hamner, 2001; Lowi, 1993; Wolf, 1997). According to Conca et al. (2006), this bargaining-driven research contains an inherent assumption that the principled content of cooperation could result from existing patterns of power and interest, making the presence/absence of cooperation (rather than normative orientation) a dependent variable. Legal scholarship, on the other side of the spectrum, has placed more emphasis on the evolution of legal principles for shared river basins, analysing decisions of the International Court of Justice (ICJ) and other precedent-setting treaties or globally articulated frameworks of legal principles such as SADC's 2000 Revised Protocol on Shared Watercourses, and the 1997 UN Convention (Conca et al., 2006). This polarization articulates a need to merge both IR and legal scholarship to investigate how principled content – both hard and soft law – affect the conflict-cooperation problematique of transboundary water governance.

Swimming upstream and downstream
the hydropolitical discourse

Within its varied theoretical foci, the hydropolitical discourse has rarely consciously adopted non-realist theorizing, but rather, many scholars of hydropolitics have written from a-theoretical or deliberately non-theoretical perspectives (Allan, 1999b; Gleick, 1993; Homer-Dixon, 1994; Ohlsson, 1995; Payne, 1996). However, as Du Plessis (2000) argues, the hydropolitical discourse does seem to have charted itself subliminally through two main theoretical traditions of IR, that is the dominant tradition of rationalism and the marginal tradition of reflectivism albeit concealed under policy analysis and issues of security. These two rival overarching traditions can subsequently be divided into sub-divisions; rationalist theories comprising of realism (and neo-realism) and institutionalist theories (liberal and neo-liberal); while reflectivist theories comprise of feminist theory, critical theory and postmodernism (Du Plessis, 2000).

The great debate between rationalism (neo-realist/neo-liberal synthesis) and reflectivism rests on incommensurability. For instance, processes and institutions are given a behavioural conception by rationalism, whereas reflectivism explains interests and identities. According to Du Plessis, there is an absence of repressive tolerance in the form of a similar self-understanding of the relationship among positions. There is also a reciprocal lack of recognition with regard to legitimate parallel enterprises, since these are believed to be linked to contending social agendas and projects. Rationalists and reflectivists see each other as harmful, and at times, almost 'evil'. According to reflectivists, mainstream theories are co-responsible for upholding a repressive order (Du Plessis, 2000).

IR and subsequently, the hydropolitical discourse, have therefore, accepted an unchallenged set of positivist assumptions (Meissner, 2004) despite a slow and incremental increase in the use of alternative theoretical perspectives. In many respects, the absolute acceptance of this positivist epistemology has suffocated debate over the characteristics of the world and how it can be explained.

Therefore, the temporal progression of IR (from one great debate to another) has a tendency to organize itself through 'a constant oscillation between grand debates and periods in-between where the previous contestants meet' (Waever, 1996: 175). The discipline of IR has long awaited the arrival of a new rival perspective, since reflectivism has become de-radicalized and re-conceptualized; indicating a move towards linkage principles (Waever, 1997). Du Plessis and Meissner argue that in fact, reflectivism is now no longer the dissident perspective, nor is it the 'other' perspective (Du Plessis, 2000; Meissner, 2004). Meissner (2004) has attempted to do exactly this by theoretically merging the two theoretical approaches through social constructivism.

This study aims to elaborate on Meissner's social constructivist approach, with a focus on the impact of norms and norm development on transboundary water governance. Waever reiterates this perspective arguing that the culmination of these principles is the increasing marginalization of extreme rationalism (formal rational choice) and anti-IR approaches (de-constructivists), as well as the emergence of a middle ground where neo-institutionalists from the rationalist side come together with the constructivists from the reflectivist side (Waever, 1997).

Indeed it might be argued that the rise of constructivism has propelled IR theory development forward due to its bridge-building capabilities. On the IR theory spectrum, Smith reiterates that certain forms of constructivism fall '. . . between both rationalist and reflectivist approaches' because '. . . it deals with the same features of world politics that are central to both the neo-realist and the neo-liberal components of rationalism, and yet is centrally concerned with both the meanings actors give to their actions and the identity of these actors' (Smith, 1997: 183). In this regard, it represents a 'synthesis' between rationalism and reflectivism (Kubálková et al., 1998; Smith, 1997).

Mainstream theories

Rationalism includes a spectrum of similar and also vastly different theories. However, they do share a number of generic characteristics. They are first 'scientific' (or positivist) and offer rational and explanatory renditions of international relations (Du Plessis, 2000). According to Meissner (2004) and Du Plessis (2000), explanatory theories are those that view the world as 'external' (and existing objectively) to the theories that explain world politics. In other words, subject and object must be separated in order to theorize properly. Furthermore, since rationalism 'assumes that images in the human mind can represent reality through observation', it also assumes that theorists are able to separate themselves from the world 'in order to "see" it clearly and formulate statements that correspond to the world as it truly is' (Du Plessis, 2000: 19). Therefore, some feature of the world, that is war, peace, political boundaries are judged to be either true or false. There is no attempt to explain how these concepts came into being (how they were constructed) but merely why they exist (if they do) and how valid they are in explaining something. They are therefore positivist, rational, foundationalist and explanatory as well as what Cox refers to as problem-solving: theory that takes the world as it finds it, including the prevailing social and power relationships and institutions, and uses them as a basis or foundation for further action (Cox and Sinclair, 1996).

Realism and neo-realism explain the inevitability of conflict and competition between states since these theories emphasize the insecure and anarchical nature of the international environment. It is however also assumed that there can be cooperation under anarchy, and that states can minimize international anarchy by constructing rules and institutions for their coexistence (Burchill, 1996). Liberal institutionalism, for example, emphasizes the benefits of transnational cooperation. Akin to neo-realism, neo-liberal institutionalists also regard the state as a legitimate representation of society. They too accept the structural conditions of anarchy, but emphasize the gains to be realized from cooperation between states (Dunne, 1997a).

To summarize therefore, rationalism takes the identities and interests of actors as a 'given' (Du Plessis, 2000). It furthermore ignores major features of a globalized political world system, and argues that the state is the primary actor in world politics. Cooperation and conflict are prioritized, and actors are viewed as rational, value maximizers (Smith, 1997).

Having briefly outlined the rational course, it is therefore no wonder that the hydropolitical discourse is charted predominantly via this route. If one is to consider conflict and security issues as primary components of war, it seems logical that the securitization of water resources be state-centric. Sovereignty and territorial integrity, as collaterals, are also emphasized in rationalist undertakings (Du Plessis, 2000). And while pluralism is not excluded, since non-state actors are regarded as key stakeholders in the hydropolitical discourse, most contributions speak from the vantage-point of state actors and none explicitly represent the alternative non-state view (ibid.).

Tributary theories

According to Du Plessis, if rational choice theories such as neo-realism and neo-liberalism are mainstream, then reflectivist theories are tributaries (in keeping with the water theme) of contemporary theorizing along which the hydropolitical discourse is charted (Du Plessis, 2000). While the reflectivist spectrum is vast, these theories are united by their rejection of state-centric realist and neo-realist conceptions of war and peace, neo-liberal institutional approaches to cooperation in anarchy, as well as the positivist assumptions that have dominated the study of IR (ibid.).

Tributary theories have a self-reflective nature and are an assemblage of post-positivist theories. These include normative theory, feminist theory, critical theory, postmodernism and historical sociology (Linklater, 2000; Meissner, 2004; Smith, 1997). Critical conceptions are based on the assumption that theory is always created for someone and for some purpose, and that theory cannot be divorced from a standpoint in time and space (Cox and Sinclair, 1996). Tributary theories therefore question the apolitical nature of positivist theorizing, and are concerned with hidden aspects such as the social and political purposes of knowledge and the dissemination thereof, the interests and agendas of the observer/researcher – and how all of this affects the images that actors construct of the world (Burchill, 1996).

Now while post-positivist theories do not add up to one theory of reflectivism, several commonalities are noteworthy to be mentioned. As Du Plessis (2000) argues, the meta-theoretical stance of reflexivity in IR involves three core elements: 'a self-awareness regarding the underlying premises of "own" theorizing; the recognition of the inherently politico-normative dimension of paradigms and the normal science traditions they generate; and that reasoned judgements can be made about the merits of contending paradigms in the absence of objective standards' (Du Plessis, 2000).

Essentially, this outlines the most fundamental difference between post-positivist theories and positivist theories – those for whom knowledge is socially constructed, and those for whom it is not (Cox and Sjolander, 1994; Du Plessis, 2000).

With the exception of a few hydropolitics scholars, reflectivist discourse is, to a significant extent, marginalized and at times silent on water governance conceptualizations. Swatuk and Vale do however, go against the grain when they question the water capture effect of the Homer-Dixon thesis. They persuasively do this by deconstructing the discourse by identifying critical problems within it as well as the policy decisions that it advocates (which they claim are racist, modernist, statist, capitalist, liberalist, technicist/militarist, exclusive and supportive of the status quo). As such, they propose a strategy for subverting this discourse as a prerequisite for reconstructing it, which entails a paradigm shift of thinking, language, focus and practice (Du Plessis, 2000; Swatuk and Vale, 2000). The significance of their argumentation is twofold. First, it is implicitly argued that the water domain is essentially a product of the theoretical foci of the prevailing hydropolitical discourse itself, and that consequently, 'water-theory' is in fact constitutive of the reality it aims to explain (Du Plessis, 2000). Secondly, it is explicitly argued that the discursive elite, that is those who are in dominant policy-making positions, and who determine the nature, form and content of the prevailing hydropolitical discourse, act as gatekeepers in order to dominate, legitimize and sanction the prevailing discourse (ibid.). This in turn leads to the creation of a dominant paradigm for the hydropolitical discourse.

IR theory's application to the hydropolitical discourse

In the following section, a selection of theoretical traditions and theories will be outlined and the degree to which they are state-centric and concerned with normative issues will be reviewed. These theories are (1) Realism (or more specifically, regional security complex theory (RSCT) and the HPC); (2) Conventional liberal-pluralist perspectives such as neo-liberal institutionalism and (neo)-functionalist regime theory and; (3) Political ecology. Following a discussion of each theory's basic tenets and relevance to the impact of norms and norm development on joint management of water resources, constructivism will be outlined as the most appropriate in terms of its ability to conceptualize the complexity of transboundary water governance.

The realist perspective

Realism is added to the discussion because it still is one of the dominant theoretical perspectives in international relations today and is therefore regarded as the orthodoxy (Halliday, 1994; Nye, 1993). While, for the purpose of this discussion, realism is described as a singular theoretical perspective (because they share several basic assumptions), on the contrary, it contains an array of competing theories that disagree on core issues (Meissner, 2004; Walt, 1997). Moreover, realism is reviewed not to refute it as a viable theoretical framework, but rather to show its complimentary if incomplete nature to norm development and hydropolitics.

The shared assumptions that realist theories hold include statism, self-help and survival (Meissner, 2004). First, the state is regarded as the primary actor and unit of analysis. It is rational and unitary, and therefore interstate relations become the focus of realist analyses (Du Plessis, 2000; Dunne, 1997b). According to Viotti and Kauppi (1999) non-state entities are secondary because governments representing states are the only institutions that can formulate, implement and enforce laws. Realist analyses are therefore overly state-centric and do not directly include non-state actors or normative issues (Lynn-Jones, 1999).

Secondly, realists assume that sovereignty takes precedence and that it must first be established before civil society can function (Meissner, 2004). Power therefore flows in a one-dimensional path from state to civil society (ibid.). This is problematic for an analysis of regional and transboundary water resource management, particularly because of the contentious nature of managing transboundary rivers. As previously mentioned, the overarching tension between the compartmentalization of states who claim sovereign rights over resources in their territory versus the indivisible/ uninterrupted continuum of water, complicates the realm of hydropolitics. Moreover, the fact that realists divorce the domestic sphere from the international realm is also problematic for an analysis of global norm development moving from the international domain into regional, national and sub-national spheres.

Thirdly, realists contend that power is used by states to further national interests (which are viewed as fixed and static variables) and achieve goals (Brown, 1997). Akin to arguments made by Finnemore (1996), I argue not that norms matter and interests do not, nor is it that norms are more important than interests. The argument here is that norms shape interests, which are by nature socially constructed. Additionally, while realist assumptions of states pursuing national interests are not disputed, what is ignored is how other non-state actors also pursue their interests. In other words, norm entrepreneurs use organizational platforms to convince a critical mass of state leaders to embrace new norms.

Fourthly, realists believe that the international system is inherently anarchical and that states seek to maximize their power in order to provide security within this anarchical system (Brown, 1997; Lynn-Jones, 1999; Meissner, 2004). Each state is therefore obligated to protect its physical, political and cultural identity from other states (Dougherty and Pfaltzgraff, 1990; Meissner, 2004; Morgenthau, 1974). Due to realism's state centric approach to IR, the theoretical framework is too narrow to solely explain the phenomena of international norm development in hydropolitics.

Security Complex Theory (SCT)/Regional Security Complex Theory (RSCT): A neo-realist-constructivist hybrid

The securitization of water resources, particularly in water scarce regions of the world has led several scholars (Buzan and Waever, 2003; Schulz, 1995; Turton, 2003a, 2003b, 2003c, 2003d, 2008a, 2008b) to analyse hydropolitics within a SCT framework.

A leading contributor to this body of literature, Barry Buzan (1991), first introduced the idea of SCT in his early work entitled 'People, States and Fear'. Here, Buzan argued that since security is a relational phenomenon, it became clear that the national security of any given state is embedded within an international pattern of security interdependence (ibid.). Therefore, comprehensive security analysis necessitated more attention to how the regional level of political interaction mediates the interplay between states and the international system as a whole (ibid.). By concentrating on regional sub-systems, two important levels of analysis between system and the state are possible (ibid.). The first is the sub-system itself, whereas the second is the pattern of relationships among the various units. Consequently, Buzan, Waever and de Wilde (1998: 201) define a security complex as 'a set of units whose processes of securitisation, desecuritisation, or both, are so interlinked that their security problems cannot reasonably be analysed or resolved apart from one another.' Some scholars argue that while securitization of water is not necessarily a desirable outcome of water resource management (Turton, 2001a, 2001b; Wester and Warner, 2002), the concept does help to understand political linkages between states in shared international river basins (Turton, 2001a).

Security complexes thus emphasize the interdependence of both rivalries and shared interests, threats and vulnerabilities, which are inherently greater over shorter distances thus assuming greater priority (ibid.). In short, security complexes are generated by the interaction of anarchy and geography, where the political structure of anarchy confronts all states with a security dilemma, but this is almost always mediated by the effects of geography (Buzan, 1991).

In a later work by Buzan and Waever entitled 'Regions and Powers' the authors advance their earlier analysis of RSC into a RSCT, arguing that regionalization has been the result of particular global dynamics and that the operational autonomy of regions has been triggered by the advent of 'non-military actors', thereby emphasizing the centrality of territoriality in the study of security dynamics (Buzan and Waever, 2003). Here, the authors attempt to advance the neo-realist framework by problematizing its ideational grid and incorporating into it elements of Wendtian constructivism, for example, a conceptualization of power; particularly, the agents of power (ibid.). They try to combine this, in their neo-realist framework, with their re-evaluation of the notion of polarity. The authors make the interesting observation that while regions do not display an actor quality (with the exception of the EU), it is the projection of power and the extent of its reach (both materially and ideationally), which defines polarization in international interactions (ibid.).

In this regard, Buzan and Waever unpack the main elements of their RSCT. First, regions are the appropriate levels of analysis of security studies. Secondly, regions provide a useful organization of and structure for empirical studies. And finally, regions provide analytical scenarios for testing possible developments in the future. Therefore, RSCT sketches a global map of RSC, whose patterns of amity and enmity are dependent upon both proximity and specific roles (enemy, rival and friend).

Most critiques of RSCT find the marriage between constructivism and neo-realism problematic. On the one hand RSCT acknowledges that security should be defined from the bottom-up by local (i.e. regional) actors and that 'security is what states make of it' (Buzan and Waever, 2003: 49). Yet on the other hand, the fact that the state is still the central unit of analysis makes analysing non-state-centric situations superfluous.

Additionally, in a typically state-centric neo-realist vein, the RSCT tends not to stray from traditional security issues, that is territoriality and territorial proximity as defining features of regions (Hoogensen, 2005). Thus, deterritorialized security issues such as economic security, which are often times raised from globalist perspectives, cannot override territorial security considerations when speaking of regions (ibid.). Furthermore, even in a supposedly weak regional security complex, or proto-complex such as southern Africa, as defined by Buzan and Waever, South Africa, the regional power, has projected its security interests further than the boundaries of southern Africa by becoming involved in peacekeeping and mediation in Burundi, Liberia, Sao Tome and Haiti (Hammerstad, 2005). While this is not necessarily a problem for RSCT, since it does allow for great powers to act outside of their region, the combination, however, of the introspective nature of threat perceptions in the region and the regional power's interest beyond the region, results in a weak complex, where the domestic level of analysis is dominant (ibid.). And finally, the focus of state behaviour and interests undermines the important role that norms play in influencing behaviour, redefining interests and contributing to a normative community of interests. There is therefore, a need to reflect on the increasingly important constitutive role that non-state actors, ideas, norms and values play within security complexes.

Buzan and Waever's analysis of Sub-Saharan Africa as a weak security complex is yet another contested area of their research. RSCT tends to rely on strong institutions present in states and according to the authors, this region has never obtained a strong foothold, and the dynamics of sub-state entities are strongly pronounced (Buzan and Waever, 2003). Non-state security threats such as HIV/AIDS and population growth are brushed over and presented as a set of state interactions with external power penetration or overlay (Hoogensen, 2005). According to Hoogensen, the African example suffers as a result (ibid.). For example, Buzan and Waever state that 'with such a poorly developed political apparatus, and with such fragmented civil societies, Africa is incapable of giving adequate voice to its own security agenda' (Buzan and Waever, 2003: 252). Thus, Africa's security needs should be expressed by 'others' given that Africa is incapable, as a region, of expressing those needs itself. In short, it has no ability to express security needs from the bottom-up. Hoogensen raises two pertinent questions; is it not likely that a security agenda is expressed in Africa, but that this agenda is not 'heard' by the dominant security discourses? And is it not also possible that, if we remove the preoccupation with state boundaries, a wide variety of 'unheard' security articulations within a variety of regions (from Africa to the Arctic) will become audible? (Hoogensen, 2005). Development of these kinds of points would have better helped RSCT establish the importance of the region as a unit of analysis beyond the state.

The Hydropolitical Complex (HPC)

Using the work by Buzan (1991), Buzan et al. (Buzan and Waever, 2003; Buzan et al., 1998) and Schulz (1995) as a point of departure, a conceptual model was developed that factors in the hydropolitical dimension of international relations, particularly as it pertains to the southern African region (Turton, 2003a, 2003d; Turton, 2005a). The rationale for this, according to Turton (2005), is based on the fact that international rivers provide permanent linkages between different states within the Southern African Regional Security Complex as originally defined by Buzan (1991). These linkages are so interconnected that they cannot be understood only in terms of geography, and a study that focuses purely on the river basin level misses this complex reality. However, while Turton's HPC and Schultz's Hydropolitical Security Complex, particularly that of the Tigris-Euphrates Security Complex, are both deviants of Buzan's Regional Security Complex, Turton's HPC is where interstate relations around water converge on a normative trajectory that moves towards amity. In contrast, Shultz's Hydropolitical Security Complex is when norms diverge and the trajectory is one of enmity instead.

In addressing some of the shortcomings of realist theories, a variety of liberalist perspectives have been offered. Conventional liberal-pluralism is a theoretical umbrella term in international relations that is theoretically discernible from, and contrasted to, realism (Stone, 1994). Moreover, it comprises of a number of theories including: regime theory, liberal internationalism, idealism, liberal institutionalism, neo-liberal internationalism, neo-idealism, functionalism, neo-functionalism, to mention but a few. It therefore does not constitute a unified theoretical approach and can most justifiably be referred to as a paradigm (Dunne, 1997a; Viotti and Kauppi, 1999). Generally speaking the liberal-pluralist perspective of world politics rests on the foundation of liberal ideas and values outlined below.

The liberal-pluralist perspective

First, the liberal-pluralist perspective postulates that states are not the only or the most important actors in international relations. Instead, non-state actors such as interest groups and individuals can also exhibit varying degrees of autonomy (Meissner, 2004; Stone, 1994). These non-state actors, it is argued, play increasingly prominent roles in influencing governments on the determination of national interests (Viotti and Kauppi, 1999: 199). Secondly, liberal-pluralists contend that a highly complex, interdependent and interconnected system exists between actors (Heywood, 1997).

Thirdly, liberal-pluralists prioritize autonomy over sovereignty as a settled norm, to accommodate a range of non-state actors (Meissner, 2004). Fourthly, they argue that states are permeable and not solid, unitary actors (Heywood, 1997; Meissner, 2004). Each state is composed differently in terms of types of government, constituencies etc., and these characteristics can change over time (Meissner, 2004; Stone, 1994). States therefore consist of citizens, interest groups, local authorities and government departments, all of whom constantly compete with one another (Meissner, 2004). In this regard, if states are viewed as unitary actors, then there can be no variety or analysis of sub-national and transnational actors who are able to influence the state (Viotti and Kauppi, 1999). Fifthly, liberal-pluralists believe that domestic and international politics cannot be separated in reality or in analyses thereof, since the realms are interdependent (Meissner, 2004). And finally, they assume that cooperation in the international system is natural because the current international system is perceived as liberal (Meissner, 2004; Stone, 1994).

Liberal-pluralism in the broader context, offers a more useful explanation of the effect of global environmental multilateralism and state sovereignty on regional water resource management than does realism because it acknowledges the plurality of the state. But while it increases the scope of international water politics by attributing agency to non-state actors (by arguing that institutions can change state behaviour), very few liberal-pluralist perspectives attempt to link non-state actors with identity and interest creation (Smith, 1997). Additionally, liberal-pluralists hold international institutions as benevolent forces, when in fact, they may act in pursuit of rational self-interest which may be at odds with those for peace and/or cooperation. Alternatively (and arguably, particular to environmental institutions), they may be hollow, ostentatious institutions created merely as lip service to the environmental problematique that is to be seen as global good citizens conforming to the norm set of transboundary cooperation, with no desire to reform domestic policy. Additionally, realists argue that liberalist arguments can be grounded in realism – and raw economic and military power still trumps sociocultural and other broader notions of power.

In reviewing several liberal-pluralist theories in terms of their applicability to norm development of regional water resource management, what is evident is the utility and indeed, necessity of accommodating non-state actors, prioritizing intersubjectivity, and understanding behaviour as being driven by both material and ideational factors.

Neo-liberal institutionalism

Neo-liberal institutionalism in IR comprises of those theories that regard international institutions as the primary actors in coordinating and fostering international cooperation. Neo-liberal institutionalists begin on a very similar theoretical starting block as realists, except, where realists assume that states focus on relative gains and the potential for conflict, neo-liberal institutionalists assume that states concentrate on absolute gains and the prospects for cooperation. These scholars argue that the potential for conflict is overstated by realists and suggest that there are countervailing forces, such as repeated interactions, that propel states towards cooperation.

Regarding cooperative or collaborative responses to water-related (in)security and water-induced conflict, neo-liberal institutionalism seems to be a strong candidate for theoretical frameworks. It emphasizes the notion of regime development, which is based on stakeholder decision-making and has a discrete legalistic-institutional foundation (Du Plessis, 2000). The concept of 'good governance' is therefore prioritized, again highlighting the centrality of the state, but also adding liberal-democratic capitalistic values as collateral (Mochebelele, 2000 cited in Du Plessis, 2000). The key participants in this respect are mostly collectivities representing the state as a political entity, as well as epistemic communities governed by technical experts in the water field (Du Plessis, 2000) which are in turn funded by governments.

Additionally, neo-liberal institutionalism, as previously mentioned of all liberal-pluralist perspectives, regards international institutions as benevolent forces created by morally good principles. In other words, neo-liberal institutionalism assumes away too much regarding the make-up of institutions and multilateralism than this study can afford.

(Neo-)functionalist regime theory

While regime theory will also not form part of this study's theoretical framework, it is worth briefly describing its importance to the water discourse, as well as to offer a justification for why its utility as a theoretical framework for this study is limited. While literature in the area of regime theory is not focused on transboundary water governance, Turton argues that there is plenty that can be applied to hydropolitics in international river basins. According to Turton (2003d), who uses regime theory extensively in his research, the role of regimes in building confidence between riparian states and thereby reducing insecurity in the face of increasing water deficit is a significant contribution to explaining successful water resource management and cooperation. The significant role of crisis is particularly pertinent here, with the avoidance of crisis becoming a major security concern, potentially leading to regime creation (Alcamo, 2000). Thus, Turton uses regime theory to analyse desecuritization processes (and thereby cooperation) to the same degree that he uses SCT and RSCT to analyse securitization (and thereby conflict).

One basic tenet of regime theory is that regimes (defined as a set of implicit and explicit principles, norms, rules and procedures around which actors' expectations converge in a particular issue-area such as human rights, nuclear non-proliferation, environmental concerns) provide for transparent state behaviour and a degree of stability in an anarchical international system (Krasner, 1983). Another central principle of regime theory is that the chances of successful regime formation are higher the more limited and well defined the issue is (Gupta et al., 1993). Now while Turton argues that this makes it very relevant to the international dimension of the SADC water sector (Turton, 2003d) due to the alignment of riparian states' interests, that is water management as an issue-area due to the interdependence of Orange-Senqu River basin states on each other for economic development, this does not prove to be as relevant to the Nile River basin. Advancing the collective action characteristic of what Elinor Ostrom (1991) terms 'common property resources' (CPRs), Waterbury (2002) presents the case that non-cooperation is perhaps more likely than cooperation, due to disparate national interests and rivalry. Waterbury clarifies that rivalry is asymmetrical. In other words, transboundary watercourses '. . . do not constitute common pool resources that can be exploited jointly and simultaneously by the riparians in the basin' (ibid.: 23). He goes on to argue that this is not a doomsday (water war) prediction due to the regional dynamics characterized by chronic instability and 'political ineptitude' of major stakeholders Ethiopia, the Sudan and Uganda to engage in this manner. When combining this logic with the intrinsic hydraulic difficulty of permanently excluding Egypt from access to water and compelling it to secure its Nile water uses by a multilateral legal framework, it becomes evident how easy it is to achieve non-cooperation! (ibid.). Waterbury further argues that non-cooperation or perhaps, non-multilateral action poses no 'tragedy of the commons' problem requiring emergency resuscitation because no crisis of that degree exists (Waterbury, 2002). This argument of regime formation differs to that presented by Young (1994), that is the view that a crisis or shock might precipitate a formation of regimes. Yet another explanation to the formation of regimes, however, is the one offered by Haas (1994) and Adler and Haas (1992). They are not overly concerned with interests and dramatic events but argue instead, that a regime can originate out of communities of shared knowledge or epistemic communities. The emphasis is on how these experts play an important role in the articulation of complex problems, such as water management issues or pollution control.

While this investigation does not aim to refute the role regimes play or undermine its importance in acting as socializing agents, regime theory says little about how norms become legitimized and internalized within regimes. Moreover, a moral judgement that regimes foster cooperation does not add to the depth of this study since it lays out a unidirectional path with cooperation as the ideal like all other liberal-pluralist perspectives. Since norms are dynamic variables, so too would socializing agents such as regimes have to change. Such a theory that regards regimes as static, monolithic entities, proves insufficient as an overarching theoretical framework. Also, although norms do feature in a secondary capacity, this theory is too narrow to explain how actors go about lobbying and advocating for the embracing of new norms. In other words, the agential nature of norms is not discussed in great detail nor how they can in fact, affect the identities of states.

Political ecology

Political ecology is the only reflectivist theory reviewed in this study, due to the under-representation of reflectivist applications to transboundary water governance. As espoused by Atkinson (1991), political ecology is a normative theory that offers an alternative perspective to neo-liberalism (Atkinson, 1991; Toke, 2000). Simply put, political ecology, as a normative approach, looks at what ought to be rather than at what is (Viotti and Kauppi, 1999), and is therefore, evaluative and prescriptive in nature (Meissner, 2004).

Additionally, political ecology has several basic assumptions that make it depart from mainstream positivist theories. First, theorists of political ecology reject the notion that only the state-system or other global political structures can respond effectively to environmental problems (Meissner, 2004). Furthermore, they expand this view by arguing for global-scale political transformation rather than institutional tinkering, such as the establishment of regimes (Paterson, 2001). Secondly, it is assumed that increased economic development through industrialization is detrimental to the natural environment (Heywood, 1997).

Thirdly, political ecology theorizing states that 'limits to growth' run parallel to rapid economic and population expansion. 'These aspects are straining the earth's resources and carrying capacity that will soon reach its limits' (Meissner, 2004: 38). In this regard, there is a definite limit to the amount of growth a society can experience (Paterson, 2001). Fourthly, political ecologists argue that development is essentially 'anti-ecological' as it destabilizes sustainable practices. These practices create inequality by turning common spaces into private property (Paterson, 2001). Fifthly, theorists of political ecology reject sustainable development since it is yet another way for the 'ruling elite to co-opt environmentalism' (ibid.: 282–5). Sixthly, political ecologists also assume that humans have become separated and indeed alienated from nature, through economic processes such as capitalist consumerism and a division of labour (Atkinson, 1991; Turton, 1999a). They therefore advocate for a change in political and social institutions in order to diffuse the social tensions that result from the currently existing inegalitarian social relations (Atkinson, 1991; Meissner, 2004).

Seventhly, political ecologists are anti-anthropocentric, meaning that they reject anthropocentrism, which contends that the well-being and needs of humans have precedence over nature's interests and needs (Heywood, 1997). Being anti-anthropocentric is therefore a type of ecocentrism, which places nature first in ethical and philosophical considerations of human activity. Eighthly, ecocentrism counteracts the anthropocentrism of state action (Meissner, 2004). It acknowledges human as well as non-human interests (Toke, 2000), and assumes a holistic approach (Meissner, 2004). Ninthly, it is also argued that political power should not be centralized at the state level, but rather decentralized within the state and centralized at the regional and global levels (ibid.). Lastly, political ecologists emphasize the important role of non-state actors, and regard interest groups, such as NGOs with an environmental agenda, as critically important in affecting a reversal of the ecological crisis facing humanity (Meissner, 2004; Turton, 1999a).

The relationship between political ecology theory and hydropolitics is relevant for this study because it recommends that societies become self-regulating (Atkinson, 1991; Meissner, 2004; Turton, 1999a). A self-regulating society can only be realized if it is 'simpler' in its functions and the relationship between humans and nature more transparent (Atkinson, 1991). This could be achieved if the population of a given political entity are allowed to question the decisions that are made by political decision-makers (Turton, 1999a). Political ecology is, however, a very narrow explanatory tool since (a) It does not say much about how norm entrepreneurs convince policymakers to embrace new norms or how norms develop and affect behaviour and interests (b) It does not explain the importance of global norms as entities that may or may not determine interests in environmental issues and (c) It does not propose an alternative to the state system it renounces (Meissner, 2004). Most importantly, it prescribes a normative judgement on that which it analyses, with a bias towards environmentalism. This links back to the applicability of the global norms set. Political ecologists may be able to provide us with a normative framework to assess the suitability of contending norms, but the criteria used to determine 'good' norms from 'bad' norms is in itself normative, and may mask or prejudge the existing landscape of norms and their interaction in time and space.

A constructivist lens

In order to bridge the divide between mainstream and tributary perspectives and to accommodate the complexities of ideational contents such as norm development in transboundary water governance, constructivism is used as the umbrella theoretical framework to analyse what Keck and Sikkink have described as '[s]ociological traditions that focus on complex interactions among actors, on the intersubjective construction of frames of meaning' (Keck and Sikkink, 1998: 4). According to Finnemore and Sikkink, 'constructivists focus on the role of ideas, norms, knowledge, culture and argument in politics, stressing in particular the role of collectively held or "intersubjective" ideas and understandings on social life' (Finnemore and Sikkink, 2001: 392). According to Bernstein, the reflectivist/constructivist agenda in IR arose from the dissatisfaction that mainstream views 'seemed to forget that international institutions are not simply a vehicle through which states cooperate, but that the cooperation they enable is for some purpose or goal' (Bernstein, 2001: x). Since I focus on the international ideational contents of regional water policy, this is an important theoretical pillar, that is, how water governance has been socially constructed in a specific political process over time and why it has been constructed the way it has.

It is however noteworthy to reiterate that due to constructivism's difficulty in explaining change, I will draw from other theoretical perspectives, and where necessary, fill in the gaps where current theory fails to do so. In spite of this shortcoming, constructivism does attempt to understand social relations by explaining the construction of the sociopolitical world by human practice (Meissner, 2004). In this regard it is successful in its bridge-building properties. Simply put, the constructivist approach applied here emphasizes the importance of normative as well as material structures (indeed the impact of the ideational on the material), the role of identity in shaping political action and also the complementary constitutive relationship between agents and structures.

It is also imperative to mention that constructivism comprises a wide range of perspectives that differ in many ways. Indeed, some scholars argue that constructivism as a single theoretical approach does not exist (Teti and Hynek, 2006). Other authors have categorized constructivism into different classifications including conventional/classical, neo-classical, naturalist, postmodernist etc. This study draws on Meissner's three-pronged classification system adapted from Reus-Smit's analysis that is systemic, unit-level and holistic constructivism (Meissner, 2004; Reus-Smit, 2001). While systemic constructivism follows a neo-realist path of adopting a 'third image' perspective, focusing on unitary state actors, unit-level constructivism is the opposite, focusing instead on the relationship between domestic, social and legal norms (Meissner, 2004). Holistic constructivism, however, aims to bridge the two realms and will therefore be used as an explanatory tool.

Other scholars make the distinction between transnational and societal constructivism, contending that transnational constructivism (with its roots in sociological institutionalism as used by Finnemore) focuses on the influence of internationally shared norms (i.e. norms that are shared by international society or by subsets of that society, such as regional or function-specific international organizations) (Boekle et al., 1999). Indicators for transnational constructivism may therefore include international law, resolutions of international organizations and final acts of international conferences (ibid.). In contrast, societal or domestic constructivism emphasizes the importance of norms that are shared within domestic society (ibid.). The effect of such norms can be investigated through indicators such as constitutional and legal order, party programmes and election platforms, parliamentary debates and public opinion data (ibid.). What we see in the case of transboundary water governance is how blurred these lines of distinction become when international norms are localized or resonate with longer standing domestic norms, or when local norms piggyback on broader international norms to convince a larger audience of their appropriateness within a particular context.

Additionally, constructivists treat actors as social entities whose identities are constituted by the social environment in which they act; view the interests of actors as endogenous to social interaction and as a consequence of identity; and regard society as a constitutive realm that determines actor identity (Du Plessis, 2000). In this respect the ideas of Alexander Wendt are of particular significance. His basic position is that human beings are purposeful actors (thus departing slightly from Boekle, Rittberger and Wagner's critique of value maximizing actors) whose actions reproduce and transform society, and that society is made up of social relationships which structure the interaction between human beings (Wendt, 1992). Since the world is pre-organized and pre-structured, it shapes and moulds actors, but actors are also international agents who act in this world and who re-create or transform the structures it contains. Using this logic, Wendt's reformulations are apt. Instead of focusing on structures or agents, he prioritizes the interrelationship between them; rather than theorizing on material facts and eternal imperatives, he emphasizes practices, processes and the social creation of meaning; and he puts the neo-realist picture into motion by historicizing it and moving it closer to actions, thought and human life.

Therefore, constructivism is indeed 'constructed' differently from scholar to scholar. Wendt's (1995) version of classical constructivism, on the one hand, attempts to locate state identities in the overarching cultural structure of the state-system. His version of constructivism does not dispute the neo-realist claim that states are self-organizing units to which it is possible to attribute identities and interests. On the other hand, more radical constructivists dispute the epistemological assumptions underpinning this particular approach (Kratochwil, 2000). Kratochwil, for instance, criticizes this very notion of Wendt's social theory argument, claiming that because it relies on (at least to some degree) a version of 'scientific realism', it is overly reliant on already problematic foundationalist notions such as the emphasis on the state as the main actor (ibid.). Kratochwil's critique is very useful today, especially with the upsurge of non-state actors active in decision-making processes in the international system. Despite these differences, most constructivists do however adopt what Mark Hoffman (1991) has called a 'minimal foundationalism'. This implies that, while accepting the contingent nature of knowledge and recognizing the importance of particular historical and cultural contexts, most constructivists argue that consensual standards (i.e. generally accepted norms and values) must govern the derivation of plausible interpretations of social reality (Hoffman, 1991). Simply put, the existence of norms, the construction of new norms and the development/revision of old ones are what influences our (states' and non-states') interpretation of social reality and thus dictate how we act. It is from this point that this study develops its constructivist argumentation, and more particularly, the impact of global norm construction and development in transboundary water governance.

Constructivism's main assumption is that there is no objective reality. A major critique presented by Boekle, et al. (1999) of neo-realist and neo-liberalist perspectives is their critique of the concept of 'utility maximizing', which forms the basis of rationalist argumentation. According to the rationalist perspective, ideas, values or norms can only operate as instruments for asserting and justifying given interests (ibid.). In contrast, constructivist strands elevate these to independent variables (ibid.). Through this theoretical lens, norms guide the actions of actors (ibid.). The assumption of the independent influence of norms is therefore, juxtaposed with the concept of the self-regarding, rational, utility-maximizing actor that neo-realism and neo-liberalism advocate. In contrast, actors take decisions on the basis of norms and rules which are created and influenced by subjective factors, historical-cultural experience and institutional involvement (Schaber and Ulbert, 1994, cited in Boekle et al., 1999).

According to this view, in contrast to the two 'neos' (neo-realism and neo-liberalism), constructivism does not portray world politics and the international system in which it operates as fixed, material structures, but rather as socially constructed, in which factors such as norms, culture, rules and identity play a defining role (Onuf, 1989). The rules of the system are therefore produced by the interactions of states and they in turn shape state practice.

Moreover, constructivist strands also differ from mainstream theories in its views on the development of norms and the path they take in this regard. Mainstream theories link the impact of norms predominantly with the variables 'power' or 'interests' (Boekle et al., 1999: 8). In neo-realist explanations, for instance, norms only affect actor behaviour when compliance with them is either enforced by powerful actors, or when they are complied with by weaker actors who fear sanctions (Krasner, 1993). In other words, norm acceptance is a function of hegemonic interests or coercive force. From this perspective, it is not norms per se, but the power behind them, that results in norm-compliant behaviour (Boekle et al., 1999).

In contrast, Boekle et al. (1999) argue that constructivist norms do not occur as a result of actors' interests, but rather precede (and define) them. The effect of norms on behaviour is therefore, not only regulative (i.e. 'constraints' or 'incentives' that increase or reduce the cost of certain modes of behaviour) (ibid.: 8). Norms are also constitutive, that is 'norms legitimise goals and thus define actors' interests' (Klotz, 1995: 26). By legitimizing certain goals, norms act as 'motives' and in turn, as 'motives', norms help to establish the goals, which states should legitimately attempt to meet (Boekle et al., 1999: 8). By taking on this character, norms provide states with the scope to define their interests in accordance with the goals that have been assigned as legitimate (ibid.).

Norm construction and the 'logic of appropriateness'

Constructivism also emphasizes the influence of norms in defining and shaping actors behaviour. For constructivists such as Boekle, Rittberger and Wagner, the 'logic of appropriateness' is apt in this regard. These authors stipulate that contrary to a rationalist perspective, where actors anticipate the consequences of their actions in order to choose the alternative which will maximize their self-regarding utility, a 'logic of appropriateness' takes socially shared, value-based expectations of behaviour as its foundational point of reference (Boekle et al., 1999). The logic of appropriateness states that behaviour is, intentional but not wilful. Rather, it involves fulfilling the obligations of a role in a situation defined by a norm (March and Olsen, 1989).

The intersubjectively shared nature of norms deserves to be highlighted since this is essentially how new norms arise. If and when enough actors, both state and non-state, have a shared belief about that which is considered to be morally acceptable behaviour and act on it, then it becomes a norm. Moreover, due to the increasingly interdependent, pluralist and multilateral nature of the international system, actors are becoming more obliged to obey international norms, particularly those surrounding human rights and the environment.

Having said this however, much of the theoretical tools and equipment of constructivism are better at explaining stability than change. According to Finnemore and Sikkink, claims that actors conform to 'logics of appropriateness', do not adequately address how these logics might change (Finnemore and Sikkink, 1998). Thus, while the 'logic of appropriateness' sheds light on how norms are constructed and adhered to, it explains very little of how it is reconstructed, or which logics are more important than others and why. As argued by Boekle et al. (1999: 6), 'A much-stated criticism of . . . [Constructivism] is the fact that an actor is frequently confronted with many value-based expectations of behaviour, with the result that a distinction between relevant and irrelevant expectations of behaviour is made difficult or becomes arbitrary.' In the constructivist view, the strength of a norm depends on two properties: on its commonality (i.e. the amount of actors in a social system who share a value-based expectation of behaviour), and on its specificity (i.e. the degree to which a norm distinguishes appropriate from inappropriate behaviour) (Boekle et al., 1999). This study, however will illustrate that these two properties are too limiting. In addition to commonality, who the actors are who persuade of appropriate behaviour is also important; as is the power they hold. In addition to specificity, the degree to which a norm is congruent with pre-existing norms, is also critically important to its ability to become socialized.

Constructivism and hydropolitics

What is the relevance then of constructivism to hydropolitics and transboundary water governance? First, since constructivism is not completely state-centric, it allows for the construction of a truly multi-actor model, including both state and non-state entities. Because water governance is not only the purview of the state, a constructivist approach enables a shift in focus to include non-state actors. External actors (whether state or non-state) within transboundary river basins are also becoming more visible and influential. A constructivist approach is therefore useful in helping to understand their impact on other actors within the basin and on the environment at large. Additionally, a constructivist lens promotes a 'derritorialized' view of water resources, and therefore frees analyses from the territorial trap[7] (Agnew, 1994). Water resources need not be viewed and researched as bounded by sovereignty and state authority, but can exist within a transnational normative sphere albeit influenced by global norms of global capitalism and water privatization, global norms of human rights, regional norms of economic and democratic development or national norms of reform. This view provides a more holistic account of the power asymmetries at play, some of which are state related, but many of which are not.

Secondly, norms may constrain state action, thereby demonstrating that normative social structures could lead to changes in policy preferences. Norm development is therefore a critically important link between furthering our understanding of state behaviour and the articulation thereof in policy.

Thirdly, an inclusion of the international, regional, national as well as sub-national levels is needed in this analysis of norms. The amalgamation of levels is useful in understanding how global norms get domesticated and internalized regionally and domestically, as well as how norms, developed at other levels of scale, interact with each other and international norms.

Fourthly, the intersubjective nature of norm development is best captured by constructivist approaches that highlight ontological intersubjectivity (of reality), as well as epistemological intersubjectivity (of knowledge), and complexity. Indeed, the range of truths that are produced in multi-level water governance, regarding what is morally acceptable, or the most appropriate way of behaving, reflects various collective understandings and complexities. Constructivist approaches are therefore better at explaining how reality, knowledge, and therefore ways of behaving are intricately constructed based on collective understandings that are shared within groups of individuals, than realist or liberal approaches.

Indeed, a major drawback of both realist and liberal approaches is their reductionist treatment of complex governance systems. The scientific method of reducing complex systems into their individual components in order to achieve a better understanding of society is followed in both theoretical approaches. However, in so doing, the essence of complex systems is not adequately addressed (Meissner and Jacobs, in press). The philosophy of reductionism does not have to be followed to explain complex systems in society. It is here where Turton and Hattingh (2007: 341) put forward their argument that '... the only way to inform decision-making processes about complex issues ... is by having redundancy in the scientific field. This will enable the best possible decision to be made, by recognising the unintended consequences of specific actions (Tenner, 1996), and qualifying the impacts, proposing mitigation actions, alternative management options and identifying possible trade-off.' They therefore reject the notion of exclusive reductionism and state that traditional knowledge is part of a scientific process that should give input into decision-making processes. They argue further that in order to understand complex reality there needs to be a 'synergy of transdisciplinarity between the reductionist style of science . . . and the integrative style of science . . .' (Turton and Hattingh, 2007: 340). Based on this, the nature and function of governance systems can be better understood through the application of constructivist approaches. Since constructivist analyses advocate an epistemology of scientific relativism, one need not reduce complex systems in an atomistic manner to explain them (Meissner and Jacobs, in press.).

Finally, according to Hogan (2005), a constructivist paradigm allows for a shared water 'ethos' to move discourse to a common ground of ideas and norms that enables parties to bypass volatile political issues. But to what extent has this actually occurred in the Orange-Senqu and Nile River basins, and has the process been lateral, top-down or bottom-up? In other words, has a clear normative trajectory cascaded down from the global level and been disseminated at the regional and domestic levels, or has a process of normative aggregation (Conca, 2006) occurred (from country to country within a basin) and lateral diffusion of norms across the Orange-Senqu and Nile River basins occurred instead? Or alternatively, has the process been bottom-up where local, culturally specific norms filter up to the national level to influence behaviour at higher levels of scale? Fourthly still, as Conca (2006: 104) argues, is it the case that no link between these two levels of institution building is evident and that basin-specific accords may reflect a rival set of norms, or may turn out to be a heterogeneous collection of agreements with no consistent collective normative structure? Indeed, a closer look at how norms develop in specific regions, how they promote the creation of regional and collective identities and how they succeed or struggle in becoming socialized in different contexts provides useful insights into interstate and inter-actor cooperation on collective environmental issues.

Notes

1   Adding to the counter-argument of poorly developed international water law is the fact that the international community has devised principles for international watercourse management in order to reduce the likelihood of conflict as well as to resolve existing disputes (Giordano and Wolf, 2002). Over the past century, as Giordano and Wolf argue, these principles have been refined and codified in the 1997 UN Convention on the Law of the Non-Navigational Uses of International Watercourses. Moreover, as the Orange-Senqu and the Nile River basins both exemplify, basin communities, building on their own rich treaty history, have accelerated the development of cooperative institutions to manage shared rivers (ibid.). This point alludes to the functionality of

legal instruments in facilitating effective transboundary water governance. As conflict prevention tools, legal instruments have been very effective, however, as a means to facilitate dialogue, build trust and confidence and stipulate volumetric allocations, for instance, legal instruments have proved less definite in some areas.

2   Oregon State University (OSU) compiled a quantitative dataset of every reported interaction between two or more nations, whether conflictive or cooperative that involved water as a scarce or consumable resource, or as a quantity to be managed where water was the driver of events (Wolf, 2005: 9–10). The result was that cooperative interactions between riparian states over the past 50 years have outnumbered conflictive interactions by more than two-to-one: 507 conflict-related events versus 1,228 cooperative events (Giordano and Wolf, 2002). Of the 507 conflict-related events, 37 were acute disputes (those involving violence), of which 30 were between Israel and one of its neighbours (Wolf, 2005). This study showed that violence over water is not strategically rational, hydrographically effective or economically viable.

3   IWRM is an evolving concept and as such several definitions and conceptualizations are used today (Moriarty, Butterworth and Batchelor, 2004). The most commonly used is that adopted by the Technical Advisory Committee of the Global Water Partnership (GWP), who have defined IWRM as a process that promotes the coordinated development and management of water, land and related resources, in order to maximize the resultant economic and social welfare in an equitable manner without compromising the sustainability of vital ecosystems (GWP, 2000). Operationally, IWRM approaches apply knowledge from several disciplines and multiple stakeholders to devise and implement efficient, equitable and sustainable solutions to water and development problems. As such, IWRM is a comprehensive, participatory planning tool that involves the coordinated planning and management of land, water and other environmental resources for their equitable, efficient and sustainable use (Calder, 1999).

4   In the transboundary water resources sense, benefit-sharing refers to a paradigm or policy tool that identifies the gains of interstate cooperation beyond merely the sharing of water, but incorporates the sharing of opportunities that water brings to a country, a basin and a region.

5   Norms of water-sharing, in this case, refer to standards of appropriate behaviour regarding the volumetric allocation of water between countries.

6   A benefit-sharing normative framework, in this case, refers to standards of appropriate behaviour relating to the joint identification of benefits that result from the use and access to the shared resource that is hydropower projects providing electricity to one country, and royalties/payment to another.

7   Agnew (1994) refers to the prioritization of the state or the 'state as actor model', as the 'territorial trap', based on three theoretical pillars: the reification of sovereignty as complete state control over a fixed unit of territorial space; the severing of domestic and foreign politics; and the state as prior to and a container of society.

2

Actors, Factors and Processes of the
Normative Landscape

Normative literature on transboundary river basin management within the field of transboundary hydropolitics has recently undergone major development, with extensive empirical research conducted by Ken Conca and his former team at Maryland University in the United States. This team has produced evidence that refutes claims made of the emergence of an international regime for the management of transboundary river basins that is based on a converging set of core normative elements, via a global-framework (which they define as top-down norm dissemination) or a basin-cumulative path (which they define as bottom-up norm aggregation) (Conca, 2006; Conca and Wu, 2002; Conca et al., 2003; Conca et al., 2006). Their core message is that there is no evidence of normative deepening, but there is some evidence of convergence around specific issue-clusters that do not challenge the notion of state sovereignty in regime negotiation. Moreover, a history of interstate cooperation tends to mitigate future conflict. Therefore, a good indicator for gauging whether a river basin is 'at risk' (Wolf et al., 2003) is ascertaining whether there has been a history of inter-state cooperation in that basin, reflected in regimes, treaties or negotiated agreements.

In addition to the Maryland School's comprehensive analyses of the principled nature of cooperation explicitly articulated in treaties and other negotiated legal agreements, norm convergence should also be examined in the *non-regulatory* landscape.

Actors: norm emergence, norm
entrepreneurs and framing

This study draws from, as well as critiques, the three-stage norm cycle model developed in a seminal article by Finnemore and Sikkink (1998), in which they suggest that norm effects depend on three evolutionary stages of norms. The first step in Finnemore and Sikkink's norm life cycle is norm emergence. Within this step, the authors argue that norm entrepreneurs working from organizational platforms present new ideas as potential norms and persuade a critical mass of their moral appropriateness. Norm entrepreneurs are therefore agents who have distinct notions about appropriate behaviour in their community (Finnemore and Sikkink, 1998), and are able to articulate them. Furthermore, they must compete with the existing constellation of norms in order for their ideas to gain acceptance as norms (ibid.).

Elgstrom, writing on the construction of new norms regarding gender and development in EU foreign aid policy, explains how norms change interests and therefore behaviour. Her theoretical argumentation on how gender and development norms change shared understandings of reality is noteworthy for this study as well (Elgstrom, 2000). Elgstrom argues that while collectively shared understandings of reality are hard to change, it is possible to change them. Constructivism's importance here is tremendous in that it emphasizes the role of agency, the capacity of actors to redefine interests and preferences (ibid.). Different types of actors (e.g. intergovernmental organizations (IGOs), non-governmental organizations (NGOs) and transnational advocacy networks) can therefore exert 'moral influence' on state interests and contribute to major changes in norms and behaviour (Elgstrom, 2000). Indeed, Finnemore and Sikkink reiterate this point by highlighting how international organizations, in particular, use expertise and information to change the behaviour of other states (Finnemore and Sikkink, 1998). Constructivism thus proposes that socially constructed variables hold the status of basic causal variables that shape preferences and outcomes: moral persuasion leads to norm spread, causing changes in preferences and interests that result in behavioural change (ibid.). There is, therefore, a need to identify:

- Who the norm entrepreneurs of a global norm are as well as who their target audiences are.
- Within a specific domestic environment, the make-up of the norm entrepreneurs or advocacy coalitions who try to push domestic norm-based change through the state and how they do so.

Due to the technical manner in which transboundary water resource management is carried out today, norm entrepreneurs exist largely in the epistemic community, both domestically and internationally. An epistemic community is created by a dense network of activists, policymakers, academics and entrepreneurs, who are influential in setting the agenda and defining the interests related to water resource management. Moreover, due to the highly technical nature of water engineering, hydrology and other environmental, ecological and soil and land management sciences, this network comprises of an exclusive club of experts who dominate the production and application of knowledge (Swatuk, 2005b). Often, their conservationist or technical interests take precedence over that of local actors (farmers, pastoralists etc.) in that they are present at organizational platforms to convince policymakers to embrace global environmental norms while local actors are not (ibid.). The epistemic community is also knowledgeable of political and technical processes, and are therefore able to articulate their interests in this manner.

Additionally, several scholars posit that in the early stages of norm emergence, entrepreneurs largely rely on persuasion and framing (Elgstrom, 2000; Finnemore and Sikkink, 1998). They largely rely on persuasion to get the norms they advocate on the agenda and to convince major actors to pay attention to the issue (Elgstrom, 2000). They draw attention to issues or even create issues by using language that names, interprets and dramatizes them, that is the process of framing (Finnemore and Sikkink, 1998).

'The construction of cognitive frames is an essential component of norm entrepreneurs' political strategies, since, when they are successful; the new frames resonate with broader public understandings and are adopted as new ways of talking about and understanding issues' (Finnemore and Sikkink, 1998: 897). Similarly, Payne (2001: 39) claims that a frame is a device used to 'fix meanings, organise experience, alert others that their interests and possibly their identities are at stake, and propose solutions to ongoing problems'. The relationship between frames and norm diffusion is that while frames provide an interpretative understanding of a situation, norms indicate the most appropriate behaviour for that situation (or the 'oughtness' of what one should do) (Yanacopulos, 2004: 720).

For instance, in a securitized frame, national security concerns become associated with the management of transboundary river basins (Schulz, 1995), water resource management structures remain stunted, and hydrological data becomes classified as secret and thereby removed from the public domain. A desecuritized frame, on the other hand, allows all interested parties to collect, store and access basin-wide data (Turton, 2003a). Some norm entrepreneurs have therefore attempted to frame water resource management within a desecuritized domain in an attempt to advocate the normative appropriateness of transboundary cooperation and to persuade against perceptions of insecurity.

Socialization

The second stage of the cycle is a norm cascade. Multiple agents now begin to accept the appropriateness of the behaviour for which the new norm calls through the process of socialization. However, as implied earlier, socialization should not be perceived as a one-way process in which the actor being socialized only accepts beliefs and practices from the world and does not contribute preconceptions of his own (Boekle et al., 1999). Instead, the socializing actor may reflect on what it internalizes during the socialization process and even alter its content (Schimmelfennig, 1994 cited in Boekle et al., 1999). As such, socialization is a constantly evolving, and continuous process, as individuals need to learn new expectations of behaviour or reinterpret that which they have already internalized (Parsons, 1951).

Furthermore, Boekle et al. make a sound distinction between the process of an individual's socialization into his social environment and the socialization process of government decision-makers (or rather the socialization of states) (Boekle et al., 1999). During the socialization process of states, two analytically distinct socialization processes run simultaneously. Since foreign policy decision-makers have to operate at both the international system and the domestic system, they face two different groups of socializing agents and, consequently, undergo two different socialization processes (ibid.). Transnational socialization refers to the process whereby government decision-makers internalize international norms, that is norms that are shared by states, while societal or domestic socialization describes the process whereby government decision-makers internalize domestic norms, that is norms that are shared by the citizens of their state (ibid.).

Transnational socialization

States are the constitutive units of international society and consequently, of transboundary water resource management, and are therefore considered to be the most important socializing agents (ibid.). While international organizations are not constitutive units of international society, they do play important roles as socializing agencies in that they represent associations of states (ibid.). Moreover, they are essential as socializing agencies because they express 'value communities' made up of states (ibid.). As Boekle et al. (1999: 9) argue, 'States acknowledge the expectations of appropriate behaviour formulated by international organisations as standards of appropriate behaviour if they regard themselves as part of the value community of the member states and seek recognition as an equal member by the other member states' (ibid.: 9). And since international organizations are regarded as incubators for value communities, they also function as 'norm teachers' who, as previously indicated in Chapter 1, teach states new norms of behaviour and help disseminate them (Finnemore and Sikkink, 1998; Finnemore and Sikkink, 2001; Keck and Sikkink, 1998).

In addition to states and international organizations, transnational advocacy coalitions also play an important role in transnational socialization processes by diffusing and imparting norms, aiming at the widest possible dissemination and acceptance (Boekle et al., 1999). Transnational advocacy coalitions also act as norm entrepreneurs in that they develop existing norms by verifying compliance (Finnemore and Sikkink, 1998) as well as help establish new norms (Keck and Sikkink, 1998). This is particularly the case with environmental advocacy groups such as Greenpeace and Habitat for Humanity.

States acknowledge the norms of international society as standards of appropriate behaviour because their identity as states depends on their membership in international society (Schimmelfennig 1994, cited in Boekle et al., 1999). For instance, states are only considered sovereign upon the recognition of such by other states (Biersteker and Weber, 1996; Thomson, 1995). In short, states are constantly concerned with legitimacy or their reputation as recognized (i.e. norm-compliant) members of international society that is as 'good' global citizens (Finnemore and Sikkink, 1998).

Additionally, domestic contexts also affect the degree to which international norms are accepted. Cortell and Davis (1996), have pioneered research on the domestic salience or legitimacy of an international norm, and have sought to conceptualize a framework for measuring domestic salience. They present two national-level factors that are imperative to the success of socialization processes and provide explanations for important cross-national variations in compliance with and interpretation of international norms (Cortell and Davis, 1996, 2000). These are (1) The domestic salience or legitimacy of the norm, and (2) The structural context within which the domestic policy debate transpires (ibid.). Several scholars share this opinion. Risse-Kappen (1994) argues, for instance, that the ability of transnational actors to promote norms and influence state policy is dependent on domestic structures understood in terms of state-societal relations, while Checkel (1999) reiterates that the effects of global norms are fostered by domestic structures as well as a norm's congruence with domestic political culture. This argument helps to explain the variations in norm diffusion among riparian states, and similarly, how 'internationally promulgated norms clash with pre-existing national understandings' (Cortell and Davis, 2005: 3).

Additionally, while contemporary international norms literature has emphasized the role of persuasion and social learning among political leaders in the process of socialization, in environmental affairs, it is typically not sufficient for political leaders to be persuaded of the appropriateness of a norm for it to alter the behaviour of a particular state (Cass, 2005). The norm must be thoroughly integrated into domestic political discourse and eventually be incorporated into the foreign and domestic policies, laws and practices of the state (ibid.). As Flockhart (2006) argues, a failure to institutionalize the norm set in national law indicates norm failure at the state level. While national leaders play a fundamental role in this process, in most cases the norm must be accepted by enough domestic actors for it to significantly alter national behaviour (Cass, 2005). Flockhart (2006) advances this argument by differentiating between norm adoption at the state level and norm adoption at the national level, that is, when a significant proportion of the political elite (defined as those individuals who occupy key roles within state structures) adopt the norms set versus when a significant proportion of the population conforms with the institutionalized norm set.

This differentiation between 'political elites' and 'the people' is a critical distinction in understanding differences in global norm socialization where there are apparent similarities in degrees of domestic salience at a state level that is institutionalization of normative principles into national law and practice of all riparian states. Flockhart (2006) divides the domestic level into what she refers to as 'we-concepts', which indicates that the domestic context operates within these two distinct political cultures; a 'state culture' at the elite level and the widely accepted 'political culture' at the mass level. The author is careful to qualify that this does not necessarily imply that these two concepts in the form of 'state' and 'nation' will always be separate, but suggests that this might be the case where the two domestic levels have different ideas on what constitutes norm appropriate behaviour. This aids in understanding differences in seemingly similar socialization processes. Simply put, domestic salience of the transboundary cooperation norm set may seemingly be effective in both South Africa and Namibia at the state level, but when the domestic context is unpacked in both riparians, differences occur between state/elite and nation/people norm acceptance ratios. In other words, even though successful norm adoption may occur at a state level by political elites, the norm may not be internalized and accepted at a national level, which would be indicated by persistent failure in a significant proportion of the population to conform to the institutionalized norm set (ibid.). The reasons for this vary. It may be as a result of a lack of awareness of the existence of the norm at the nation/people level, a lack of public participation at political fora where these norms are debated and accepted, the resistance due to incompatibility with pre-existing local norms or that the norms are too vague to be applicable on the ground.

Mechanisms of norm convergence

In addition to considering the landscape in which the norms are diffused, the method by which norms become socialized is also likely to have a significant impact on the success of the socialization process. In a broad sense, socialization methods include three strategies for socialization. The first is persuasion, which encourages norm conforming behaviour through a social process of interaction and communication that changes attitudes without the use of either material or mental coercion (Finnemore and Sikkink, 1998, 2001; Flockhart, 2004). Norm entrepreneurs use this strategy along with framing to get the norms they advocate on the agenda and to convince major actors to pay attention to the issue (Elgstrom, 2000). They draw attention to issues or even create issues by using language that names, interprets and dramatizes them, that is the process of framing (Finnemore and Sikkink, 1998).

The second strategy used is social influence and/or sanctioning, which elicits norm-conforming behaviour through the distribution of social rewards and punishments (Flockhart, 2006). The importance of power asymmetries is critically important in this regard. Once norm entrepreneurs persuade state leaders to accept the appropriateness of an international norm, state leaders then become socializing agents in their own right, but use social influence in attempts to get a significant proportion of the population to accept the norm (ibid.). Additionally, mechanisms of coercion through which values and norms are internalized are not the only manifestations of the role of power in relation to norm convergence. Power also enters via a social theory of international politics, as dominant normative understandings and discourses that help to construct subjectivity (Adler and Bernstein, 2005; Guzzini, 2005), institutionalize practices and construct and transform social structures (Adler, 2005). In other words, power takes on an 'epistemic authority, the ability to socially construct dominant understandings and discourses' (Adler, 2005: 178). And very importantly, according to Mattern (2005), power also enters in the discursive ability of agents during a crisis situation, to force other agents to change for the sake of restoring their mutual 'we-feeling'. The latter point is particularly pertinent in the presence of regional hegemons who are able to use their discursive ability to create a sense of regionalism, as in the case of South Africa.

A third causal pathway to norm convergence is that of complex social learning, which varies from the rationalist strategies mentioned above. According to Checkel (2001), complex social learning is a process whereby agent interests and identities are shaped through and during interaction. This idea resonates with Adler's understanding of institutionalization, which is based on 'cognitive evolution', defined as a 'collective learning process that consists of the expansion in time and space of the background knowledge that constitutes practices and, thus, also in the expansion of "communities of practice" – the material representation of background knowledge in like-minded groups of individuals who practice the same practice' (Adler, 2005: 176).

It is imperative to note that socialization is not an outcome nor does it have to be successful (Schimmelfennig, 2000). The fact that it may not be a smooth process is a significant point for this investigation since it would be improbable to expect an easy transition from international norms to the domestic level, even when there is apparent conformity with the new norm. Pockets of resistance of varying strengths and oppositional capacities to the new norm should always be expected. This is evident in the example of the Nile River basin where no Nile riparian state has since signed or ratified the UN Convention on the Law of the Non-Navigational Uses of International Watercourses with only Kenya and Sudan voting for the Convention (Ramoeli, 2002). Instead, various states have resisted the acceptance of one or several principles found in the UN Convention. That said, however, there has been a broad-based and gradual indication of norm-compliant behaviour in the Nile River basin. It is therefore evident that norm convergence is a slow and incremental process of change.

Societal/domestic socialization

Not only do domestic political contexts affect the internalization of global norms, so too do domestic norms impact on domestic political processes. In a constructivist vein, Boekle et al. (1999) list three reasons why the behaviour of (foreign policy) decision-makers is influenced by domestic norms: (1) decision-makers have already internalized domestic norms through processes of political socialization to which all the citizens of a state are subject; (2) before representing their state in international society, politicians typically have had national political careers for a period of time whereby they have internalized more specific domestic expectations of appropriate behaviour; and (3) decision-makers conform to domestic norms because this corresponds with the way they see themselves as representatives of their society in the international environment. 'If a government does not comply with the societal expectations of behaviour addressed to it, it runs the risk of losing its recognition by [domestic] society as its legitimate representative' (ibid.: 10).

Foreign policy decision-makers and the state which they represent are therefore subject to both transnational and societal/domestic socialization processes. On the one hand, they have to comply with international norms; while on the other hand, the nation state expects its representatives to satisfy domestic norms at the international level (ibid.). If however, a situation arises where global and domestic norms contradict each other, a constructivist prediction is just as impossible as when these norms are completely absent on both levels or do not reveal sufficient commonality and/or specificity for them to be regarded as significant (ibid.). Boekle et al. (1999) attribute this potential dilemma to the fact that constructivism does not offer any criteria for evaluating whether decision-makers are influenced more by global norms or by domestic norms. 'If there are conflicting societal and international norms, a constructivist explanation is indeterminate because in such situations, decision-makers are free to choose the norm which best justifies their behaviour. Theoretically, therefore, it cannot be ruled out that actions are in fact guided by an interest with no normative base and are justified only ex post by recourse to a norm which matches the behavioural option chosen' (ibid.: 11).

Norm internalization

The final stage in the cycle is internalization. Here, the new norm becomes taken for granted, and conformance with its dictates is no longer (or at least rarely) questioned. If socialization is successful, the actor internalizes the expectations of behaviour, that is beliefs and practices imparted by its social environment (Boekle et al., 1999; Finnemore and Sikkink, 1998; Schimmelfennig, 2000). The actor does this by acknowledging the institutionalized modes of thought and behaviour as correct, and makes them 'its own', thus aligning its existing interests and preferences with them (Boekle, et al., 1999).

This does not, however, mean that internalization is devoid of deviant desires or behavioural preferences, but rather that internal sanctioning mechanisms are sufficiently effective to prevent deviant preferences from evolving into norm-violating actions (Axelrod, 1986; Schimmelfennig, 2000). Indeed internalization exists on a continuum of degrees, going from '. . . a situation in which the actor has to rely heavily on the effectiveness of internal sanctioning mechanisms to a situation in which such mechanisms are not needed because the social beliefs and practices are unchallenged' (Schimmelfennig, 2000: 112). To reiterate, not only do different states react differently to the same global norm but different 'parts of the state' (elite, epistemic community, public etc.) may react differently to the norm. Similarly, the mechanisms by which norms are internalized within states and the combination of conditions under which global norms are influential, vary greatly from state to state.

The challenge of conventional approaches to norm development

In an attempt to construct a multi-level normative framework for water governance in the two case-study areas, it is also useful to plot the pathways of 'conventional' norm development analysed in both the first wave of scholarship on normative change and the second wave as defined by Acharya (2004).

The first wave of scholarship comprises of three elements: norms being propagated are 'universal' or 'cosmopolitan' norms for example the struggle against racism, the campaign against landmines; transnational agents are the key norm entrepreneurs be they individuals or social movements; and it focuses heavily on Nadelmann's (1990: 481) 'moral proselytism' which resembles 'norm colonization' or the conversion of local contexts that regard resistance to cosmopolitan norms as illegitimate or immoral. As such, it is concerned mainly with top-down norm diffusion from the global level, conceptualized by the downward arrows in Figure 2.1.

In examining the first wave, Acharya points out two unfortunate tendencies of this type of scholarship. First, it gives causal primacy to 'international prescriptions' and

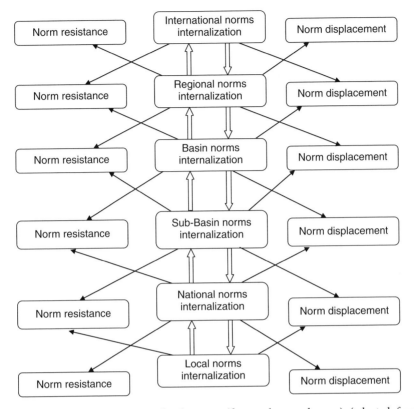

Figure 2.1 Conventional norm development (first and second wave) (adapted from Acharya, 2004)

therefore undermines the important agential role of 'norms that are deeply rooted in other types of social entities – regional, national, and sub-national groups' (Legro, 1997: 32). As Checkel observes, this focus on the global, creates an implicit dichotomy between good global norms and bad regional or local norms (Acharya, 2004; Checkel, 1999). For subscribers to this school of thought, universal norms advocating some sort of 'good' are considered to be more desirable, and subsequently, more likely to prevail than norms that are localized or particularistic (Finnemore, 1996; Finnemore and Sikkink, 1998). Secondly, Acharya argues that first-wave scholarship establishes a moral superiority, by regarding norm diffusion as a process of 'teaching by transnational agents' and in so doing, downplaying the agency role of local actors (Acharya, 2004).

The second wave of scholarship on normative change looks beyond international prescriptions and prioritizes the role of domestic political, organizational and cultural variables in conditioning the reception of new global norms (Acharya, 2004, 2007; Checkel, 1999, 2001; Cortell and Davis, 1996; Legro, 1997; Risse-Kappen, 1994; Williams, 2009). Concepts that fit with this wave of scholarship are: congruence, which describes the degree of fit between international and domestic norms (and not only the degree of fit between competing international norms) (Florini, 1996). Secondly, it includes Legro's notion of organizational culture, which is defined 'as a heuristic filter for perceptions and calculation' (Legro, 1997: 33, 36) that actors employ when evaluating and responding to external norms. And thirdly, it includes Checkel's concept of cultural match which examines situations where prescriptions reflected in an international norm are convergent with domestic norms, as reflected in discourse, the legal system and bureaucratic agencies (Checkel, 1999). As such, second-wave analyses examine the downward arrows but also the upward arrows in Figure 2.1.

However, Acharya argues that this wave is also limited in its ability to capture dynamic contexts. Since they are 'confined to the domestic arena' they can be 'unduly static' in their analyses of how historically constructed domestic norms prevent agent learning from occurring (Acharya, 2004). In response, Acharya (2004, 2007) advocates for a dynamic process of matchmaking through framing, grafting and localization. This chapter builds on Acharya's conceptual framework to look at the relationships between norms constructed at different levels of scale with different contexts and the ways in which both norms and contexts are transformed as a result of the other. This chapter attempts to construct the normative framework based on this premise of norm, as well as context-specific dynamism.

The Maryland School

The Maryland School (so referred because of the large and influential body of research that was spear-headed by this centre at the time that Ken Conca was based there) has made a valuable contribution to the field of hydropolitics focusing on the principled content of international river basin management, by using empirical datasets to investigate whether a cooperative international approach to the management of water is emerging. In other words, these scholars have attempted to examine the relationship between basin-specific politics and global principled developments and subsequently, whether norm diffusion of the global norm set of transboundary cooperation has taken place and been socialized at the basin level. The dataset compiled and analysed comprised of basin-specific interstate agreements for the period 1980–2000 (Conca, 2006; Conca et al., 2006). Through coding methods, content was analysed using the global norm set of transboundary cooperation (or as referred to by the Maryland School, emerging principles of international water law) as the yardstick (Conca et al., 2006). Central goals for the study included (1) Determining whether governments are converging on common principles, norms and values, when they articulate a governing framework for a shared basin, and (2) Examining whether any such convergence follows a parallel trajectory to the trends in soft international water law (Conca, 2006; Conca et al., 2006).

Several core datasets were pooled together to compile a single analytical dataset, such as the Systematic Index of International Water Resources Treaties, Declarations, Acts and Cases by Basin (FAO, 1978), the Transboundary Freshwater Dispute Database (TFDD) at Oregon State University and the FAOLEX legal database (Conca, 2006; Conca et al., 2006). Conca identifies more than 150 basin-specific treaties that set out the rights and responsibilities of riparian states sharing a specific international river basin (Conca, 2006; Turton, 2005a; Turton, 2008b). By analysing these basin-specific treaties, a set of protonorms[1] were compiled. These include the global norm set of transboundary cooperation, norms of water privatization/marketization, techno-rational norms of integrated water resource management constructed by water policy experts, norms of human rights and the preservation of local cultures and ecosystems.

Two main claims on norm convergence were therefore tested in the Maryland study:

- Top-down norm dissemination from the international level:
  Convergence on the global norm set of transboundary cooperation across individual basin-specific treaties, which involves highly varied political, economic and ecological landscapes, could be read as significant evidence of a global normative pull, that is the top-down process of norm dissemination (Conca, 2006; Conca et al., 2006).
- Bottom-up norm aggregation:
  Alternatively, the causal relationship could be the opposite of the first claim, meaning that the global framework simply reflects accumulated practice in the basin-specific treaties. Simply put, it may be the case that a bottom-up process of aggregation and lateral diffusion of norms is at play (Conca, 2006; Conca et al., 2006).

The third claim summarized their findings:

- Norm contestation:
  There is no link between these two levels with basin-specific accords reflecting a rival set of norms (Conca, 2006; Conca et al., 2006).

Claim 1: Top-down norm dissemination

According to Conca and his team, top-down norm dissemination rests on the premise that a set of principles formulated at the global level would be adopted at the basin level (Conca, 2006; Conca et al., 2006). Evidence of this process occurring would be reflected in basin-specific treaties that provide greater depth, breadth and specificity of these global principles in basin-specific agreements as opposed to mere acceptance at a global level (i.e. signing an international agreement). Using the TFDD and FAOLEX as primary sources of data, Conca et al. (2006) extracted 62 river management agreements worldwide, which they then subjected to a rigorous statistical analysis with reference to the 8 core principles of the 1997 UN Watercourses Convention in terms of breadth, depth and specificity (ibid.). As introduced in Chapter 1, the eight core principles are (ibid.):

- Equitable use.
- Avoidance of significant harm to other riparian states.
- Sovereign equality and territorial integrity.
- Information exchange.
- Consultation with other riparian states.
- Prior notification.
- Environmental protection.
- Peaceful resolution of disputes.

Statistical analysis of the dataset revealed that several of the eight core normative elements seem to be emerging, but each was coalescing around different river basin configurations in different ways (Conca, 2006; Turton, 2005a; Turton, 2008a, 2008b; Turton and Ashton, 2008). On the one hand there was a distinct correlation around the issue of openness and transparency, such as the commitment to information exchange, prior notification and the peaceful resolution of disputes. Of noteworthy importance, none of these indicators correlated with the core principles relating to the state's right to water. Similarly, indicators such as specific water allocation formulae, or whether domestic waters were exempt from the provisions of the agreement, coalesced with that of equitable use. From this assessment, the Maryland scholars concluded that one subset of the dataset under investigation is rooted in principles of openness and sustainability, whereas a second distinct subset is rooted in the state's right to water (Conca, 2006). It is noteworthy to mention, that according to Conca (2006), emergence of these principles does not reflect deepening and consequently, norm diffusion, of the norm set of transboundary cooperation.

Considering that the UN Watercourses Convention dates only to 1997 and as such is still a relatively new framework, Conca et al. (2006) qualify that it is still possible for these principles to diffuse to the basin level. However, the principled content of the convention emerged and evolved over a period of roughly a few decades prior to this and was formalized as early as 1991 in the ILC articles (Conca et al., 2006). If global norm diffusion was taking place and exerting a significant normative pull on basin-level agreements, the expected result would be diffusion and deepening of the global norm set of transboundary cooperation in the 1990s, relative to the 1980s, in terms of becoming more widespread over time, and deepening in the sense of greater specificity of the responsibilities or obligations created for states (ibid.).

Conca et al. (2006), therefore found little evidence that the ILC process and the UN Watercourses Convention has exerted a direct, tangible, unidirectional pull on the principled content of basin agreements. What is apparent instead is that most of the core principles appear as well established early in the study period as they are by its end with no evidence of deepening of principles within basin-level agreements. Only one principle, that of consultation, showed signs of deepening, which indicated that forming a permanent basin commission became the predominant specific mechanism for regular consultation. The relative specificity or intrusiveness of the other principles did not change over time (ibid.).

Claim 2: Bottom-up norm aggregation

In terms of bottom-up norm aggregation, Conca et al., argue that evidence of this claim would be reflected in a notable increase of new international basins subscribing to normative elements present in other international basins and one would see a marked increase in basin-specific agreements. In other words, norm aggregation would take place horizontally by spilling over from one basin to another, and thereby form a unified global normative approach/framework. However, these scholars found relatively few international basins as being the subject of significant water-related agreements in the past two decades. Moreover, short-term fluctuations notwithstanding, they found that the rate at which international agreements were reached was not increasing over time. Agreements that did emerge, however, were concentrated in basins with a prior history of river cooperation, but that this tendency to cooperate was not spreading to new basins (ibid.). Additionally, few agreements include representation by *most* riparians, and less still include *all* riparian states.

The interpretations of the Maryland School are that there is a strong tendency for cooperation to be concentrated in international river basins where a prior history of cooperation already exists (Conca, 2006). However, there is no strong evidence of the diffusion of these norms. More significantly, most of these norms seemed to be well established already at the beginning of the study period, suggesting that they did not evolve more over time. Additionally, Conca argues that, while the 1997 UN Convention goes well beyond merely codifying existing principles at the basin level, some of the core themes namely, universal participation, equitable use and the avoidance of significant harm, appear only sporadically in specific basin-level agreements (ibid.). There is, therefore not sufficient compelling evidence to convince the Maryland School that a common normative structure is emerging in the sphere of interstate cooperation, and according to their findings, there is no evidence to suggest that international legal principles are taking on greater depth, or even moving in an identifiable direction (ibid.).

Claim 3 (Findings): Norm contestation and dynamism

The Maryland School's main finding was therefore not a unidirectional progression towards a global regime for international rivers but, rather, a more complex and dynamic pattern of principled evolution (Conca, 2006; Conca et al., 2006). However, statistical coalescence in terms of correlations were found on two different normative frameworks (one stressing shared river protection, the other stressing the state's rights to water) (ibid.). Moreover, these authors argue that an uneven normative evolutionary process is occurring where some key principles appear to be subject to a global normative pull and take on deeper meaning, become more widespread and show signs of progressive development over time, such as the principles of environmental protection, consultation and peaceful resolution of disputes; but many others do not, such as that of equitable utilization. Additionally, 'periods of momentum are reversed, and the meaning of principles may be rendered more shallow and vague over time rather than deeper and more precise' (Conca et al., 2006: 281). The no harm principle, for example, enjoyed a modest increase in the 1990s, yet it remains poorly specified, and ambiguous in basin-specific agreements. These and other non-linearities make the term 'norm diffusion' a poor metaphor, according to the Maryland School.

Beyond quantitative analyses

While the findings by the Maryland School have proved highly significant in advancing the discourse on the principled content of cooperative management by making it the dependent variable, rather than simply the probability of agreement formation (ibid.), several limitations become evident, particularly as they pertain to the quantitative method used.

According to Turton (2005a), the 62 agreements used for analysis by the Maryland School covered 36 international river basins, or roughly one-seventh of the global total of international river basins. Only one-quarter, or 16 of these 62 agreements, are the first agreements for the particular river basin (Turton, 2005a; Turton, 2008b). The remaining 46 agreements used were not first-time agreements, indicating that there was evidence of prior agreement in the same river basin (ibid.). This suggests that at least three-quarters of the agreements analysed occurred in basins with a previous cooperative history between riparian states (ibid.). According to Conca (2006), it therefore does not appear that the idea of creating an instrument of shared governance by means of a regime is rapidly diffusing aggregately to new, previously uncovered basins. In other words, there is no evidence that norms are being diffused aggregately via horizontal trajectories (bottom-up) to other basins.

In his critique of Conca's empirical findings that regimes are not emerging via a basin-cumulative path, Turton makes the case that the dataset used to achieve that result, might have been too small to generate truly conclusive findings (Turton, 2005a; Turton, 2008b). First, of the total 62 agreements, 46 are bilateral agreements (three-fourth) while 16 (one-fourth) contain 3 or more parties (Conca, 2006). Significantly, two-thirds of the bilateral agreements are in basins where there are more than three riparian states (Turton, 2005a), that is to say, some riparian states have been (deliberately) excluded from a particular agreement. In this regard, multilateral agreements are over-represented in the dataset (ibid.). Two-thirds of the world's international river basins are bilateral (176 of the 263 known basins or 67%), yet more than three-quarters of the agreements written during the study period from 1980–2000 (49 of 62 or 79%) were in multilateral basins (having 3 or more riparian states within their hydrological configuration) (ibid.). This indicates that due to the temporal frame, more multilateral basins were analysed than was realistically proportionate.

Secondly, within these multilateral basins, Conca concludes that a bilateral regime is more common. However, according to Turton, in the six southern African 'Basins at

Risk' as defined by Wolf et al. (2003) (i.e. Orange-Senqu, Limpopo, Incomati, Kunene, Okavango, Zambezi), multilateral basin-wide regimes now exist in all of the basins. Even in the most complex basin in the region due to the multiplicity of riparian states and stakeholders involved – the Zambezi – the ZAMCOM Agreement, was signed (by Angola, Botswana, Malawi, Mozambique, Namibia, Tanzania and Zimbabwe) on 13 July 2004 and entered into force in 2011 after the last party, Zambia, signed on to the Agreement. Conca et al. (2006) does concede that the presence of an agreement tells us nothing about its capacity to 'swim upstream' normatively against the prevailing distribution of power and interests, and therefore provides little evidence of cumulative bottom-up norm diffusion.

One then needs to look for normative influence and spread beyond basin agreements, and in other sociopolitical fora, other than legal texts. Indeed, a qualitative analysis is also important to examine the effects of non-regulatory variables that influence actor interests, identities and behaviour. For instance, several other frameworks exist of which the Zambezi basin and its riparian states form part, indicating that merely analysing one agreement and its content is too narrow an analytical tool to measure bottom-up norm diffusion. The Revised SADC Water Protocol, for instance, can be regarded as being '. . . a surrogate regime in the case of the Zambezi, mitigating against conflict potential and providing the necessary legal recourse when needed' (Turton, 2005a: 37) since the ZAMCOM Agreement was being negotiated long before the first SADC Water Protocol came into force. It was then decided that since the SADC Protocol could include all SADC states and not only the eight Zambezi riparians, the ZAMCOM negotiations would be temporarily halted to allow for the Protocol to be drafted. This illustrates that norm convergence has not followed a strictly linear path in southern Africa, but definitely shows signs of normative diffusion and convergence, where convergence penetrates different levels of scale simultaneously (i.e. basin to region or region indirectly to global).

Processes of norm convergence

How then is it possible to analyse patterns/evolution of principled content and indeed norm convergence from the global level down, from the local to state to regional level, and laterally, from basin to basin? The causal pathway to convergence, and therefore, compliance with regional regimes is a part function of social sanctioning (coercion) due to inherent power asymmetries at play in transboundary governance; and instrumental calculations (strategic social construction). This causal pathway is based on the assumption that explanations based on norms and identities cannot be separated from a discussion on material and structural factors when it comes to the question of where norms come from and why they are sustained. Indeed, power and interests may not explain everything, but they often account for why certain norms emerge and are sustained to influence policy as opposed to others. However, there is also something to be said for a non-instrumental causal pathway.

According to Checkel, this occurs 'Where state compliance results from social learning and deliberation that lead to preference change. In this view, the choice mechanism is non-instrumental and the environment . . . is one of social interaction between agents, where mutual learning and the discovery of new preferences replace unilateral calculation' (Checkel, 2001: 560). Following these causal pathways, this study plots norm convergence through three main tracks: global norm convergence from the top-down through diffusion and localization; regional norm convergence via lateral tracks of state-to-state or from state-to-basin-to-region; and bottom-up norm convergence from the local to national levels.

Global norm diffusion from the top-down

Conca's analysis of top-down norm dissemination (claim 1) rests on the premise that a set of principles formulated at the global level would be adopted at the basin level in basin-specific treaties that provide greater depth, breadth and specificity of global principles (Conca, 2006; Conca et al., 2006). Top-down norm diffusion in this study refers to processes whereby global norms and norm sets are directly and *indirectly* integrated into regional and basin-wide legal and institutional frameworks.

In addition to tracking the development of these norms, an analysis of whose interests are met and whose are redefined when global norms are socialized is also important. This involves an understanding of which power relations are at play. These normative trajectories may not be linear, and so evidence of their influence must therefore be sought in other areas outside of conventional basin-specific treaties. Moreover, evidence of their influence is not only reflected in the verbatim acceptance of these norms, and as such, global norms may be transformed into something different when localized. Indeed, as Williams (2009) points out, global norms are not automatically accepted as is in different regional contexts and subsequently, the commitment to them will vary depending on the local context.

Amitav Acharya has described the process of norm localization as a congruence-building process that occurs as a result of the 'contestation between emerging transnational norms and pre-existing regional normative and social orders' (Acharya, 2004: 241). Norm localization also argues that successful norm diffusion depends on the degree to which external norms provide opportunities for localisation or the degree to which they resonate with historically constructed domestic norms (Acharya, 2004; Checkel, 1999; Williams, 2009). Here, Acharya prioritizes the agency role of local agents or 'insider proponents' (Acharya, 2007). Although external pressures are still significant 'in the construction of regional orders . . . local responses to power may be more important' (ibid.: 642). These insider proponents will build congruence between transnational norms and local beliefs and practices through framing (the process where norm entrepreneurs use language that names, interprets and dramatizes e.g. securitized water) and grafting[2] (a tactic norm entrepreneurs use to institutionalize a new norm by associating it with a pre-existing norm in the same issue area, which makes a similar prohibition or injunction). Acharya argues that the process of norm localization '. . . may start with a reinterpretation and re-representation of the outside norm, including framing and grafting, but may extend into more complex processes of reconstitution to make an outside norm congruent with a pre-existing local normative order' (Acharya, 2004: 244).

Williams aptly suggests that African international society should, in this sense, be thought of as 'a partly autonomous society because it is embedded within a wider, global society of states that influences how African states think about sovereignty, statehood and security' (Williams, 2009: 396). Understanding this degree of autonomy is crucial because regional identities are constructed more from within than without (Acharya, 2007).

Regional norm convergence

In addition to processes of norm convergence from the global level down, norms are also constructed at the regional level and emerge through state-to-state or state-to-basin-to-region tracks. This type of convergence is based on multilateral cooperative agendas and the movement towards a community of interest around particular issue clusters. Conca's view of norm convergence at the regional level (claim 2 bottom-up norm aggregation or cumulative norm convergence) describes the way in which one basin's normative framework influences another, reflected in an increase of new international basins subscribing to normative elements present in other international basins. In contrast, given the uniqueness of each basin. I have chosen to focus on how two different basins construct a regional normative framework, either through state-to-state tracks or state-to-basin-to-region tracks.

Bottom-up (local to national) norm convergence

While Conca's analysis does not delve into this track in detail, this study argues that local sub-national norms are crucial to the way in which global and regional and basin-wide norms are accepted, localized or resisted. For example, the 'embedded wisdom' based on the sacred and equitable (and sustainable) use of water, inherent in local cultural practices has had very real implications for conservation policies at a national level.

Norm dynamism/contestation

Similar to Conca's conclusion of norm dynamism, that is a more complex and dynamic pattern of principled evolution (Conca, 2006; Conca et al., 2006), norm dynamism in this study refers to the outcome or combination of various normative tracks. While Conca's results focus on 'norm fights' or the contestation between various norms and norm sets, the emphasis here is rather on coexistence and complementarity. This implies that normative frameworks change, and are changed, by various contexts which result in outcomes unique to particular river basins and regions.

Notes

1 According to Conca, a protonorm is defined as a norm that has become sufficiently recognizable and well established, so as to become available for application to watershed governance in basins and watersheds that are beyond the direct reach of the agreement concerned (Conca, 2006).

2 Grafting is also referred to as 'incremental norm transplantation' (Farrell, 2001).

3

The Orange-Senqu River Basin and the Local Past

The Orange-Senqu River is known by a variety of names based on who you are, and where you live. It is often referred to as the Oranjerivier in Afrikaans, the Gariep River in Nama and the Senqu River in Sesotho, some of the most widely spoken languages along various parts of the river. In South Africa, the name *Gariep* (meaning great) is often used, which originates from the terms *Nu* (meaning black) *Gariep* and *Gij'Gariep* (meaning 'tawny' or 'yellow' as a result of its muddy colour), which are the precolonial Nama (which forms part of the Khoisan linguistic family) names for different parts of the river. It is also sometimes referred to by the name of any one of its major tributaries: the Caledon, Senqu, Kraai, Vaal, Hartebees or Fish Rivers (Earle et al., 2005). In this book, the term Orange-Senqu is used, as this is the internationally recognized term used in all multilateral agreements regarding the river today.

The river's multiplicity of names also reflects the multiplicity of actors, interests and demands on the river. Although the process of naming the Orange-Senqu has been a contentious one at times, it is significant and is analogous to the process of norm convergence at play in the basin, where actor identities have been reconstructed and interests have converged on a normative trajectory to one more fitting of the basin as a whole rather than a component thereof. Now, different interests have converged and the name itself has become a combination of different identities – *Orange* and *Senqu*. This chapter documents norm convergence in the Orange-Senqu Basin, paying particular attention to the development of a community of interests in the basin and the importance of local dynamics in facilitating the socialization of particular norms and explicitly steering state and/or basin behaviour towards a multilateral cooperative agenda in which the majority of actors have bought.

An overview of the Orange-Senqu River basin

The Orange-Senqu River flows through four riparian countries in southern Africa: Lesotho, South Africa, Botswana and Namibia. It originates in the rocky Highlands of Lesotho and flows westward for roughly 2,300 km (Heyns, 2003), to its mouth in

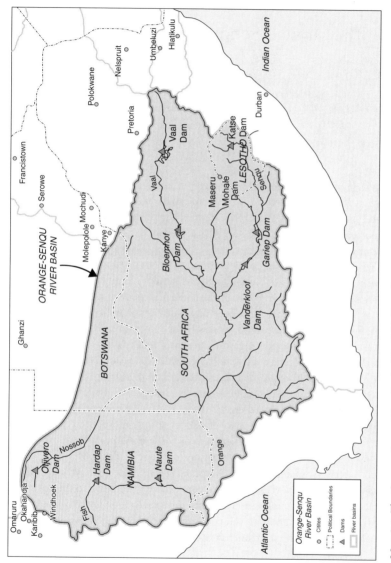

Map 3.1 The Orange-Senqu River basin (Hatfield Consultants Africa, 2011)[1]

the Atlantic Ocean, where it forms the contiguous border between South Africa and Namibia (see Map 3.1). The basin spans a wide range of ecological zones from the mountainous area of the Lesotho Highlands, through the savannah grasslands and rugged hills of South Africa's central plateau, to the desert conditions in the western part of the basin in Namibia (Bohensky et al., 2004; ORASECOM, 2012). As such, rainfall also varies from high rainfall in the eastern parts of the basin (over 2,000 mm per annum) to Namibia's hyper-arid area where rainfall is less than 50 mm per annum.

The Orange-Senqu River basin is also the largest river basin south of the Zambezi River with a catchment area of approximately 1 million km^2 (DWA, 2011) and an estimated natural runoff of more than 12,000km^3/yr (ibid.). The latter figure represents the average river flow that would occur if there were no developments of any kind in the catchment (ibid.). However, very little of this total run-off reaches the mouth, estimated to be in the order of 5,500 km^3/yr (Earle et al., 2005). This is due in large part to extensive water abstraction in the Vaal River basin, most of which is for domestic and industrial purposes in South Africa; immense evapotranspiration; the construction of large dams; and inter-basin transfer schemes that deliver/divert water to neighbouring river basins (Mare, 2007). See Table 3.1.

Still, irrigated agriculture is the biggest user in the Orange-Senqu River basin, accounting for roughly 54% of water use, while 10% goes towards environmental demands contrasting with the 2% that goes to urban and industrial supply (see Figure 3.1; DWA, 2011). In addition to the water demands mentioned above, evaporation losses (32%) from the Orange-Senqu River and run-off to the ocean through the mouth and canals (2%) account for 34% of water use, depending upon the flow of water (and consequently the surface area) in the river (ibid.).

The Orange-Senqu is therefore the most developed (and modified) river in the region, comprising of 31 dams having a storage capacity of more than 12 × 106m^3 (24 in South Africa, 5 in Namibia and 2 in Lesotho) (Heyns, 2003). The most notable development is the Lesotho Highlands Water Project (LHWP), the largest international inter-basin transfer (IBT) scheme in the world, which transfers water from Lesotho to South Africa's Gauteng Province, watering big cities such as Johannesburg and Pretoria (Basson et al., 1997).

Table 3.1 Physical characteristics of the Orange-Senqu River basin

Orange-Senqu River basin – major features	
Total basin area	1 million km^2
Area rainfall (mm/y)	Average: 330; range > 2000 to < 50
Estimated natural run-off	12,000 km^3/yr
Water demand	Irrigation – 54%, environmental demands – 10%, urban and industrial use – 2%, evaporation and run-off to the ocean through the mouth and canals – 34% (as supplied from the Gariep and Vanderkloof) (DWA, 2011)
Population	19 million (year 2002)
Water availability	<1000 m^3 per capita

Source: Earle et al., 2005; Mare, 2007

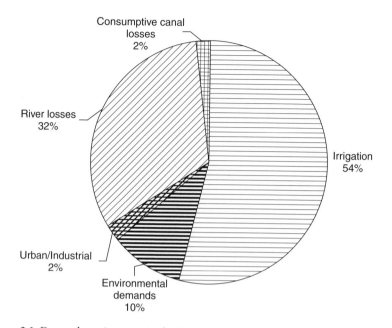

Figure 3.1 Demand requirements in the Orange-Senqu River basin (DWA, 2011)

Table 3.2 Contributions to the Orange-Senqu River basin by country

Item	Lesotho	South Africa	Botswana	Namibia
Area in basin (%)	3.4	64.2	7.9	24.5
Area in basin (km²)	34,000	642,000	79,000	245,000
MAR (%)	41	55	0	4

Source: ORASECOM, 2012

The contributions of the riparian states to the basin in terms of mean annual run-off (MAR), as well as the area of the basin falling within each state vary considerably (as shown in Table 3.2). Lesotho provides the basin with 41% of its water, from a mere 3.4% of the total basin area, while 64.2% of the basin falls within South Africa, 24.5% in Namibia and 7.9% in Botswana (ORASECOM, 2012). Moreover, virtually the entire population of Lesotho is resident in the basin (see Map 3.1 and Table 3.2), which intricately links its national interests to the Orange-Senqu River basin.[2]

Also, Lesotho is highly dependent on royalties from South Africa for inter-basin water transfer for economic development, and together with garments, the export of water forms the majority of its export revenue.

South Africa has the largest area of the basin within its territory (an estimated 642000 km²), contributes the most water in terms of MAR and is also the largest user, accounting for between roughly 82% (Earle et al., 2005; ORASECOM, 2012) and 97%

of annual total use (Lange et al., 2007). In terms of national strategic importance, the Orange-Senqu River basin is the most important river basin in South Africa and includes the Vaal River basin which is the largest and most important tributary of the Orange-Senqu River (DWA, 2011). The Vaal River supplies water to the industrial heartland of southern Africa, including the Greater Pretoria and Johannesburg areas (Basson et al., 1997; Turton, 2003a). Additionally, it also supplies water to some of the largest gold and platinum mines in the world as well as many of the world's largest coal reserves (ibid.). The industrial areas supported from the Vaal River are also responsible for producing more than 50% of South Africa's wealth as well as more than 80% of the country's electricity requirements (DWA, 2011). Six of South Africa's nine provincial regions are in some or other way affected by the basin and some of the largest and most ambitious water projects to be undertaken in Africa are situated here (ibid.).

Interestingly, Botswana contributes no streamflow and uses none of the surface water in the basin, but is still considered to be a riparian state due to the ephemeral Nossob and Molopo Rivers. The Molopo River is suspected to have contributed to surface run-off contributions historically but is now blocked by the Kalahari Desert dunes downstream of its confluence with the Nossob River (Heyns, 2003). The Nossob and Molopo Rivers therefore, do not reach the Orange-Senqu, but it is suspected that Botswana contributes groundwater from the Molopo River and its dependency is related to groundwater aquifers.[3]

Some scholars have argued that Botswana has made use of its legal rights to engage in basin issues as a 'normal' riparian state, and by doing so, has created an avenue for potential future water supply from the LHWP, which is technically feasible but too expensive to be realistic at the time of writing (Turton, 2008b). Other policymakers argue that Botswana's interest in the Orange-Senqu might be by way of trying to give support to other key areas[4] such as strategic interests in the Limpopo River basin, on which it is highly dependent (Earle et al., 2005).

Namibia is the most downstream riparian state with a high reliance on the Orange-Senqu for agricultural activity in the south of the country (Kranz et al., 2005a) even though a relatively small proportion of its population (8.9%) live in the basin's territory. Namibia has an extremely arid hydroclimate, a high level of water stress and is also unique in that all its perennial rivers are transboundary (see Bohensky et al., 2004 and Falkenmark and Widstrand, 1992 for water stress scale). These characteristics make it particularly vulnerable to external dynamics regarding the river, and Namibia therefore relies heavily on international water resources to meet internal demand (GEF, 2005; Kranz et al., 2005a). Specifically, Namibia relies on South Africa for future water storage developments to increase its assurance of supply. In the southern parts of Namibia, the greatest development potential lies in irrigation, and this subsequently creates the highest demand for water (Kranz et al., 2005a).

Water availability is therefore a main transboundary issue in the region. Of the four riparian states of the Orange-Senqu River, three are classified among the driest countries in the SADC namely, South Africa, Botswana and Namibia. As already noted, South Africa is highly economically dependent on the Orange-Senqu River, with a staggering 100% of the gross domestic product (GDP) of Gauteng Province dependent on inter-basin transfers involving the Orange-Senqu River system (Basson et al., 1997; Turton, 2003a). Future water demands are also expected in Lesotho where urban and industrial development in the rapidly urbanising lowlands is expected to contribute to marginal increases in the demand on the resource (Kingdom of Lesotho, 2004; Kistin and Ashton, 2008; Kranz et al., 2005a).

Finally, institutional capacity, be it in the form of river basin commissions and regional water structures, or whether it is defined as a legal framework in the form of formal treaties and protocols, or technical cooperation in the form of informal working groups and technical task teams or generally warm relations, has had a long history in the basin. Negotiations over cooperative management have been ongoing between various combinations of the riparian states since the 1890s, which has resulted in a wide range of bilateral and multilateral interstate or government-led commissions and agreements, to project-based organizations and treaties, to technical committees (Turton et al., 2004). This cooperative framework has been, to a large extent, determined by the hydropolitical history of riparian relations (Ashton and Turton 2005; Meissner, 2004) and the domestic context of national regime types (Jacobs, 2010a).

The basin is therefore considered to be the most institutionalized river basin in the SADC region and is regarded by many as the role model for transboundary river basin management. It has the most comprehensive history of successful water regime creation in the entire SADC region due to a high dependence on the resource-base for long-term economic growth by virtually all riparian states. Scholars have argued that water resource management has been placed within a political frame where it can be debated, rather than in a security frame where security specialists deal with it in a highly secretive and non-transparent manner (ibid.). Arguably, political framing (desecuritization) of water has facilitated a smoother socialization process of the global transboundary cooperation norm set by encouraging debate and the dissemination of knowledge at the state level and within epistemic communities. Alternatively, the domestic context could be more conducive to the socialization of global principles since versions of these principles (such as equitable utilization, cooperative governance, communication and so forth) have existed in historical agreements that predate global agreements. In essence, the domestic context allows for 'normative fit' with global principles.

A brief hydropolitical history of the Orange-Senqu and the winds of change

Several key factors have greatly influenced national and regional approaches to transboundary cooperative water governance in the basin. These include: colonial and apartheid legacies; South Africa's position as regional hegemon, and the subsequent apprehension of neighbouring states to this position; riparian disputes between South Africa and Namibia (border dispute); SADC intervention (South Africa and Botswana) in Lesotho (Operation Boleas); the origin of SADC; and the post-independence water sector reforms in South Africa, Namibia and Lesotho in the 1990s and that continue to this day. These factors, combined with localized military conflicts or civil wars during the last three decades further illustrate the strategic and sensitive nature of water in the region (Ashton and Turton, 2005; Turton, 2003d, 2004; Turton and Earle, 2005).

During the colonial period, the political geography and demarcation of states, as well as the structuring of national water sectors, within the region was a product of colonial legacies (Ashton and Turton, 2005). Arbitrary state borders were set with little consideration of how this might have impacted and/or divided social, cultural and ethnic groupings (ibid.). Oftentimes, previously common pool rivers were used to delineate political boundaries, thus politicizing the nature of water. The Orange-Senqu River, for example, forms the contiguous border of South Africa and Namibia, making the likelihood of a border dispute emerging (Meissner, 2001; Turton, 2005a; Turton, 2008b). It is therefore no wonder that a century-long dispute has been on-going over territorial and other ancillary (water-related) rights along the lower Orange River, or stated more specifically, the exact location of the border within the river (Meissner 2001). This translated into a 2-km-wide window of uncertainty depending on the size and timing of large and small flood events (Ashton, 2000b). The dispute had enormous repercussions for officials who had to decide on the positions of prospecting mining leases of offshore minerals such as oil, gas and diamonds, as well as for delineating the catch areas of commercial fisheries (ibid.).

The demarcation, made in 1890, by the British colonial administration, identified it as the high water level on the northern bank (Ashton, 2000b). This effectively meant that the entire river fell within South African territory, and therefore, deprived Namibia of independent access to the water (Ashton, 2000b; Hangula, 1993; Heyns, 1995). Promises were made to revisit this demarcation, and that the border would be moved to the middle of the river. Several scholars argue that this was an unfulfilled promise tactfully used during the run-up to Namibian independence (Ashton, 2000a, 2000b; Maletsky, 1999; Meissner, 2001).

Despite attempts by both of the original colonial powers and, subsequently, by the South African Government since 1910, the dispute lasted for decades (Ashton, 2000b). Only in 1991, shortly after Namibian independence, did South Africa agree to change the position of the boundary from the northern bank to the centre of the main river channel or the *thalweg*, the universally accepted term for a border demarcation, meaning the deepest continuous line along the watercourse (ibid.). This decision allowed Namibia to claim its fair share of all resources in, and related to (minerals, fisheries, oil), the Orange River (ibid.). The decision has, however, not been without complications. In particular, it has resulted in considerable confusion as to the validity of existing alluvial mining leases in the bed of the river, and has denied some local residents on the South African side, the right to graze their livestock on islands that have now become part of Namibian territory (Meissner, 2001). As such, the issue is still, not fully resolved.

However, despite predictions that the border dispute had the potential to tarnish South Africa's hydropolitical image, it has never escalated into a major issue that could threaten international relations between South Africa and Namibia (Turton, 2005a, 2005b). There are a range of possible answers for this, but one is arguably due to the role South Africa played in Namibia's political history, as the UN mandated trustee of South West Africa.

Based on these and other happenings throughout history, it is easy to see how colonialism could have a major impact on the hydropolitics of southern Africa. Moreover, by the early 1960s, the desire for independence was acutely felt by all southern African states (Turton and Earle, 2005). The Portuguese colonies of Angola and Mozambique achieved their independence through wars of liberation, while the British colonies of Southern Rhodesia,[5] Northern Rhodesia,[6] Nyasaland,[7] South Africa and also South West Africa (through the 'Struggle' from 1966 to 1989), achieved theirs through various forms of anti-colonial struggle (ibid.). Although Bechuanaland,[8] Basutoland[9] and Swaziland were never British colonies, and operated as fully functional monarchies, they were British Protectorates, appeals which they made during the time of Zulu national expansion and Boer settler land invasions in the previous century (ibid.).

The British withdrawal from the various colonies in the 1960s, combined with the domino effect of newfound independence therefore gave new impetus to the various liberation movements operating at the time (ibid.). More specifically, it opened up new areas and access to safe bases from which they could train guerrilla fighters, and regroup if needed (ibid.). These events, combined with the resultant armed struggle contributed to the securitization of water, which was based on a strong military response to any threat, supported by destabilization via economic means (Gutteridge, 1983).

On the other hand, the wave of independence that spread across the region, laid the foundation for greater regional cooperation and coordination in the water sector (Ashton, 2002; Heyns, 2002; Ramoeli, 2002; Turton, 2003a, 2003d). The origins of SADC actually predate these developments and go back to 1980. Its foundational objectives included the establishment of an institutionalized common front against apartheid South Africa, and to combat against South Africa's military aggression and economic hegemony. It was only after the abolition of apartheid that South Africa was allowed to join regional political institutions, as part of the process of resuming its position among sovereign states, and the spirit of 'community' (Kranz and Vidaurre, 2008). This historical development has had its effect on the nature of regional hydropolitics today, with neighbouring states adopting an arguably cautionary approach to South Africa's leadership role in several multilateral fora and institutions. However, over the past decade, South Africa has been successful in slowly reducing the distrust with which it was perceived (Turton, 2003c).

Additionally, the post-independence period had further implications for the hydropolitics of the region. This is best encapsulated in Operation Boleas. In 1998, in the aftermath of the 1986 military *coup d'état* in Lesotho, and South Africa's political transition in 1994, political instability broke out in Lesotho following allegations of elections fraud. A call was made to SADC by the then Prime Minister of Lesotho, Pakalitha Mosisili, requesting military assistance. In response, SADC decided to send in a peacekeeping force made up of soldiers from South Africa and Botswana. When Operation Boleas entered Lesotho's borders it came under heavy and unanticipated fire, causing it to split into two (Turton, 2003d). One element focused on Maseru, while the other moved in to secure the infrastructure related to LHWP and particularly, the securing of Katse Dam. This is therefore cited, by some, as an example of a water conflict, as the intervention was perceived as South Africa's protection of its national interest, identified to be the strategic water reserve of Katse Dam, which is 'a major water source supplying South Africa with fresh water' (Berman and Sams, 2000: 185). However, other scholars disagree with this interpretation emphasizing the fact that the issue had less to do with a water conflict than it had to do with apartheid politics (Meissner, 2004). Additionally, South Africa insisted that the intervention was justified by the Lesotho Prime Minister's request and was sanctioned by SADC. Whichever point of view you choose to accept, the event unfortunately caused strained relations between South Africa and Lesotho as evidenced in various newspaper articles at the time (Lawrence, 1998; Mills, 1998; Mopheme, 1998).

It was under these pressures, the end of the Cold War as well as the wave of political independence that spread across all countries in the region that social and economic reforms began to take place (Kranz and Vidaurre, 2008). This directly influenced the reformulation of water policies and legislation, most notably, South Africa's water reform process since its first democratic elections in 1994 (Kranz and Vidaurre, 2008). The hydropolitical history of the basin depicts a central aspect of riparian relations, that is, a high degree of technical cooperation despite high levels of political distrust experienced between states as a result of colonialism, apartheid and Cold Water politics. This environment greatly influenced cooperative strategies in the 1990s and beyond. This is not to say that cooperation was born out of disputes and distrust, but rather that they played a significant role in shaping the nature of cooperation today, that is, a comparatively high degree of institutional development. In fact, cooperation in the Orange-Senqu has been hailed as a model for effective governance.

Institutional and legislative development

An obvious way for states to cooperate over the management of shared waters such as the Orange-Senqu River is by negotiating international agreements (Hiddema and Erasmus, 2007), which ensures the sovereignty of states and allows them to reconcile national legal and jurisdictional aspects with regional legal and jurisdictional infrastructure. The most significant international, regional and basin-wide legal instruments for the Orange-Senqu River basin includes the 1997 UN Convention, which has not yet been entered into force (and will only come into force once 36 parties have ratified it), the 2000 SADC Revised Protocol on Shared Watercourses, as well as the Agreement between Botswana, Lesotho, Namibia and South Africa on the establishment of the Orange-Senqu River Commission (ORASECOM) signed in 2000. Several significant bilateral agreements are also significant and have contributed to the high level of technical collaboration experienced in the basin despite the sociopolitical histories of riparian states.

The adoption, and thereafter, socialization of international norms and principles into the national law of riparian states is noteworthy. The incorporation of such norms to be implemented by the states involved can occur in several different ways and need not only follow paths of socialization indicated by Conca and the Maryland School as discussed earlier (Conca, 2006; Conca and Dabelko, 2002; Conca and Wu, 2002; Conca et al., 2003; Conca et al., 2006). Socialization can occur when an international institution is mandated with powers to take the necessary decisions and develop detailed tasks, which member states are required to implement. Alternatively, an international legal framework can be adopted and the onus is then on member states to interpret it and implement it through their own legislation (Hiddema and Erasmus, 2007).

International context

At the international level, the 1997 UN Convention offers much value as a legal framework as well as an indicator of top-down norm diffusion since it shows which countries have committed themselves in principle to the normative principles of transboundary cooperation such as equitable utilization, prior notification and the no harm doctrine. The UN Convention is codified international water law, although since it is not yet in force, it acts only as a framework agreement. It does however, allow for ad hoc watercourse agreements to be adopted for other regional watercourses (Hiddema and Erasmus, 2007) and acts as a guideline for these specific bilateral and multilateral regional agreements relating to the use, management and preservation of transboundary water resources (Eckstein, 2002). Additionally, it has the objective of helping to prevent and/or resolve conflicts over international water resources and promoting sustainable development and the protection of water supplies (ibid.).

In terms of its progression towards ratification, the UN Convention was passed by the UN General Assembly on 21 May 1997 (UN, 1997a) by a 103 vote with 3 against (Turkey, China and Burundi), 27 abstentions and 33 member states absent (Eckstein, 2002; Thompson, 2006; UN, 1997b). By the end of the signature period (20 May 2000), the UN Convention acquired eight ratifications, and an additional ten had signed the Convention (Eckstein, 2002; Thompson, 2006). Also, no SADC member states voted against the Convention.

The UN Convention therefore represents substantial progress in the development of international water law since it addresses issues such as the non-navigational uses of international watercourses, measures to protect, preserve and manage international watercourses and flood control, water quality, erosion, sedimentation, saltwater intrusion and ecosystems within watercourses (Thompson, 2006).

However, many controversial issues have not been reconciled, arguably owing to the few states that have ratified it as opposed to voting for it. Many states that voted against the text of the Convention, or abstained, argued that the document was not yet ready for a vote. Additionally, the numbers voting 'for' the Convention belie a voting pattern that manifests the complexity of the subject matter, as well as the fragility of the coalition favouring the 1997 UN Convention (Eckstein, 2002). States adopted positions that reflected their national interests and riparian positionality (Eckstein, 2002; Thompson, 2006). Upstream states support rules that give them control of the water that originate in their territory (e.g. Ethiopia), while downstream states accept the doctrines of prior appropriation or vested rights, and in some cases, absolute territorial integrity, embracing a stance that would give them unaltered flow of the water that enters their territories (Eckstein, 2002; Thompson, 2006). Considering the fact that it took more than 25 years of continuous work, 13 reports and 5 special rapporteurs to finalize the text, it is clear that the UN Convention is still highly contentious and reflects competing interests of states that are embedded within a political context. Top-down norm dissemination, has therefore not occurred in the manner whereby states accept and ratify the UN Convention and thereafter integrate these principles into the text of regional agreements.

While no SADC member states voted against the Convention, only two SADC member states have ratified it. At a superficial examination of the impact of global frameworks on local contexts, this may lead one to infer that the UN Convention has not had much influence in the southern African region. After all, while South Africa and Namibia are both parties and signatories to the UN Convention, they are two of only eight African signatories (UN, 2011). As of November 2011, the UN Convention has 16 signatories and 24 parties that have ratified it (leaving it with 9 more before it can enter into force) (UN, 2011).

However, despite the limited amount of southern African signatories, all SADC member states indirectly adhere to the principles contained within the UN Convention, due to their ratification of the Revised SADC Protocol, which was modelled after the UN Convention and which contains very many similarities and applications of the global framework at the regional level (Malzbender and Earle, 2008).

A degree of norm dissemination has also occurred in SADC where states have side-stepped the 'clumsiness' of the UN Convention text. Article 2 of the UN Convention defines a watercourse as a 'system of surface waters and groundwaters constituting by virtue of their physical relationship a unitary whole and normally flowing into a common terminus' (UN, 1997a: Article 2). It also recognizes that as an international watercourse, parts of it are situated in different states (UN, 1997a: Article 2). This differs to the Helsinki Rules, which refer to an international drainage basin. The reconciliation of the terms watercourse versus drainage basin or international water versus transboundary and shared water is not insignificant. While they appear to be similar, the terms international watercourse and international drainage basin are in fact very different. According to Thompson (2006) a major difference is that the Helsinki Rules would consider the water that falls on the drainage basin and is used before flowing into a common river as beneficial water use for the state benefiting from the water, while the UN Convention would not consider any water from the outside of the watercourse as part of the water to be equitably utilized. This could greatly affect practices such as rain fed agriculture, natural forests and usage of groundwater resources, particularly in areas where rivers traverse along states with climate variability, as is the case in southern Africa.

Similarly, Article 3 of the UN Convention exhibits inconsistencies for various parties. It states that watercourse riparian states may enter into one or more agreements, called 'watercourse agreements', that are applicable to them, and adjust the provisions of the Convention to the characteristics and uses of a particular international watercourse or part thereof (Hiddema and Erasmus, 2007). Article 3 also stipulates that existing treaties are not affected by the Convention, but states who are party to such agreements are encouraged to harmonize the treaties with the basin principles of the Convention (UN, 1997a: Article 3). Here, states also found a contradiction in terms between the need to 'harmonize' or adjust existing treaties to be in line with the Convention's principles, and the need in future agreements to 'adjust' the same principles to certain watercourse characteristics (Eckstein, 2002). India, for instance, remarked that 'Article 3 had not adequately reflected a State's autonomy to conclude agreements without being fettered by the Convention' (Eckstein, 2002: 84; UN, 1997b). In contrast, Ethiopia, who abstained from the vote, argued that by adjusting the principles in future agreements, one risked undermining the Convention, and that future watercourse agreements should be harmonized with the Convention not the other way around (Eckstein, 2002; UN, 1997b). Israel, on the other hand, abstained because it concluded that the Convention should not affect existing agreements since states had complete freedom to negotiate and enter into new agreements, provided that those agreements did not adversely affect other states (Eckstein, 2002; UN, 1997b).

The most contentious issues on the UN Convention were those raised in Articles 5, 6 and 7, the main reason for objection (including those who voted for the Convention) being that the text failed to establish a balance between the rights and obligations of upper and lower riparian states (Eckstein, 2002). Article 5 contains the foundational provision with respect to 'equitable and reasonable utilisation and participation', while Article 6 explains in more detail the factors relevant to equitable and reasonable utilization. It provides a list of factors relevant to the assessment of water use, which watercourse states must consider when evaluating what can be classified as equitable and reasonable utilization (Eckstein, 2002; Hiddema and Erasmus, 2007). Article 7 speaks to taking precautionary measures to prevent significant harm to other watercourse states (UN, 1997a).

During the negotiations of the UN Convention, there was strong contestation on what the exact relationship between the no harm obligation and the equitable and reasonable principles is (McCaffrey, 2001a, 2001b). The clash of the terms equitable and reasonable utilization on the one hand, and no harm on the other hand, is largely as a result of upstream riparians traditionally favouring the doctrine of absolute territorial sovereignty over resources located in their jurisdiction, while lower riparian states favoured the principles of prior appropriation which posits that current users of water have precedence over future or planned uses (Eckstein, 2002).

A definition of equitable utilization as it pertains to the UN Convention is therefore noteworthy. Ideally the states in question should consider the interests of other riparian states and incorporate this into their water resource development plans (Eckstein, 2002), and also negotiate and agree on the utilization of the watercourse under discussion (Hiddema and Erasmus, 2007). In the case of the Orange-Senqu, for example, this would entail that South Africa consider Namibia when assessing the repercussions further downstream for any infrastructural development on the Vaal.

Several scholars have interpreted the text of the Convention, particularly Article 7.2 and have argued that the equitable and reasonable utilization principle takes precedence over the no harm obligation (Eckstein, 2002; McCaffrey, 2001a; McIntyre, 2007; UN, 1997a). McIntyre (2007: 26) states that 'it is apparent that the principle of equitable utilisation takes priority over the obligation to prevent significant harm.' Similarly, McCaffrey (McCaffrey, 2001a: 255) argues that 'it appears to be that 7.2 gives precedence to equitable utilisation over the no-harm doctrine, and is thereby consistent with actual state practice.' Article 7.2 stipulates that 'where significant harm nevertheless is caused to another watercourse, the States whose uses cause such harm shall . . . take all appropriate measures, having due regard for the provisions of articles 5 and 6 . . . to eliminate or mitigate such harm' (UN, 1997a: Article 7.2). The explicit reference that measures need to be taken with due regard to the equitable utilization principles confirms this principle's precedence over the no harm obligation. However, as Eckstein (2002: 85) argues, this shift may suggest an increased level of support for reconciling various interests of watercourse states in the development of their transboundary waters, but it also overshadows a continued determination by the opposition to prevent the inclusion of more definite obligations to be added to the UN Convention. Seen differently, this is an example of resistance to the equitable and reasonable utilization norm.

The UN Convention also contains procedural obligations of cooperation. In order to respect obligations to each other on the protection of ecosystems, watercourse states should interact, coordinate their policies and activities and act jointly (Hiddema and Erasmus, 2007). McCaffrey (2001b: 404) observes that '. . . cooperation between states in relation to international watercourses is not only necessary, but probably required by general international law'.

The procedural obligations therefore contain a general duty to cooperate, to disseminate and exchange information, the requirement of prior notification as well as the obligation to consult (Hiddema and Erasmus, 2007; UN, 1997a). Additionally, some of its provisions are binding as customary international law, that is watercourse states should not be deprived of their equitable benefits when it comes to a shared watercourse (Tanzi, 2001). The SADC Protocol on Shared Watercourses, adopted in 1995 was revised into the SADC Revised Protocol in 2000 to incorporate virtually all of these normative principles. These regional agreements are meant to make the normative principles set out in the UN Convention more regionally specific. The influence of the UN Convention on subsequent legal developments can therefore be found not in the amount of SADC signatories it has, but the degree to which it has influenced the negotiation of regional agreements, and is therefore incorporated into regional texts.

Despite the limited amount of southern African signatories, all SADC member states indirectly adhere to the principles contained within the UN Convention, due to their ratification of the Revised SADC Protocol, which was modelled after the UN Convention and which contains very many similarities and applications of the global framework at the regional level (Malzbender and Earle, 2008). The UN Convention's utility is therefore in the degree to which it supports the interpretation of some provisions of the SADC Protocol. For example, the UN Convention provides more clarity and meaning to Article 3.6 of the Revised SADC Protocol, which obliges states to exchange available information and data regarding the hydrological, water quality, meteorological and environmental conditions of shared watercourses (ibid.). Secondly, the UN Convention provides more detailed rules for data-poor areas or in situations where information is not readily available (ibid.). Thirdly, the Convention also stipulates that 'if a watercourse State is requested by another watercourse State to provide data or information that is not readily available, it shall employ its best efforts to comply with the request but may condition its compliance upon payment by the requesting State of the reasonable costs of collecting and, where appropriate, processing such data or information' (UN, 1997: Article 9.2). Similarly, 'Watercourse States shall employ their best efforts to collect and, where appropriate, to process data and information in a manner which facilitates its utilisation by the other watercourse States to which it is communicated' (ibid.: Article 9.3). In this regard, the UN Convention could provide further elaboration for the SADC context if there is ever an uncertainty regarding the format in which data is presented as well as the responsibility of costs for the collection and processing of data (Malzbender and Earle, 2008).

Additionally, equitable and reasonable utilization is another such ambiguously phrased norm which could benefit from the provisions provided in multiple legal frameworks, to give it greater meaning. The interpretation of Article 3.8 of the SADC Protocol, for example, which lists factors for the determination of 'equitable and reasonable utilisation', could receive support and greater elaboration through Article 10.2 of the UN Convention (ibid.). The latter UN article outlines the concept of vital human needs in the determination of 'equitable and reasonable utilisation' (UN, 1997: Article 10.2). According to Malzbender and Earle (2008), the concept of vital human needs is growing in importance in international water law as a key factor to consider in the relationship between different uses, but it is not explicitly mentioned in the SADC Protocol. If the UN Convention entered into force and became legally binding on SADC member states, the vital human needs factor would be strengthened in the application of the SADC Protocol (ibid.).

Additionally, Malzbender and Earle (2008) recommend that the ratification of the UN Convention would be of great relevance for basins shared with non-SADC member states in that it would provide a legal framework and established principles and rules beyond the scope of the SADC Protocol, which is only applicable to SADC member states (ibid.). Examples of basins that comprise of SADC member states and non-SADC member states include the Nile (of which two SADC member states are riparian: DRC and Tanzania); the Congo (of which four SADC member states are riparian: DRC, Angola, Tanzania and Zambia); the Pangani and Umba (of which one SADC member State is riparian: Tanzania).

Global norms have therefore followed a non-linear progression from the top down, where norms and principles are instead accepted at the global level through codification, than the regional level where they are incorporated into legal frameworks (Jacobs, 2010a). The strategic nature of water in the SADC region has arguably given preference to the need to consolidate regional frameworks first.

Regional context

The SADC legal framework reflects the international context in terms of the adoption of the global principles of equitable utilization, no harm and information exchange.

When ascertaining the degree to which norms/principles have been accepted and socialized and examining the trajectory these norms have followed in the SADC region, it is important to understand the historical development of the SADC water protocols and SADC itself.

In an attempt to combat South Africa's military aggression and economic hegemony, 1980 saw the formation of the Southern African Development Co-ordination Conference (SADCC), by nine southern African states including Botswana and Lesotho. Namibia later joined after it became independent in 1990. In 1992, the SADCC was superseded by the Southern African Development Community (SADC), of which South Africa became a member after its 1994 democratic election (Conley and Van Niekerk, 2000; SADC, 1995). SADC is today a regional organization and has adopted a number of protocols to promote cooperation between the 15 member states of the region. For the Orange-Senqu riparian states, the 1995 Protocol on Shared Watercourses (SADC, 1995) and the 2000 Revised Protocol on Shared Watercourses (SADC, 2000) are valuable legal instruments, which allow for the evaluation of norm convergence at a regional level.

The first SADC Protocol on Shared Watercourse Systems (as it was then called) was signed in 1995 and was the first protocol following the signing of the SADC Treaty in 1992 (Ramoeli, 2002). Its origin and history date back to 1993 when SADC was implementing the largest of its basin-wide programmes, the Zambezi River Basin System Action Plan (ZACPLAN) (Ramoeli, 2002; Turton, 2008b). Drafted initially as one of the ZACPLAN projects (ZACPRO, 2), which aimed to establish a basin-wide legal and institutional framework to better facilitate management of the Zambezi River basin, SADC then decided that instead of developing a legal instrument for a single river basin, it should first develop a region-wide legal framework which all river basins in the region could adopt (Ramoeli, 2002). As a result of this decision, the SADC Protocol on Shared Watercourse Systems was drafted and subsequently adopted in 1995 by ten SADC member states: Botswana, Lesotho, Malawi, Mozambique, Namibia, South Africa, Swaziland, Tanzania, Zambia and Zimbabwe. Mauritius later signed the Protocol when it joined SADC in 1996 (Ramoeli, 2002).

The revision of the 1995 Protocol was influenced by two main factors: (1) some member states had reservations about the contents of the Protocol and the summit approved that these concerns be addressed; and (2) the adoption of the UN Convention in 1997. Following these developments, the Protocol was then revised and the SADC Revised Protocol was signed by member states on 7 August 2000. The SADC Revised Protocol came into force in October 2004 after two-thirds of the signatory states ratified it (Hiddema and Erasmus, 2007).

According to the SADC Water Division based in Gaborone, several differences exist between the old and revised protocols:

- While the 1995 Protocol was based on the Helsinki Rules and Agenda 21, the Revised Protocol reflects the UN Convention and in many ways is a direct replica of it (Hiddema and Erasmus, 2007; Ramoeli, 2002; Thompson, 2006).
- While the 1995 Protocol does not include clear objectives, the Revised Protocol expressly states the objectives of fostering closer cooperation with the intended

outcome of achieving sustainable and coordinated management, protection and utilization of shared watercourses as well as advancing the SADC Agenda of Regional Integration and poverty alleviation (Hiddema and Erasmus, 2007). Additionally, the Revised Protocol encourages the establishment of shared watercourse agreements and institutions, to advance sustainable, equitable and reasonable utilization, sound environmental management, harmonization and monitoring of legislation of the states involved as well as the promotion of research, technology development, information exchange and capacity building (Hiddema and Erasmus, 2007; SADC, 2000). This is an explicit prioritization of norm convergence and cumulative regional integration through policy alignment.

- While the 1995 Protocol stresses territorial sovereignty of a watercourse state, the Revised Protocol emphasizes the unity and coherence of each shared watercourse. This has strong implications for this investigation because it indicates a higher priority given towards regional cooperative agendas as opposed to unilateral national agendas, thus implying (if not providing evidence for) a regional move towards norm convergence.
- While the 1995 Protocol provides a general regulatory framework, the Revised Protocol, in Article 6 thereof, provides allowance for the creation of future watercourse agreements with respect to entire shared watercourses, a part thereof or a particular project, programme or use (Hiddema and Erasmus, 2007). This is aligned with the stipulations of the 1997 UN Convention, which allows for more flexibility, particularly regarding the creation of ad hoc arrangements with respect to specific international watercourses such as the Orange-Senqu River (Hiddema and Erasmus, 2007).
- The Revised Protocol provides clearer regulations than does the 1995 Protocol regarding planned measures, environmental protection, management of shared watercourses, prevention and mitigation of harmful conditions and emergency situations (Hiddema and Erasmus, 2007; SADC, 2000).

The Revised Protocol therefore espouses much the same principles as the 1997 UN Convention:

- Unity and coherence of each shared watercourse
- Respect for the existing rules of customary or general international law
- Conservation and enhancement of the environment to promote sustainable development
- Cooperation with regard to the study and execution of projects
- Equitable and reasonably utilization
- Protection of the watercourse for the benefit of current and future generations
- Prevention, mitigation or compensation of significant harm to other Parties

The entry into force of the Revised Protocol means that the previous SADC Protocol has been repealed (SADC, 2000: Article 16). The Revised Protocol is therefore the source of applicable treaty law for the four states bordering the Orange-Senqu River (since they have all ratified this instrument) (Hiddema and Erasmus, 2007).

The format of the SADC Revised Protocol starts by defining a watercourse as 'a system of surface waters and ground waters constituting by virtue of their physical relationship a unitary whole normally flowing into a common terminus such as the sea, lake or aquifer' (SADC, 2000). The Orange-Senqu River is one such international watercourse. A watercourse state is a state 'in whose territory part of the watercourse is situated' (ibid.). Lesotho, South Africa, Namibia and Botswana are, therefore, all watercourse states with respect to the Orange-Senqu River. Following definitions, the SADC Revised Protocol contains general principles in Article 3, specific provisions in Article 4, a detailed institutional framework for implementation in Article 5, provisions on shared watercourse agreements in Article 6 and a provision on dispute settlement in Article 7 (Hiddema and Erasmus, 2007; SADC, 2000).

In Article 3, the priority given to norm convergence is once again expressed: 'The State Parties recognize the principle of the unity and coherence of each shared watercourse and in accordance with this principle, undertake to harmonize the water uses in the shared watercourses and to ensure that all necessary interventions are consistent with the sustainable development of all Watercourse States and observe the objectives of regional integration and harmonization of their socio-economic policies and plans' (emphasis added) (SADC, 2000: Article 3). Additionally, it stipulates that state parties should cooperate closely and liaise with each other on all projects likely to have an effect on the regime of the shared watercourse, and for equitable and reasonable utilization to be respected and adopted in these processes (Hiddema and Erasmus, 2007). The exact definition of equitable and reasonable utilization is clearly outlined in Article 3.8, being virtually identical to that stipulated in the UN Convention (Hiddema and Erasmus, 2007).

The concept of harmonization, contained in Article 3.1, is critically important as is the process of carrying it out provided in Article 6. One way in which the protocol calls for harmonization is through the establishment of shared watercourse agreements or institutions (such as the Orange-Senqu River Commission). Watercourse states should 'undertake to establish appropriate institutions such as watercourse commissions or authorities or boards that may be determined' (SADC, 2000: Article 5.3). Additionally, as stated in Article 6.3, 'Watercourse States may enter into agreements, which apply the provisions of this Protocol to the characteristics and uses of a particular shared watercourse or part thereof' (ibid.: Article 6.3). Similarly, Article 2 suggests that in order to obtain 'closer cooperation for judicious, sustainable and co-ordinated management, protection and utilisation of shared watercourses . . . this Protocol seeks to promote and facilitate the establishment of shared watercourse agreements and Shared Watercourse Institutions for the management of shared watercourses'.

This sentiment encouraging the formation of shared watercourse institutions (or river basin organizations/commissions) is elaborated upon in Article 4.3. Article 4 provides in detail for 'specific provisions' on planned measures, notification thereof, environmental protection and preservation, management of shared watercourses, prevention and mitigation of harmful conditions and emergencies (Hiddema and Erasmus, 2007). 'Planned measures' are not explicitly defined but the obligation is that states:

> Shall exchange information and consult each other and, if necessary, negotiate the possible effects of planned measures on the condition of a shared watercourse. Timely notification must be given to other watercourse states if a particular Party implements or permits the implementation of planned measures which may have a significant adverse effect on a particular watercourse state or states. The duty to notify is accompanied by the further obligation to allow a state that has been notified a period of six months within which to study and evaluate the possible effects of the planned measures and to communicate the findings. (SADC, 2000: Article 4.1c)

During this six-month period the notifying state wishing to implement planned measures 'shall not implement or permit the implementation of the planned measures without the consent of the notified States' (SADC, 2000: Article 4.1d). Moreover, information and technical data must also be exchanged (ibid.: Article 3.6).

The Revised Protocol also provides guidelines for the management of such shared watercourses in Article 4.3. In this regard, and upon the request of a watercourse state, states who share a watercourse should 'enter into consultations concerning the management of a shared watercourse, which may include the establishment of a joint management mechanism' (ibid.: Article 4.3a). Once again, these provisions in Article 4 are identical to the procedural obligations outlined in the UN Convention.

In addition to calling for the establishment of river basin organizations (RBOs) or Shared Watercourse Institutions (SWIs), Article 5 also calls for an 'institutional framework for implementation' on the SADC level (Hiddema and Erasmus, 2007). SADC now has a fully functional water sector comprising of a number of organs, such as the Committee of Water Ministers, and the Committee of Water Senior Officials, for example (Hiddema and Erasmus, 2007).

In addition to the concept of 'harmonization' explicitly mentioned in the SADC Revised Protocol, another is the promotion of regional integration. Regional integration is one of SADC`s overall objectives and is a process which requires focused cooperation, joint decision-making and suitable institutional arrangements between states. When sharing the utilization of a single watercourse such as the Orange-Senqu River, integration, at least at a basin-wide level, seems unavoidable. The Revised Protocol provides the necessary framework; to be fleshed out in a specific arrangement between the states involved. However, the exact process and consequences of this differs from basin to basin. Moreover, regional integration is an incremental process based on the cumulative transformation of unilateral national agendas and norm sets into a multilateral agenda based on the identification of benefits to be shared on and beyond the basin (in the region), thus bypassing sovereignty as a constricting force while not attacking it.

Basin-level context

Institutional development on the Orange-Senqu River has been fragmented but successful where it has occurred reaching a level of sophistication and success not found in other river basins in southern Africa (Turton, 2003d). Moreover, institutional arrangements have evolved over time and reflect the changing political, social and economic transformations that have occurred in the region (Kistin and Ashton, 2008: 391). The historical context within which these development and institutional agreements were formed is therefore, of great significance. These development projects were established in a time when public participation and environmental investigation/accountability were not routinely performed (Tompkins, 2007). Additionally, the political context was heavily influenced by the South African apartheid government, and was subject to the controversies and issues generated by that context (Tompkins, 2007). As a result, the older institutions established in the Orange-Senqu Basin reflect the context in which they were formed, with an emphasis on technical cooperation to overcome the political incapacity to engage.

Today, there is a comparatively high level of collaboration not only between states in the basin, but also between sovereign states and non-state entities (Meissner, 2000a). Technical cooperation is particularly dominant in the basin (ibid.). Additionally, in parallel with technical collaboration, political institutions and agreements have also been enacted (ibid.). Yet, while collaboration in the Orange-Senqu River basin has been predominantly of a technical nature (as opposed to political), recent multilateral collaboration makes for easier lateral norm convergence from state-to-state, and regional norm convergence from state-to-basin-to-region since the mechanisms and organizational platforms which foster and facilitate norm diffusion are already in place.

In addition to the Revised SADC protocol and the 1997 UN Convention, the four Orange-Senqu riparian states have established six bilateral agreements and one multilateral basin-wide treaty of noteworthy importance (Hiddema and Erasmus, 2007; Kistin and Ashton, 2008; Kranz et al., 2005a; Tompkins, 2007; Turton, 2003d) (see Figure 3.2). Four of these agreements are relevant to the current management of the basin:

1. The 1986 bilateral treaty between South Africa and Lesotho, providing a framework for the LHWP and the establishment of the Joint Permanent Technical Commission (JPTC), referred to today, as the Lesotho Highlands Water Commission;
2. The 1992 bilateral agreement for the establishment of the Vioolsdrift and Noordoewer Joint Irrigation Scheme (VNJIS) and the Joint Irrigation Authority (JIA) between South Africa and Namibia;
3. The 1992 bilateral agreement also between South Africa and Namibia that resulted in the establishment of the Permanent Water Commission (PWC); and
4. The 2000 multilateral agreement establishing the Orange-Senqu River Commission (ORASECOM) between all four riparian states (Kistin and Ashton, 2008).

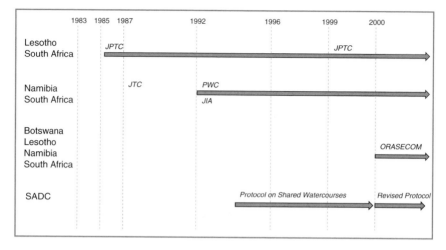

Figure 3.2 Schematic timeline showing the emergence of different water management institutions in the Orange-Senqu Basin over time (adapted from Turton, 2003d)

In terms of the composition and synergy between the mandates of these various institutions, Kistin and Ashton (2008) summarize the various institutional responsibilities in Table 3.3.

The 1986 LHWP treaty, a key bilateral agreement between South Africa and Lesotho, is a project-based treaty and establishes provisions for the construction and management of the LHWP. Similarly, the 1992 bilateral VNJIS agreement by the Joint Irrigation Authority (JIA) is also project-based and establishes provisions for the operation and management of the scheme and is specific to the VNJIS. Additionally, it dedicates 20 million m³ annually to the scheme with 11 million m³ going to famers in South Africa, and 9 million m³ designated for those in Namibia (Kistin and Ashton, 2008). As Kistin and Ashton (2008) note, these fixed allocations do not provide flexibility for over time.

The agreements establishing the PWC and ORASECOM on the other hand, create joint institutions to advise parties on the development and utilization of shared waters (ibid.). As is evident, bilateral agreements and treaties have dominated co-riparian relations in the Orange-Senqu River basin until the ORASECOM Agreement, the only multilateral basin-wide agreement that was reached in 2000 (ORASECOM, 2000).

In terms of institutional responsibility, the project-related institutions, the LHWC and the JIA, are granted substantial powers to design and carry out policies and procedures relating to the investigation, negotiation and recommendation to parties regarding water allocation (Kistin and Ashton, 2008). As the two commissions, the PWC and ORASECOM serve as advisory bodies whose mandates are wider in scope than the project-based institutions, and were specifically designed with an advisory function to parties on 'such matters as may be determined', by the parties (ibid.). This brings with it both positive and negative consequences in that these broad mandates

Table 3.3 Composition and mandate of Joint Institutions for Water Management in the Orange-Senqu River basin

Institution	Composition	Mandate
ORASECOM	The Council consists of three delegates from each of the riparian states and is supported by a Technical Task Team comprising specialists drawn from each country. A permanent secretariat for the Commission was established in October 2007.	To serve as a technical advisor to the Parties on matters relating to the development, utilization and conservation of water resources.
PWC	Three delegates from each party.	To serve as a technical advisor to Parties on the development and utilization of shared waters; monitor and advise the JIA.
JIA	Four delegates from each party, at least three of which must be landowners within the district. The fourth space in each delegation is currently filled by a representative from the respective Departments of Water and Agriculture who also serves as liaison to the PWC.	To operate and maintain the Irrigation Scheme and control the abstraction of water from the Orange River.
LHWC	Three delegates from each party.	To be responsible and accountable for the project; monitor, advise and audit the LHDA and TCTA; determine appropriate policies, procedures and expenditure limits.

Source: Kistin and Ashton, 2008

give the existing institutions scope for changes in management and the institutional capacity to absorb flexibility and variability in climate, development and political contexts. However, ORASECOM particularly, has no formal oversight, advisory or coordinating powers with respect to the pre-existing bilateral agreements (ibid.) albeit it the umbrella body to which preceding bilateral agreements should report on any issues pertaining to the basin.

The Permanent Water Commission (PWC)

The PWC, initially named the Joint Technical Committee (JTC), was a bilateral agreement between Namibia and South Africa established in 1987 (while Namibia was still an autonomous region of South Africa). Today, the PWC advises the governments of Namibia and South Africa on the use and (primarily infrastructural) development of the lower Orange River (Tompkins, 2007). The commission focuses on the Vioolsdrift and Noordoewer Irrigation Schemes (the PWC also evolved from the VNJIS) (ibid.). In 1992, shortly after Namibia's independence in 1990, a bilateral agreement between Namibia and South Africa established the PWC.

The Lesotho Highlands Water Commission (LHWC)

The LHWC is a bilateral governmental body that evolved from the JPTC established under the 1986 Lesotho Highlands Water Treaty (LHWC, 1986; Tompkins, 2007). This organization is responsible for joint matters pertaining to Lesotho and South Africa with regard to the implementation of the LHWP and specifically, monitoring the performance of the two implementing agents of the LHWP, namely the Trans-Caledon Tunnel Authority (TCTA) and the Lesotho Highlands Development Authority (LHDA). Other responsibilities include the appointment of auditors and consultants, operating and maintenance plans, tendering procedures, the allocation of costs between the parties and the quantities of water to be delivered (Mohammed-Katerere, 2001).

On the South African side, the TCTA acts as the implementing agent of the South African government and manages and maintains the delivery tunnel North which transfers water across the border (i.e. under the Caledon River) to the Ash River Outfall in the Vaal catchment as well as all other aspects of the infrastructure in South Africa.[10] The TCTA operates on a much smaller scale than its counterpart in Lesotho because it is only responsible for the water from the Lesotho border until it reaches the Vaal Dam.[11] The LHDA, on the other hand, is responsible for the management of all aspects of the project that fall within Lesotho, including infrastructure, hydropower as well as social aspects, such as the resettlement and compensation of displaced communities, of water supply to resettled communities, public participation and civil society inclusivity in decision-making processes relating to the LHWP, irrigation and tourism (Tompkins, 2007).

The responsibilities of the TCTA are therefore comparatively less than that of the LHDA and this is reflected in the 1986 LHDA treaty (LHWC, 1986). While there are specific management provisions for the LHDA in the 1986 Treaty the functions of the TCTA, 'are provided for in considerably less detail and no attention is given to downstream responsibilities' (Mohammed-Katerere, 2001). While it can be viewed as a matter of the practical implications of functions for each state (more infrastructural development in Lesotho implies a greater responsibility for the LHDA), it can also be regarded as an indication of the significant power asymmetries between the two states (Tompkins, 2007). This also raises key issues presented by several policymakers and scholars of the exclusion of Namibia and Botswana from the Treaty despite the fact that the LHWP has a very significant impact on the downstream waters of the Orange-Senqu Basin (Heyns, 2003; Tompkins, 2007).

The Lesotho Highlands Water Project (LHWP)

The LHWP is the largest water infrastructure project in Africa (Tompkins, 2007) and contains the largest inter-basin transfer scheme in the world. Its raison d'être arguably dates back to the 1950s and was further concretized in a significant Commission of Inquiry into Water Matters conducted by the South African government in 1966, which predicted that the demand for water from the industrial and economic heartland of South Africa's Gauteng region and the water demand to meet population growth would escalate beyond the country's water supply (Ashton et al., 2008; Commission of Inquiry, 1970; Tompkins, 2007). Based on these predictions, the Government of South Africa set out to find alternative sources of water to supply Gauteng. Phakoe refers to the origin of the LHWP as a 'double coincidence of needs,' that is South Africa's growing need to provide more water to meet its industrial and population needs, and Lesotho's need to tap into its bountiful water resources in order to reduce poverty and foster economic development.[12]

The LHWP therefore, manages water transfers from Lesotho to South Africa, and hydroelectric power generation in Lesotho. Negotiations were conducted for 30 years during the apartheid era in South Africa before the Lesotho Highlands Water Treaty was signed in 1986, between South Africa and the then military government in Lesotho (de Jonge Schuermans et al., 2004). The Treaty includes provisions for the quantities of water to be delivered, the calculation of royalties, examines country shares in the common revenue pool of the Customs Union and also makes provisions for cost sharing, loans, income tax and insurance (Tompkins, 2007). The main objectives of the project, as categorized by Tomkins (2007: 11) are to:

1. Transfer surplus water from the Lesotho Highlands to South Africa for royalties;
2. Generate hydropower in Lesotho; and
3. Promote economic development of both states.

Initial international funding was provided by the World Bank, along with numerous aid agencies and the European Investment Bank, through Lesotho, as a result of sanctions imposed on apartheid South Africa (Hilyard, 2002). Despite the negative perceptions of World Bank involvement, various institutional representatives expressed the opinion that it brought credibility and security to the project, and as a result, attracted other foreign investment. Additionally it set up a trust mechanism as a result of sanctions against South Africa, and increased local capacity.

According to a former Chief Executive of the LHDA:

> The World Bank has been very, very instrumental in shaping, not only the behaviour of LHDA, but also the governments of Lesotho and South Africa, and of course LHDA. When you look at the total financing of the project, you'll find that for example, the World Bank (WB) contributed less than 5%. . . . But what they brought into the whole scheme was credibility, and security. It opened room for other multinational corporations and financiers to see, the WB have come in

here, they've done appraisal reports, they negotiated, they played match-maker. It was a difficult period . . . [and] they even helped us set up a very complicated trust system. South Africa, at that time, could not directly borrow capital on world financial markets because the Apartheid regime was a pariah state . . . So a complicated trust mechanism was set up, but of course, it has been dismantled now because South Africa, since 1994, has been the darling of the world . . . So that's what the WB has done, they brought credibility. First they did their homework, they were satisfied that it was a good project. It had economic, political and social viability. So they brought it capital and other organisations then came in. But not only that, the WB went beyond that. They set up a system of supervision. They brought a panel of experts, social and engineering. These people would come in and advise the governments and LHDA. So everybody knew that whatever has been done it has been looked at by experts in the field. Over and above that, the WB came here twice a year. Supervision which was designed in the project, half yearly for all the period, came here and actually checked . . . [T]he half yearly supervision continued right up until the end [of Phase I]. It was mandatory. It was a requirement, twice every year until the end. Every 6 months they'd come in and check, progress. So, as you can imagine, kept a lot of pressure, so we behaved well as a result. . . . And one other thing, the WB was not shy to say that they were using this project as a guinea pig, as a test, because some theories had never been tested before. So they were experimenting. But the experiment worked so well, and we succeeded. Now, we are a pioneer. People come to us to learn how to manage environmental flows.[13]

Today, the overall plan for the scheme has four phases comprising of several dams, over 200 km of tunnels, and a 72-megawatt hydropower plant for the supply of electricity to Lesotho (LHWP, 2011). Phase I was divided into two projects. First, Phase IA, completed in 1998, saw the construction of the Katse Dam (1,950 million m³), a 45-km transfer tunnel, the 72 MW Muela Hydropower Station and Tail Pond, a 15-km delivery tunnel south and a 22-km delivery tunnel north (ibid.). Secondly, Phase IB consisted of the construction of the Mohale Dam (958 million m³) and a 30-km-long transfer tunnel between the Mohale and Katse Dams (ibid.). These developments were completed in 2003.

Additionally, Phase II was approved in August 2011, and involves the construction of the 165-metre high, 2.2 billion m³ capacity Polihali Dam at Tlokoeng, at the confluence of Senqu and Khubelu Rivers in the Mokhotlong district in Lesotho, as well as support infrastructure such a 38-km tunnel, roads, and the 1000-MV Kobong pump storage scheme (Lesotho Review, 2011). When completed, Phase II will augment the existing LHWP supply of water to the Vaal River water system in South Africa as well as the existing hydropower generation capacity in Lesotho (ibid.). Several environmental and social programmes are also expected to start or be extended, such as housing projects and the construction of the national referral hospital (Lesotho Review, 2011; LHWP, 2011).

Phase III is proposed to include the construction of the fourth and final dam, the Tsoelike Dam (2,223 million m³) and pumping station (LHWP, 2011). The fourth and final phase concludes the LHWP with the construction of the Ntoahae Dam and Pumping Station (ibid.).

Several positive outcomes have been evident in the execution of the LHWP. The overall dam construction, which commenced in 1989 has resulted in an increase in employment for Lesotho and has subsequently provided substantial revenue to the government of Lesotho through import duties (Tompkins, 2007). The first water delivered from Phase IA in 1998 supplies the Government of Lesotho with roughly R20 million per month in royalties (ibid.). Moreover, simultaneous power production from the Muela power plant has resulted in Lesotho becoming self-sufficient in electricity.

However, the LHWP has also been extensively criticized due to the massive social upheaval caused by the project in Lesotho by various local, regional and international civil society groups, the most notable being the INGO, International Rivers and a local NGO, Transformation Resource Centre (TRC). Although a relatively small amount of households (1,000) had to be resettled in Phase I, approximately 27,000 lost access to valued resources in the areas inundated by the two dams as well as downstream of these (TRC, 2006). Moreover, some sources cite that despite US$62,000 being spent per household resettled from the Katse Dam, and over US$30,000 per household for Mohale Dam, the resettlement process has been plagued by problems including corruption, lack of adequate basic services in resettled areas, inadequate compensation for displaced people and tension between resettled people and residents of the resettlement areas (de Jonge Schuermans et al., 2004).

Moreover, another unforeseen consequence of inter-basin transfer schemes of this nature involves significant amounts of 'water theft', unlawful use or illegal abstraction of the waters on the South African side. In the Vaal River system the amount of water lost to unlawful use has been cited to be equivalent to 200 million m³; the amount of water that can be supplied to approximately 8.5 million households using 100 litres per day (Hendricks, 2008). The central premise of this issue is that farms are located in areas that are riparian to those streams which are being used for conveyance. A common argument used is that farmers are merely abstracting water which would have been available to them through the natural flow in the river. Given that the streams being used for conveyance have flowed through private agricultural land, and under old South African water law, based on 'riparian rights', farmers owned this water too. However, the quantity of water that is currently being abstracted outweighs that which would have been possible had the conveyance streams operated under natural flows that is without the increased flow due to the transfer scheme. This concept is noteworthy because it illustrates the degree to which global norms of equitable utilization and/or regional normative principles (of integration) do in fact cascade down and become socialized at the local level, whether these norms in fact matter at the local level, whether individuals are aware of these principles or whether local norms of historic rights to the land (and therefore the water on it) still take precedence.

The Orange-Senqu River Commission (ORASECOM)

Arguably, the most significant institutional and legal framework for the Orange-Senqu River basin, exists in the ORASECOM Agreement (established in November 2000) and institutional structure, which is the first attempt to bring all Orange-Senqu riparian states together in a multilateral forum. Its mandate is to serve as a technical advisor to the Parties on matters relating to the development, utilization and conservation of water resources (Kistin and Ashton, 2008) and can, in this capacity, execute the necessary feasibility studies to support decision-making. As such it is responsible for the dissemination of information and encourages communication on basin issues between the member states by hosting an annual meeting of all state representatives. It also stipulates that states utilize the resource within their respective states equitably and reasonably (in accordance with the 2000 Revised Water Protocol). It furthermore acts within the role of funding coordinator for basin specific and joint basin projects. Moreover, the bilateral institutions are required to inform ORASECOM of any issues pertaining to the basin, changes to agreements or impacts on the waters of the basin (Tompkins, 2007). It does not, however, have any direct links (through formal mechanisms), or any formal oversight or coordinating powers with respect to the pre-existing bilateral commissions (Lesotho Highlands Water Commission between South Africa and Lesotho, or the Permanent Water Commission between South Africa and Namibia).

Additionally, the ORASECOM comprises of three delegates from each country of the riparian states, and is supported by several task teams including Communications, Financial, Legal and Technical (including a hydrogeology committee) comprising of specialists drawn from each country. A permanent secretariat was established in October 2007 comprising of four core members namely, the Executive Secretary, a water resources specialist, a finance administrator and administrative support.

In terms of the 2000 ORASECOM Agreement, its Preamble is inspired by wide-ranging sources such as the Helsinki Rules (with its acceptance of sovereignty), the 1997 UN Convention and importantly, quotes the 1995 SADC Water Protocol (ORASECOM, 2000). Arguably, its most basic objective is to 'extend and consolidate the existing tradition of good neighbourliness and friendly relations between the Parties by promoting close and coordinated cooperation in the development of the resources of the River System' (ibid.: 1).

The Agreement therefore establishes ORASECOM as an international organization with legal personality and powers (Hiddema and Erasmus, 2007). However, nothing 'shall affect the prerogative of any number of the Parties to establish among themselves river commissions with regard to any part of the River System'. This clause clearly protects the sovereignty of riparian states as final custodians of the river system. These commissions will then be subordinate to ORASECOM (ORASECOM, 2000: Article 1.4). Additionally, Articles 2 and 3 speak to notions of sovereign equality and territorial integrity by stipulating that each delegation may only consist of no more than three permanent members (ibid.: Article 2.3), and allowing each delegation to the Council one vote (i.e. one vote per country) (ibid.: Article 3.6) ensuring even representation by all riparian states and by conducting meetings on a rotational basis giving each Party a chance to host and coordinate annual meetings (ORASECOM, 2000: Articles 3.1, 3.2, 3.3, 3.4, 3.5).

Article 7 is noteworthy as it lists the obligations of the Parties or the manner in which the River System it utilized within the respective riparian territories. Article 7.2 requires states to '[U]tilise the resources of the river system in an equitable and reasonable manner with a view of attaining optimal and sustainable utilisation thereof, and benefits therefrom, consistent with adequate protection of the river system' (ibid.: Article 7.2). Equitable and reasonable utilization is specifically defined and '[I]interpreted in line with the Revised Protocol on Shared watercourses in the SADC region' (ibid.: Article 7.2). Similarly, the no harm obligation is also cited with the term being interpreted in accordance with that of the Revised Protocol (ibid.: 7.3). Prior notification and communication duties are given great importance and specifications cover several sub-sections (Articles 7.4, 7.5, 7.6, 7.7, 7.8, 7.9, 7.10 and 7.11) in Article 7.

Ecosystem protection is also articulated, whereby 'Parties shall individually and jointly take all measures that are necessary to protect and preserve the River System from its sources and headwaters to its common terminus' (ibid.: Article 7.12). Article sub-sections 7.13, 7.14 and 7.15 further elaborate on ecosystem protection and specifies obligations as it relates to pollution (prevention, reduction and control), preservation of the estuary of the River System including the marine environment, prevention of the introduction of alien species. The settlement of disputes is specified in Article 8 which stipulates that 'Any dispute between the Parties arising out of the interpretation of implementation of this Agreement shall be settled amicably through consultation and/or negotiation between them' (ibid.: Article 8.1). Additionally, Article 8.2 makes provisions for states to go to the Tribunal, as established in Article 16.1 of the 1992 SADC Treaty and shall accept the decision of the Tribunal as binding (ibid.: Articles 8.2, 8.3). Once again, the dispute resolution mechanism binds Orange-Senqu riparians to the SADC treaty and to normative principles contained therein.

As such, the global normative principles of equitable and reasonable utilization, no harm, sovereign equality and territorial integrity, information exchange, consultation with other riparian states, prior notification, environmental protection, peaceful resolution of disputes are all articulated in the ORASECOM Agreement, although the degree to which they are deepened in terms of specification varies. See Table 3.4.

Norm diffusion is also expected to be influenced by the relationship between bilateral and multilateral regimes. For example, typically, certain hydropolitical conditions favouring bilateral regimes have included situations where hegemonic states with a high resource need (such as South Africa) prefer to enter into bilateral arrangements, because under such conditions, they are more likely to have their national interests served (Turton, 2003d). On the other hand, hydropolitical conditions favouring multilateral regimes include situations where other riparian states, with high resource needs but in a low-order riparian position, prefer a multilateral basin-wide approach, with a preference for well-defined legal norms such as equitable and

Table 3.4 Agreements, Treaties and Protocols established solely between the basin states of the Orange-Senqu River

Year	Signed by	Agreement/Treaty/Protocol	Scope	Institution
1930	Lesotho, SA	Agreement between Kingdom of Lesotho and the Republic of South Africa to set up the Lesotho Highlands Development Authority	The LHDA was established to implement and operate the portion of the LHWP that falls within the borders of Lesotho	LHDA
1983	Botswana, SA	Agreement between the Government of the Republic of South Africa and the Government of the Republic of Botswana establishing the Joint Permanent Technical Committee		JPTC
24/10/1986	Lesotho, SA	Treaty on the LHWP with six protocols listed below	The signing of the LHWP Treaty by Lesotho and South Africa established the Joint Permanent Technical Commission to represent the two countries in the implementation and operation of the LHWP. The Joint Permanent Technical Commission was later renamed the Lesotho Highlands Water Commission with a secretariat in Lesotho to monitor and oversee the carrying out of the treaty.	Establishment of the Joint Permanent Technical Committee
1987	South West Africa (Namibia and SA)	Agreement between the Republic of South Africa and the Interim Government of the National entity of Southwest-Africa/Namibia concerning the control, development and utilization of the water of the Orange River	Focused on the management of the Lower Orange River between South Africa and Namibia	JTC, replaced in 1992 by the PWC
1988	Lesotho, SA	Protocol I to the treaty of the Lesotho Highlands Water Project: Royalty Manual	Expanded the methodology for calculating the net benefit of the project and specified royalty payments	LHWC

Date	Parties	Agreement	Description	Body
1988	Lesotho, SA	Protocol II to the treaty of the Lesotho Highlands Water Project: SACU Study	Examined the Lesotho share in the common revenue pool of the Customs Union (between SA, Botswana, Lesotho and Swaziland) and specifies the advance payment to Lesotho as a fixed percentage of the present value of the total cost of initial development	LHWC
1988	Lesotho, SA	Protocol III to the treaty of the Lesotho Highlands Water Project: Apportionment of the Liability for the Costs of Phase 1A Project Works	Specifies the responsibility of payment by country for the construction costs of water delivery and hydropower infrastructure	LHWC
13/11/1990	Botswana, Namibia	Agreement on the Establishment of a Joint Permanent Water Committee	Established the Joint Permanent Water Committee	JPWC
19/11/1991	Lesotho, SA	Protocol IV to the treaty on the Lesotho Highlands Water Project: supplementary arrangements regarding phase IA	Established the processes and clarified expectations of the Cost Allocation Reports, royalty payments, reimbursement, loans and insurance	LHWC
3/08/1992	Lesotho, SA	Ancillary agreement to the deed of undertaking and relevant agreements entered into between the Lesotho Highlands Development Authority and the Government of the Republic of South Africa		LHDA, South Africa
14/09/1992	Namibia, SA	Agreement between the government of the Republic of Namibia and the government of the Republic of South Africa on the establishment of a Permanent Water Commission	Established the Permanent Water Commission (PWC)	PWC
1992	Namibia, SA	Agreement on the Vioolsdrift and Noordoewer Joint Irrigation Scheme	Established the Joint Irrigation Authority (IIA)	IIA
1992	Lesotho, SA	Protocol V to the treaty of the Lesotho Highlands Water Project: Supplementary Arrangements with Regard to Project Related Income Tax and Dues and Charges Levied in the Kingdom of Lesotho in respect of Phases 1A and 1B of the project	Categorized the different types of water-related contracts in Lesotho and the need to track the amount of income tax paid; also specified ways in which income tax can be regarded as project costs	LHWC

(Contd)

Table 3.4 continued

Year	Signed by	Agreement/Treaty/Protocol	Scope	Institution
1/03/1994	Namibia, SA	Agreement on Water-related Matters pertaining to the Incorporation of Walvis Bay in the Territory of the Republic of Namibia	Walvis Bay	
1999	Lesotho, SA	Protocol VI to the treaty on the Lesotho Highlands Water Project: supplementary arrangements regarding the system of governance for the project	Redefined the functions and responsibilities of the Board of Directors of the LHDA, the TCTA and the JPTC. JPTC renamed LHWC; also redefined hierarchical structure of LHDA, TCTA and LHWC, and between the LHWC parties. Established that LHWC is the overall legal institution to which the LHDA (development organization on Lesotho side) and TCTA (development organization on South Africa side) report	LHWC
3/11/2000	Bots, Les, Namibia, SA	Agreement on the Establishment of the Orange-Senqu River Commission	Establishes ORASECOM, the first RBO to be established in terms of the Revised SADC Protocol	ORASECOM

Source: Adapted from Kistin and Ashton, 2008; UNEP, 2005

reasonable utilization and the no harm principle as central components, because these best serve their own national aspirations (ibid.).

Yet, this dynamic fails to fully explain South Africa's surge to prioritize multilateral relations in the last decade. An arguably plausible explanation for this lies in the domestic political and social contexts of riparians.

National context

At the national level, while the institutional and legal frameworks vary considerably between the four basin states the consistent factor among all the states is the transitional nature of state political and legislative frameworks evidenced in the promulgation of new acts, the revision of old ones and the development of water policy and strategies (Tompkins, 2007). The 1994 political transition in South Africa has led to an entirely new Water Act (1998) for South Africa and a change in the delivery and management of water services (following local government restructuring). These new pieces of legislation are generally compatible with the principles of the UN Convention and the Revised SADC Protocol. The new or revised national water acts also make reference to international rivers and meeting international obligations, an element not previously found in preceding national water laws. This indicates an awareness of international obligations and transboundary matters as well as a commitment to the implementation of the Revised SADC Protocol at a national level. However, unique political contexts and governance structures have altered the way in which these riparians have localized transboundary cooperation norms.

Lesotho

Lesotho's national hydropolitical legislative outlook is very much a reflection of its geopolitical position: a small and fragile state, completely landlocked by South Africa, with structural dependence in relation to South Africa (Santho, 2000). In this regard, Lesotho has faced and continues to face challenges of economic dependence and political survival, which are consequently highly dependent on exogenous factors (ibid.).

Particularly, Lesotho's relationship with South Africa has been heavily dependent on cooperative water exchange, yet tense at times (in the 1970s) as a result of Lesotho's criticism of apartheid, and South Africa's condemnation of Lesotho harbouring the then banned members of the African National Congress (ANC) (Meissner, 2004; Mirumachi, 2004). Only after the military coup d'état in Lesotho in January 1986, when Lesotho Paramilitary Force leader, Major-General Justin Metsing Lekhanya overthrew Chief Leabua Jonathan, did the process of negotiations accelerate (Meissner, 2004; Mirumachi, 2004).

Issues like apartheid, which may not be directly linked to water transfer, were therefore quite instrumental in steering, delaying and/or halting negotiations (Mirumachi, 2004). Moreover, the nature of cooperation was significantly different to what may be perceived as ideal today. Both countries used the LHWP as a tool to achieve political objectives and to further national agendas (ibid.). While South Africa used the LHWP as leverage to impose its control over ANC members, Lesotho emphasized protection of integrity and sovereignty (Meissner and Turton, 2003). As a result, a deep rooted mistrust permeated bilateral cooperative strategies on water.

Today, Lesotho has a transforming water management framework, and has produced its National Environment Policy (NEP) of 1998 and the subsequent Environment Act of 2008, as well as the Lesotho Water and Sanitation Policy of February 2007. Additionally, the Water Act (2008) was recently enacted by the Parliament of Lesotho. However, there are two significant issues that affect the successful implementation of this structure. First, the policy, legislative and institutional frameworks are in burgeoning stages of implementation and as such it will take time to be integrated into the current institutional framework (Jacobs, 2010a). Secondly, technical capacity to implement this framework is limited in Lesotho (ibid.).

South Africa

South Africa's political transformation formalized by the country's first democratic elections in 1994 brought with it a host of progressive reforms in the water sector (Jacobs, 2010b). The Water Services Act was ratified in 1997 and the landmark National Water Act in 1998 (Republic of South Africa, 1998). The 1998 NWA includes provisions for international arrangements, and provides for bilateral and multilateral bodies to implement international agreements pertaining to the management and development of water resources shared with neighbouring countries. It therefore emphasizes regional cooperation of water resources (ibid.). As such, it is regarded as one of the pioneering pieces of legislation that has influenced the international wave of reform, and as one of the most innovative and far-reaching water acts in the world (Ashton et al., 2008; Postel and Richter, 2003; Woodhouse, 2008). The establishment of the NWA has also been instrumental in influencing the national water management frameworks of neighbouring states. However, South Africa's challenge has not been the development of its progressive water reform policy, but rather the implementation thereof (Jacobs, 2010b). As Philip Woodhouse states, 'The prospect of redistribution from existing *haves* to *have nots* raises considerably the political risks and expectations attached to the implementation of reform' (Woodhouse, 2008: 3).

Additionally, South Africa is party to 25 agreements with its neighbours on shared rivers (Kistin et al., 2009), and, since 1910, it is documented that South Africa has entered into 101 international water-related treaties and agreements (ibid.). These include protocols and conventions with countries worldwide for example the Ramsar Convention (ibid.). A total of 61 of these treaties and agreements deal with shared water resources (ibid.). Some examples include: (1) Treaty on the LHWP with Lesotho in 1986 (2) The Permanent Water Commission between South Africa and Namibia in 1992 (3) The Development and Utilization of the Komati River basin with Swaziland in 1992 (4) The ORASECOM Agreement with Lesotho, Namibia and Botswana in 2000 and (5) The SADC Revised Water Protocol in 2000. South Africa has also, as previously mentioned, ratified the 1997 UN Convention. This brief policy and legislative framework could imply an outward-looking stance on cooperation, and indeed, may also display South Africa's hegemonic ambition in determining the broader ideational and normative framework within the southern African region.

Namibia

Much like South Africa's policy reforms after apartheid, Namibia also adopted water reforms after independence in 1990 although lengthy review processes delayed the implementation of legislation. The first policy reform came in the form of the 1993 Water Supply and Sanitation Policy (WSASP). This policy document was subject to a review process and several revisions. The most notable revisions included recommendations that the Namibian Water Corporation Limited (NamWater), a State Owned Enterprise be established as the major bulk water supplier, and also, that the Directorate of Rural Water Supply (DRWS) be established in the Ministry of Agriculture, Water and Rural Development to improve access to safe water for communities in rural, communal areas (Republic of Namibia, 2008). A later version of the WSASP drafted in 2008, has now replaced the policy of 1993 (ibid.).

Additionally, the National Water Policy White Paper of 2000 was developed into the 2004 Water Resources Management Act (Act No. 24 of 2004). However, soon after its promulgation, several water management and legal experts pointed out that certain technicalities hampered the practical implementation thereof.[14] It was inherently flawed with a multitude of amendments (104 to be specific)[15] and required substantial revision to enable effective implementation. The Ministry was therefore advised to revise and rewrite the entire Water Resources Management Act of 2004.

This review process, otherwise known as the Namibia Water Resources Management Review (NWRMR) was particularly politically charged reflecting a degree of norm contestation at the national level. The motivation behind this review was a decision taken by the minister at the time, in consultation with the Cabinet, that a water resources management review project will be conducted by young indigenous Namibians (Heyns, 2005). The NWRMR comprised mainly of a technical team of young Namibians with 'acceptable academic backgrounds, but unfortunately very little practical experience in the water sector', and was supported by consultants and directed by a task force of stakeholders (ibid.: 99). One significant criticism of this process was that this team operated in isolation of the Namibian Department of Water Affairs (DWA) (because the DWA was also 'reviewed') and were guided mostly by foreign consultants with little knowledge of the Namibian situation (ibid.).

The review process started in 1997 but petered out by 2002 due to a lack of further support from donors who initially funded the process.[16] According to several sources directly involved and affected by this process, the post-independence review of functional processes was initiated as a way of exposing the perceived evils perpetrated in the past and to get rid of an older generation of white professionals that symbolized a colonial past.[17] The said rationale for the reforms centred around the need to improve institutional arrangements to meet new challenges specific to Namibia, in a changing water management environment and to accommodate political views, perceptions and requirements to meet the expectations of the electorate (ibid.). Moreover, the rationale relates to several other sociopolitical issues. Primarily, 'The post-independence sentiments of the public created political imperatives to remove all unacceptable practices originating from the colonial past, including the institutions, policies and legislation that could be associated with that period' (Heyns, 2005: 99).

In 2010, Cabinet approved the Water Resources Management Bill, it was tabled in the National Assembly and finally became operational. Namibia's old Water Act (Act No. 54 of 1956), inherited from South Africa has therefore now been repealed. The 2004 Water Resources Management Act is aligned with South Africa's NWA, makes provisions for a future IWRM and planning system, promotes the equitable and beneficial use of international watercourses and is also based on the eight normative principles and practices of international water law (Republic of Namibia, 2004). It also focuses on 'international water management institutions', and provides a basis for integrating and aligning Namibia's arrangements with the future activities of regional institutions (Hiddema and Erasmus, 2007; Republic of Namibia, 2004). The Namibian government now faces conventional challenges of technical capacity to implement it.[18]

Another pertinent issue influencing Namibia's institutional and legislative framework involves access to transboundary rivers. Access to the Orange-Senqu and Okavango rivers remains of paramount importance to Namibia and as such, Namibia is party to several water agreements with its neighbours: (1) The JPTC between Angola and Namibia on the Cunene River in 1990 (2) The 1992 PWC Agreement between South Africa and Namibia on the lower Orange River (3) The Agreement on the Establishment of the Vioolsdrift and Noordoewer Joint Irrigation Scheme on the lower Orange River in 1992 (4) The Permanent Okavango River Basin Water Commission (OKACOM) between Angola, Botswana and Namibia of 1994 (5) The 1990 Joint Permanent Water Commission (JPWC) Agreement between Botswana and Namibia and (6) The 2000 ORASECOM Agreement. Like South Africa, Namibia has also signed and ratified both the 1997 UN Convention as well as the 2000 Revised Water Protocol.

Once again, this may lead to a conclusion that Namibia is particularly willing to cooperate with regards to its international watercourses. However, international agreements require further legislative incorporation, translation and implementation before they are domestically effective in Namibia (Tompkins, 2007). This alludes to a key argument presented in this book: coherent implementation of these agreements does not happen automatically nor does it occur smoothly. Moreover, the manner in which policy reform and review takes place also determines the degree to which global, regional and national normative principles are accepted and socialized on the ground. But the Namibian example further illustrates the complexities of the effect of poorly developed policy and legal frameworks which have massive effects on the sub-national uptake and socialization of certain regional and international norms. The poorly drafted 2004 Water Resources Management Act, and the subsequent politically charged problems in its review process, has indeed marred smooth institutionalization processes. However, it also reflects the importance of context in helping or hindering the development of cooperative management norms, and the instrumental role of individuals and personalized politics.

Botswana

Due to Botswana's water scarcity and limitations to access of surface water resources (particularly in the area of the Orange-Senqu Basin), the management of water resources and the protection of the environment are key national priorities (Hiddema and Erasmus, 2007; Tompkins, 2007). However, Botswana's legal and institutional framework is the oldest of all Orange-Senqu riparian states (Hiddema and Erasmus, 2007; Tompkins, 2007). While it is party to several international environmental agreements such as the RAMSAR Convention, the ORASECOM and OKACOM Agreements and the Revised SADC Protocol on Shared Watercourses, Botswana's national legislation on Water Works dates back to 5 March 1962, the Water Utilities Cooperation to 30 June 1970, the Boreholes Act to 19 October 1956 and the Water Act to 1968 (Hiddema and Erasmus, 2007). While these have been amended over time, it is questionable whether they can address new policy challenges of harmonization with regional and international agreements and transboundary challenges relating to climate change, equitable and reasonable use and information exchange (ibid.). In 2005, a new Water Bill was drafted, but this is still under review (Kranz et al., 2005b). It has however led to a Policy Brief on Botswana's Water Management, published in 2006, that aims to address key national issues such as water accounts and policy messages, most notably that water planning has to shift from a supply-oriented approach towards IWRM balancing supply and demand measures (DEA, 2006).

Summary of legislative and institutional development

To summarize, norm convergence has emerged in southern Africa and in the Orange-Senqu River particularly. Global principles found in the 1997 UN Convention have diffused down to the regional level and are included in the SADC Water Protocols of 1995 and 2000 (see Figure 3.3). An interesting characteristic of the SADC region is that while SADC states (with the exception of South Africa and Namibia) have not ratified the UN Convention, they have all accepted the SADC Protocols and in so doing, have indirectly adopted the principles of the UN Convention. Top-down norm dissemination has occurred, although not in a linear pattern. Additionally, the transitional nature of national institutional and legal frameworks since the 1990s has also resulted in lateral norm convergence from state to state, and regional norm convergence from state to basin to region, as key principles were shared and transferred in policy reforms, although fast-track policies have at times been detrimental to successful implementation.

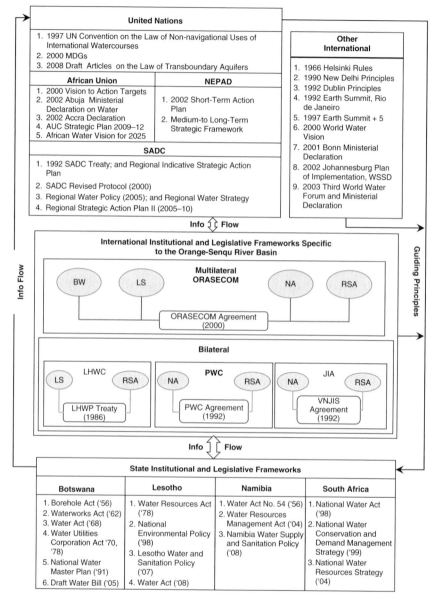

Figure 3.3 The current institutional framework of the Orange-Senqu River basin

Barriers to norm convergence do, however, exist at the basin-wide level due to resource and capacity constraints shared by all four countries. A review of legislative and institutional frameworks is therefore not sufficient to understand the intricacies of norm convergence or the trajectory of normative processes. For that, it is important to examine the practical drivers and barriers to norm convergence.

Top-down norm diffusion

Albeit a non-linear pattern of top-down norm diffusion, global principles found in the 1997 UN Convention have indeed infiltrated regional agreements such as the Revised SADC Protocol. Additionally, despite the fact that South Africa and Namibia are the only SADC states to sign and ratify the UN Convention, all other SADC states have indirectly adopted the principles enshrined within the UN Convention, due to the almost verbatim inclusion of it in the Revised SADC Protocol, to which all are party (Ramoeli, 2002; Turton, 2008b). These riparian states have therefore, de facto accepted the core principles enshrined in the UN Convention because these principles have been codified into the SADC Protocol. Thus, irrespective of whether the individual states have ratified the UN Convention or not, their accession to the Revised SADC Protocol on Shared Watercourse Systems requires them to abide by the core requirements of the UN Convention (Ashton et al., 2005). Subsequent amendments to the SADC Water Protocol have also been made, each reflecting evolving international legal norms and a subsequent evolution in normative priorities regarding international watercourses.

Regional norm convergence

Several points allude to the argument made for regional norm convergence at an institutional level. First, the transitional nature of national policy frameworks for all Orange-Senqu riparian states, has enabled them to align their policies with that of the Revised SADC Protocol but also the national policies of their neighbours.

Basin-wide agreements have been signed in all of the SADC basins that have a significant level of development (Ashton et al., 2005; Turton and Ashton, 2008); and since many of these basins are multilateral basins, this is counter to the global norm identified by Conca (2006). Additionally, the wide range of bilateral and basin-wide agreements signed by the individual states within the SADC region, and their accession to important international agreements, suggest that SADC states are committed to strengthening levels of cooperation between states and reducing the potential for disputes and conflicts to occur (Ashton et al., 2005; Turton and Ashton, 2008).

Turton and Ashton (2008) argue that ideally, this should translate into the establishment of suitable multilateral institutions that can manage the different river basins on behalf of the riparian states concerned. However, despite the evidence of growing cooperation between states, less success has been achieved in the development of multilateral institutions to manage shared water resources. While multilateral commissions have been formed for several other southern African river basins (e.g. the Cunene, Incomati, Limpopo, Orange-Senqu, Okavango, Umbeluzi and Zambezi basins), these commissions remain almost purely advisory in nature; each country still conducts its normal processes of decision-making for managing the water resources within the boundaries of its sovereign territory (Turton et al., 2005). This could either suggest that the countries concerned are reluctant to delegate part of their sovereign responsibility to another party (in this case to an institution for the management of water resources), especially where these resources are critical for their future social and economic development (Turton and Ashton, 2008). Alternatively, as is evident in the Orange-Senqu Basin, it could also be the case that due to pre-existing bilateral regimes, multilateral regimes are slower to develop and their mandates are questioned as a result of project-based bilateral agreements conducting most operational functions. Different scholars and managers have had varying opinions on the coexistence of both multilateral and bilateral agreements/institutions on the Orange-Senqu, that is PWC and LHWC, stating that the pre-existing bilaterals advise ORASECOM processes because they are older and more established, while others argue that ORASECOM acts as the central advisory forum that supersedes the bilaterals. Qualitative research revealed that power dynamics are not contentious and that no overlap of mandates exists due to the fact that most state representatives are members on both bilateral and the multilateral institutions.

Another argument presented by the Maryland School is that lateral norm convergence is not occurring nor is the deepening (or specification) of the eight normative principles in regional and basin agreements. Once again, as is evident with the ORASECOM Agreement, all eight normative principles were referenced to varying degrees. Similarly, Article 12 of the ZAMCOM Agreement makes specific reference to eight legal principles, which are sourced from wider than the UN Convention alone. The concept of deepening is first of all in and of itself questionable as to what exactly it is and why it is necessary. Also, the degree to which these principles have deepened is reflected in causal processes unique to the sociopolitical and cultural context of the basin as well as behavioural factors, not only in the degree to which it is articulated in policy.

Drivers and barriers to norm convergence in the Orange-Senqu River basin

Several drivers and barriers to norm convergence exist and act as catalysts and inhibitors to the development of a community of interest on water resources. These drivers and barriers may be enabling or inhibiting processes that shape actor behaviour, such as skills flight and the lack of sustainable knowledge transfer, trust-building or the lack of trust and technical cooperation. They may also be structural and context-specific such as, congruence and localization. These factors drive the multi-levelled development of cooperative management norms and ultimately determine the way in which regional communities of interest develop.

Barriers

Skills flight and the lack of sustainable knowledge transfer

The loss of intellectual assets threatens effective water management and also norm convergence, particularly in water-scarce countries such as South Africa where the onus is on the scientific community to find technological solutions (Jacobs, 2010b;

Turton, 2008a; Walwyn and Scholes, 2006). There has been a large skills flight in southern Africa in recent years due to a range of causal factors including: the lack of opportunities for professional development in specific countries, political unrest, increased crime, lack of confidence in the government and social mobility. Water specialists in African countries often emigrate to apply their trade in developed countries, but also move to international and multi-national organizations. Similarly, South Africa attracts significant capacity, particularly from Zimbabwe and other African countries further afield, where highly skilled people seek economic security (see Jacobs, 2010b for an argument on the influx of immigrants and its effects on service delivery in South Africa).

The repercussions for the water sector include high staff turn-over, the loss of skills and institutional memory due to the departure of experienced staff, little or no career path and succession planning, the appointment of non-technical personnel to management positions requiring technical experience, as well as the absence of well-structured educational and training programmes suitably targeted to all stakeholders in the water management chain (Jacobs, 201b; Mwendera et al., 2003). These factors have an inhibiting effect on institutional effectiveness as it requires a large degree of re-learning and re-building of trusting relationships (Jacobs, 2010b). This in turn affects the institutional capacity and effectiveness of transboundary institutions such as river basin organizations (RBOs) where to a large extent, certain individuals who have represented their countries in both bilateral and multilateral negotiations, created an institutional vacuum when they left (ibid.). The lack of sustainable knowledge transfer policies therefore impedes norm convergence due to the time it takes to re-learn and re-build a national, basin-wide or regional culture around cooperative water management.

Institutional memory loss is therefore a major obstacle to institutional development but also to norm convergence. A Water Research Commission (WRC) report concluded that institutional memory loss results in negative impacts on service delivery and opportunities for cooperation, particularly where mechanisms to institutionalize individuals' knowledge have not been put in place (Pegram et al., 2006). Moreover, the lack of sustainable knowledge transfer policies has contributed to norm resistance, not because newly employed individuals actively resist a normative pull, but because they lack an awareness of such convergence taking place. This consideration is critical to a normative understanding of the problem by emphasizing the significance of individual identities on both personal relationships and institutional capacity. As Checkel argues, the environment in which agents/states take action is social as well as material and this setting can provide agents/states with understandings of their interests and can in fact 'constitute them' (Checkel, 1998).

Lack of trust

The lack of trust between policymakers representing different countries and constituencies can also be regarded as a barrier to smooth norm convergence. It is however important to note that while political trust has not been essential for technical collaborations to take place and be successful in the Orange-Senqu River basin, and also the SADC region, it does make for better cooperative management strategies as a result of personal relationships that have formed, for example, between hydrologists, engineers and other technical professionals in different countries sharing hydrological or flood warning data. Even before 1994, and despite levels of distrust among riparian states at that time, technical cooperation existed as a means to overcome the political incapacity to engage. While political distrust was commonplace, personal trusting relationships that were built up over many years by technical professionals working together on bilateral projects contributed to the development of a basin-wide ethos of technical cooperative water management.

The second aspect of trust relates to institutional trust or the confidence that individuals have in an institution's functionality. An increase in institutional trust influences individuals to accept institutionalized norms that have emerged as part of the institutional fabric (Jacobs, 2010a). Similarly, if individuals do not have faith in the institution's functionality, very few norms will be socialized through institutional avenues. Several technical water managers in Namibia, South Africa and Lesotho, have noted that the practical cooperation on the exchange of hydrological data has disappeared with the introduction of international river basin commissions (ibid.). Examples cited were the Kavango and Zambezi, where managers argued that there was never any problem getting Kavango hydrological data from Botswana before OKACOM was established. This could be interpreted as an opposition to the formalization of information exchange channels, oftentimes which involve time-consuming processes constrained by bureaucratic red tape (ibid.). These sentiments reflect a lack of trust in multilateral institutions to effectively perform their mandates, and as such, may be a barrier to the development of a community of interests since professionals do not buy into the idea of cooperative management of water if these organizations are the ones to spearhead it. But this sentiment is not shared by all decision-makers. According to Heyns, the real problem is not so much the existence of the institution or its capacity to fulfil its mandate, but rather the capacity of state to provide the necessary hydrological information to other countries that might need it for flood warning purposes.[19]

Drivers

Technical cooperation

Technical collaboration has been previously articulated as a key driver of norm convergence in the basin. Due to the relative scarcity of water as a resource in the region, and despite the political instability and distrust, there were few alternative options that countries had other than to cooperate in this manner. Of course, this has also shaped the nature of cooperative management that has been largely dominated by 'technical experts'. In this regard, cooperative management of water has been founded on sound empirical, technically driven expertise embedded within a positivist tradition that has relied heavily on notions of objectivity, quantification, accuracy, linearity and rationality. This positivist science or 'hard science', has oftentimes been regarded as the preferred and most reliable type of knowledge on which to base decisions regarding water management and has therefore influenced the kinds of norms that have been socialized in local contexts (see Jacobs and Nienaber, 2011 for an examination of the consequences of the development of water management within the positivist paradigm).

Trust and confidence-building

Institutional or state-to-state trust is not a necessary factor for cooperation particularly that of a technical nature, but it does produce more effective cooperative management strategies. Once again, the distinction between individual trust and institutional trust is important. Transboundary river basin management is largely based on individual personalities and identities. Trust in this context is of paramount importance since good relations translate into more robust policies (Jacobs, 2010a). Institutional trust builds the credibility of the institution and how it is perceived as a functional institution which effectively carries out its mandate. Institutional trust is equally important to facilitate norm convergence because it builds institutional reputations and persuades other institutions of the moral appropriateness of certain principles and/or ways of doing things. Indeed, ORASECOM has developed a great deal of credibility both regionally and internationally and acts as the multilateral model for RBO institutional development in the region (ibid.). As such, it arguably sets the standard for best practice in the region in activities regarding multilateral institutions. Norms adopted or created by ORASECOM therefore carry greater clout than those borne out of, or advocated by less respected institutions.

Norm entrepreneurs and the significance of personalized politics

The importance of individuals to the success or failure of effective water governance in southern Africa is noteworthy as has not been given enough attention in scholarly discourse to date (Jacobs and Nienaber, 2011). As Swatuk argues, water governance in southern Africa exists within a context of differently empowered actors who negotiate and renegotiate roles and rights to resources (Swatuk, 2002b; Swatuk, 2005a). This may have positive consequences (a close-community of technical experts based on trusting relationships, a wealth of knowledge and experience in the water sector) and negative consequences (power asymmetries and an elite epistemic community, institutional memory loss when these individuals leave). These individual policymakers and technocrats, labelled by Finnemore and Sikkink (1998) as norm entrepreneurs, have succeeded in persuading their constituencies of the moral appropriateness of certain codes of conduct relating to transboundary water governance. Norm entrepreneurs are regarded as agents who have distinct notions about appropriate behaviour in their community (Finnemore and Sikkink, 1998), and are able to articulate them. Furthermore, they compete with the existing constellation of norms in order for their ideas to gain acceptance as norms (ibid.).

Due to the technical manner in which transboundary water resource management is carried out today, norm entrepreneurs exist largely in the epistemic community, both domestically and internationally. An epistemic community is created by a dense network of activists, policymakers, academics and entrepreneurs, who are influential in setting the agenda and defining the interests related to water resource management. Moreover, due to the highly technical nature of water engineering, hydrology and other environmental, ecological and soil and land management sciences, this network comprises of an exclusive club of experts who dominate the production and application of knowledge (Swatuk, 2005b). Swatuk argues that often, their conservationist or technical interests take precedence over that of local actors (farmers, pastoralists etc.) in that they are present at organizational platforms to convince policymakers to embrace global environmental norms while local actors are not (ibid.). The epistemic community is also knowledgeable of political and technical processes, and are therefore able to articulate their interests in this manner.

In essence, key individuals in the epistemic community (policymakers as well as academics) have played a significant role in 'bringing' international and national norms and principles home (see Harold Koh, 1998 for an analysis of how international and domestic legal regimes interact, and how international rules become internalized in domestic law ,and politics). Moreover, where certain of these norms have been ambiguous or deliberately vague in wording, these individuals or norm entrepreneurs have adopted the language of the norm without giving it immediate substance (Swatuk, 2005a), or have interpreted them for specific national contexts.

Similarly, individuals have been instrumental in resisting certain norms if they were not well articulated enough for local contexts. For example, in Namibia, after the new Water Resources Management Act was just promulgated in December 1994, the Head of the Department of Water Affairs and Forestry at the time, Mr Piet Heyns, convinced the Minister that the Department had insufficient human, technical and financial capacity to administer the new Act once implemented. Moreover, he highlighted the fact that the text needed considerable revision to make it practically implementable.[20] The Minister agreed and the Department started with a process to amend the Act.[21] The review processes lasted several years and resulted in subsequent revision of Namibia's Water Resources Management Act.[22]

This example illustrates the critical importance of individuals and the personalized politics of norm entrepreneurs to the success of building normative frameworks and actively lobbying for the socialization or resistance of norms. The clarity with which policies, legal and institutional frameworks are drafted, is highly influenced by an individual dimension. That is to say, key individuals play a major role in the framing of norms, the way in which they are codified, and the degree of socialization in terms of influencing others' uptake of these norms. More research is needed on the role that individuals play in influencing normative debates of cooperative water management.

Congruent norm sets

In line with the Finnemore-Sikkink logic (1998) international norms have a better chance of being accepted in local contexts if they are able to fit in with existing local normative frameworks. Similarly, Checkel (1999) refers to this as 'cultural match'. As the southern African case shows, the domestic context is conducive to the socialization of several global principles since versions of these principles (such as cooperative governance, communication and information exchange) have become prioritized in post-colonial and post-apartheid ideals of democratic governance, stakeholder participation and decentralization. In essence, the domestic context allows for 'normative fit' with several global principles. Indeed, actors throughout the SADC region support ideas that are morally appealing and that serve their political interests, without threatening pre-existing configurations of power, such as the notion of 'peace parks' (Swatuk, 2005a).

Conclusion

This chapter applied the central thesis of multi-level governance in the analysis of the Orange-Senqu River basin. At the basin level, this chapter focused on legal and institutional processes that symbolized a movement towards norm convergence. However, an evaluation of the institutional and legal frameworks within the basin is not sufficient to fully grapple with the intricacies of norm convergence. Qualitative research in the basin highlighted significant drivers and barriers to the development of a community of interests in the Orange-Senqu Basin around water resources. While it can be concluded that institutional or political trust was neither a driver nor a barrier to technical cooperation, personal trusting relationships at the individual level and personalized politics have acted as drivers (trust-building) or barriers (lack of trust) to facilitating norm convergence since the latter has been dependent on social learning and persuasion in the Orange-Senqu River basin. Sustainable knowledge transfer policies or the lack thereof is of paramount importance to the sustainability of competence and to the ability of a river basin organization to absorb institutional shocks such as skills flight. The maintenance of institutional memory in this regard, also helps to facilitate norm convergence through social learning. These drivers and barriers not only affect regional norm convergence at a basin level, but are also applicable to sub-national normative influences.

Notes

1 Data layers: USGS HydroSHEDS, ESRI, FAO Aquastat, WWF, UNEP.
2 Personal Communication with Ashton, P. (2008) Aquatic Ecologist, Council for Scientific and Industrial Research (CSIR), Pretoria, South Africa, 7 July 2008.
3 Ibid.
4 Personal Communication with Thamae, L. (2008) Executive Secretary, ORASECOM, Pretoria, South Africa, 17 September 2008.
5 This was later referred to as Rhodesia, the Republic of Rhodesia, the Republic of Zimbabwe Rhodesia and became Zimbabwe upon independence on 17 April 1980.
6 This became Zambia upon independence on 24 October 1964.

7   This became Malawi upon independence on 6 July 1964.

8   This became Botswana upon independence on 30 September 1966

9   This became Lesotho upon independence on 4 October 1966.

10   Personal Communication with Roberts, P. (2008) Former Deputy Director General: Water Resources, Department of Water Affairs and Forestry (DWAF), Government of South Africa, Pretoria, South Africa, 19 December 2008.

11   Personal Communication with Phakoe, M. (2008) Chief Executive: Lesotho Highlands Development Authority (LHDA), Maseru, Lesotho, Maseru, Lesotho, 25 November 2008.

12   Ibid.

13   Ibid.

14   Personal Communication with Heyns, P. (2008). Former Under Secretary: Department of Water Affairs, and Namibian delegate to the ORASECOM and the OKACOM, Ministry of Water Affairs, Namibia, Windhoek, Namibia, 1 September 2008; Personal Communication with Biggs, D. (2008). Former Deputy Director: Planning, MAWF, Namibian Technical Task Team Member of the ORASECOM Technical Task Team, Namibia, Windhoek, Namibia, 1 September 2008.

15   Personal Communication with Biggs, D. (2008).

16   Email Correspondence with Heyns, P. (2009). Former Under Secretary, Department of Water Affairs, and Namibian delegate to the ORASECOM and the OKACOM, Namibia, 19 November 2009–December 2009.

17   Ibid.

18   Personal Communication with Heyns, P. (2008).

19   Ibid.

20   Ibid.

21   Ibid.

22   Ibid.

4

The Nile River Basin and a
Changing Landscape

The waters of the Nile are embroiled in greater complexity than its southern counterpart, the Orange-Senqu River. First, the Nile River is longer and the river basin is larger. Secondly, the effective governance of the Nile River involves many more state actors than does the Orange-Senqu River, flowing through eleven riparian states: Egypt, Sudan, South Sudan, Ethiopia, Kenya, Eritrea, Democratic Republic of Congo, Tanzania, Burundi, Rwanda and Uganda (Abraham, 2004; NBI, 2007; Waterbury, 2002; Wolf, 1998). And finally, Nile River basin management has been entangled in colonial bilateral agreements and treaties and consequent unilateral action for longer than the Orange-Senqu River basin. All these factors, combined with political instability, tense co-riparian relations and a general lack of trust between riparian states have led to greater resistance to the global transboundary cooperation norm set in the Nile River basin, with some scholars going so far as to argue that a community of riparians does not exist in the Nile Basin (Waterbury, 2002).

Waterbury (2002) states that there are no accepted norms of group behaviour that could shame riparian states into upholding group action, and that the main frameworks that promote and sustain cooperation are contract and hierarchy. This is arguably due to the fact that externally induced norms of transboundary cooperation have not been fully socialized and internalized and have met with greater local resistance. That said however, there has been a steady increase in state-to-state and state-to-sub-basin-to-region norm convergence as well as significant bottom-up norm infiltration from local communities to the national level.

Overview of the Nile River basin

At 6,825 km long, the Nile River is the longest river in the world. Its basin covers approximately one-tenth of Africa with a catchment area of over 3 million square km (see Table 4.1). The river does not form a contiguous border between any of

Table 4.1 Physical characteristics of the Nile River basin

Nile River basin – major features	
Total basin area	3.1 million km2
Area rainfall (mm/y)	Average: 600–650mm
Estimated natural runoff	84 km3
Water demand	Irrigation, power generation and navigation
Population	160,000,000 within the boundaries of the basin and 300,000,000 live within the 10 countries that share and depend on the Nile waters.

Source: Malzbender and Earle, 2008; UNEP, 2005

the riparian states, and instead, flows through them, which has made it possible for any one riparian state to act unilaterally regarding infrastructural development on its portion of the river (Malzbender and Earle, 2008). It is generally agreed that the Nile River has several major sources: (1) Roughly 80 per cent of the water originates from the Ethiopian Highland Plateau through the Blue Nile (Abbay) and the Atbara River (Tekeze) with their sources in Lake Tana; (2) The basin of the Equatorial Lakes Plateau shared by Burundi, Democratic Republic of Congo (DRC), Kenya, Rwanda, Tanzania and Uganda, with its most distant source in the Kagera River, which winds its way through Burundi, Rwanda, Tanzania and Uganda into Lake Victoria and (3) The Bahr el Ghazal Basin whose contribution is almost negligible (El-Fadel et al., 2003; Waako, 2008).

In terms of national contributions to streamflow and to the percentage of national land mass in the basin, all the Nile water used in Burundi and Rwanda, and more than half the waters in Uganda are produced within their national boundaries. Most of the water resources of the Sudans and Egypt, however, originate outside their borders: 77% and 97%, respectively (El-Fadel et al., 2003). Egypt and the Sudans also account for over 90% of water use and have legitimated this use in historical treaties and agreements (1929 and 1959 Agreements) formed under colonialism. Similarly, less than 9% of Kenya's land mass falls within the Lake Victoria Basin, however it provides over half of the country's freshwater supply (Tadesse, 2008). Ethiopia is by far the greatest contributor of streamflow, supplying 86% of the Nile's waters and 95%[1] during the flood period (ibid.). In comparison to the Blue Nile's enormous contribution, the White Nile contributes only 14% (see Table 4.2 and Map 4.1).

Water availability is also highly varied in this basin. Nearly all of the river's water is generated from an area covering 20% of the basin, while the remainder are arid or semi-arid regions with minimal water supplies and very large evaporation losses (Karyabwite, 2000). To be specific, while the sources of the Nile have average rainfall exceeding 1,000 mm per annum, as it moves northwards through South Sudan, rainfall gradually decreases to approximately 200 mm per annum at the confluence of the Blue and White Niles in Khartoum (Tadesse, 2008). Semi-desert and desert conditions characterize the northern part of the basin, with rainfall dropping to virtually zero in northern Sudan and most of Egypt (ibid.).

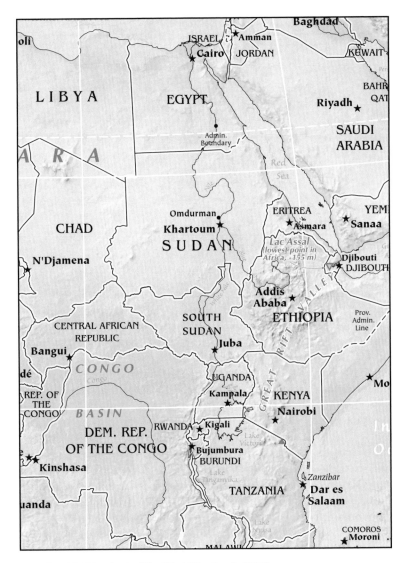

Map 4.1 The Nile River basin (The World Factbook, 2009)

The population size of the Nile River basin mirrors its biophysical enormity. It is home to an estimated 160 million people within the boundaries of the basin, while roughly 300 million live within the 11 countries that share and depend on Nile waters. Over the next 25 years, the population is expected to double, which has led some scholars and environmental activists to forecast that this projected increase in water demand could lead to a potential conflict situation (El-Fadel et al., 2003; Pottinger, 2004). For example, a World Bank study forecasted that the amount of

Table 4.2 Contributions to the Nile River basin by country

Sub-Basin	Nile riparian	Item		
		Area in basin (km²)	**Approximate basin area (%)**	**MAR (mm)**
Eastern Nile	Egypt	326, 751	10.5	15
Sub-Basin	Sudan	1 978,506	63.6	500
	Ethiopia	365, 117	11.7	1,125
	Eritrea	24,921	0.8	520
Equatorial Lakes	Kenya	46,229	1.5	1,260
Sub-Basin	Tanzania	84,200	2.7	1,015
	Uganda	231,366	7.4	1,140
	Rwanda	19,876	0.6	1,105
	Burundi	13,260	0.4	1,110
	DRC	22,143	0.7	1,245

Source: Phillips et al., 2006: 67

water available to each person in North Africa will drop by 80% in a single lifetime by 2025 (Brunnée and Toope, 2002). El-Fadel et al. (2003) further argue that the increase in population distribution in the basin is dominated by a shift towards greater urbanization, migration and over-grazing, which have contributed to deforestation and land degradation.

Additionally, the flow of the Nile has diminished significantly over the past century due to climate change, evaporation and seepage. The Jonglei Canal project was designed to resolve this problem and ameliorate the loss of water by partially by-passing the Sudd wetlands in South Sudan and deliver waters more efficiently downstream to the White Nile (Phillips et al., 2006). Construction of the 360-km Canal commenced in 1978 but was postponed indefinitely because of regional instability, most notably the civil war in 1983 (McCaffrey, 2001b; Phillips et al., 2006). Moreover, the construction of the Jonglei is ridden with contention, and the rationale for draining a wetland of major international significance such as the Sudd has received tremendous attention from various environmental advocacy groups and the international community (Phillips et al., 2006). Any future developments to continue with this project would have to strike the balance between a demand for the retention of the Sudd wetlands with downstream water needs (ibid.).

In Egypt, the problem is exacerbated due to the large-scale use of fertilizer and high levels of salinity resulting in poor water quality (Brunnée and Toope, 2002). Furthermore, the Aswan High Dam was constructed to control and conserve flood waters for use in the dry season, however, Lake Nassar, the immense reservoir created behind the dam, permits a high level of water loss through seepage and evaporation (suggested to be about 12% of flow), thus further increasing salinity of the waters (ibid.). That said however, more than 95% of the silt in the Nile originates in the Ethiopian highlands (Tadesse, 2008).

In terms of future development, Egypt has begun construction on the North Sinai Development Project, which includes the Al-Salam Canal in front of Damietta

Lock and Dam with the purpose of reclaiming 220 thousand feddans west of the Suez Canal; the New Valley Project, which is a system of canals around Sheikh Zayed Canal, fed from Lake Nasser through the Mubarak Pumping Station to irrigate 234,000 hectares in the Sahara; and the Infrastructure Project for Irrigation Improvement in the West Delta Region, all of which requires substantial abstraction from the Nile (Brunnée and Toope, 2002; Spiegel, 2005). Additionally, both South Sudan and Ethiopia have projected future development of hydro-electric and dam projects (ibid.). However, the Nile cannot meet the current volumetric demands and abstraction trajectory of both Ethiopia and Egypt, while simultaneously meeting the needs of all other Nile riparians (ibid.).

Brief hydropolitical history of the Nile River

In terms of basin-wide multilateral cooperation, several dilemmas are evident. First, a multilateral treaty agreement governing all eleven Nile riparian states is non-existent (Abraham, 2003; Mallat, 1994; Spiegel, 2005). Secondly, many treaty agreements and resulting claims were formed under British colonial rule rather than in a context of independent sovereign states, and their validity has constantly been questioned (Abraham, 2003). And finally, even the more recent treaties fail to adequately address future factors such as climate change, human intervention set to harness the flow of the waters, changes in the flow of the water itself (ibid.) and the growing pollution problem (Tadros, 1996–7).

Colonialism is arguably responsible for the beginning of modern legal and institutional tensions in the basin. Colonial superpowers realized the significance of the Nile water for the prosperity of the colonies, particularly Egypt (El-Fadel et al., 2003), and entered into water-sharing negotiations with each other. In this regard, Britain had to enter into agreements with France and with Italy to prevent their interference with British dominance over the Nile. The Protocol signed in Rome on 15 April 1891 between Britain and Italy, for instance, demarcated their respective spheres of influence in East Africa from Ras Kasar to the Blue Nile (Degefu, 2003), at a time of Italian colonization of Eritrea (Nicol, 2003b). Article III of this Protocol stipulates that 'The Italian Government engages not to construct on the Atbara, in view of irrigation, any work which might sensibly modify its flow into the Nile' (Degefu, 2003: 95). In return, Britain recognized Ethiopia as an Italian Sphere of Influence, thereby denying Ethiopia's independence (ibid.). However, Ethiopia has never accepted the 1891 protocol since it was signed by Italy on Ethiopia's behalf on the basis of the Treaty of Wechale between Emperor Menelik and the Italian Government on 2 May 1889 (ibid.). Additionally, this treaty was later annulled following Italy's defeat by Ethiopian forces at the Battle of Adwa in 1896 (ibid,).

Another highly disputed agreement regarding the waters of the Nile was signed on 15 May 1902 between Britain (acting for Egypt and Sudan) and Italy-Ethiopia, and is highly contentious to this day. This agreement prohibited Ethiopia from engaging in any construction activities of the Nile's headwaters that would 'arrest' the flow of water to Egypt (Okidi, 1990). This was brought about by the realization of the enormity of Ethiopia's contribution to streamflow, and that the British had no control over the Ethiopian portion (El-Fadel et al., 2003). While this agreement was actually drafted to regulate the frontiers between Anglo-Egyptian Sudan, Ethiopia and Eritrea (Nicol, 2003b), it contained within it a stipulation on the Nile waters in Article III:

> His majesty the Emperor Menelik II, King of Kings of Ethiopia, engages himself toward the government of His Britannic Majesty not to construct or allow to be constructed any work across the Blue Nile, Lake Tana or the Sobat which would arrest the flow of their waters into the Nile, except in agreement with His Britannic Majesty's Government of Sudan. (Hertslet, 1967: 585; Tadesse, 2008: 7)

This treaty was prepared in two languages, Amharic and English, 'both being official and equally authentic' (Degefu, 2003: 96). The disputed term was the meaning of 'arrest'. According to the Amharic version, the wording 'not to arrest the flow of the Nile' did not imply a prohibition on use. Additionally, the English version, contained a phrase, 'and the Government of Sudan'. This required Ethiopia to seek clearance not only from the colonizing power but also from the local Sudanese authorities for any planned developments on the Blue Nile (Degefu, 2003; Nicol, 2003b). However, this additional wording is absent in the Amharic version (Degefu, 2003). According to Degefu (2003), therefore, Ethiopia signed this agreement under duress, but has never ratified it. In 1935, however, the UK recognized the annexation of Ethiopia by Italy, an act that invalidated all previous agreements between the two governments (ibid.).

The 1906 agreement between Britain, France and Italy, referred to as the Tripartite Agreement is yet another important treaty signed by the colonial powers. The agreement, in Article I, stipulated that 'France, Great Britain and Italy shall cooperate in maintaining the political and territorial status quo in Ethiopia' (Tadesse, 2008: 7). In essence, this referred to the renewal of previous declarations, such as the 1902 Agreement, and affirmation of joint support in their quests for economic penetration of Ethiopia (ibid.). Specifically, it defined their interests in Ethiopia, and recognized the principles of non-interference with the flow of the Blue Nile, Sobat and Atbara (Degefu, 2003). Britain's main interest was based on strategic, political and economic considerations, particularly with regard to Egyptian cotton, a huge resource for the British textile industry. Additionally, the Suez was critically important as the gateway to India and the Middle East. Great Britain therefore 'continued to seek the protection of the Nile affluences' (ibid.: 103). France's interest was related to the railroad and its adjoining territory, which followed the Awash Valley, and which spanned 100 km to the north and 250 km to the south, from Djibouti (formerly French Somaliland) to Addis Ababa (ibid.). Italy, hoped to gain control of northern Ethiopia. While this agreement did not remove all differences among the colonial powers who competed for access to the region, it enabled Britain to buy the goodwill of the French 'extremely cheaply by accepting a railway which they did not have the financial resources to oppose and in the process staked out a future claim to a good part of Ethiopia' (Keefer, 1981: 380). However, Ethiopia immediately rejected the agreement since it denied Ethiopia of its sovereign right over its water resources.

Egypt's present rights and inequitable control over the Nile Basin were also imposed by colonial agreements. In the quest to regulate the flow of the Nile and apportion its use, British-Sudan reached an understanding with Egypt on behalf of the British-controlled territories of Uganda, Tanganyika and Kenya (a British colony), that culminated in the signing of the Nile Waters Agreement on 7 May 1929 (Othieno and Zondi, 2006; TFRD, 2007). The cotton scheme in Sudan also acted as a catalyst for this agreement since it required perennial irrigation as opposed to the traditional flood-fed method (TFRD, 2007). The British assured Egypt of its dominant share of the waters. Of the river's average flow of 84 billion cubic metres at the time, 48 billion cubic metres (or the entire timely flow from 20 January to 15 July) was allocated to Egypt, while 4 billion cubic metres was designated for Sudan, at a ratio of 12:1 (ibid.). The British concessions then legalized Egyptian hegemony over the Nile by awarding it veto rights over any upstream water projects.

Disputes over water rights during colonial times were minimized or eliminated because of overall British hegemony in the region. However, as the Nile riparians gained independence, riparian disputes became international and more contentious (TFRD, 2007). The issue of historic versus sovereign water rights was therefore further complicated by the technical question of where the river ought to best be controlled, upstream (Ethiopia) or downstream (Egypt) (ibid.).

One particular bone of contention was that voiced by newly independent Sudan in 1956, which repudiated the 1929 Agreement and demanded an increased share in the Nile waters (ibid.). The allocations were then increased to 55.5 billion cubic metres for Egypt and 18.5 billion cubic meters for Sudan, after the 1959 Nile Waters Agreement was signed between the United Arab Republic of Egypt and the Republic of Sudan for the Full Utilization of the Nile Waters, which altered the ratio from 12:1 to 3:1 and fully allocated the Nile flow between the two states (Spiegel, 2005). Under this agreement, Sudan was allowed to undertake a series of development projects, such as the Rosieres Dam, while Egypt was allowed to build the Aswan Dam which was designed to create an assurance of supply, particularly during droughts, and also harness the hydroelectric power of the river (Tadesse, 2008).

Once again, Ethiopia has never recognized the validity of the 1959 Nile Waters Agreement, while Egypt has continued to assert the no harm doctrine[2] and its historical claim to the Nile (Spiegel, 2005).

Tense co-riparian relations therefore have a long history of dispute and distrust. This differs from the Orange-Senqu River basin's history of technical cooperation despite (or as a way to overcome) political distrust. Egypt has been heavily criticized by the upstream riparian states for its reluctance to compromise on the bilateral 1929 and 1959 agreements made with Sudan and its unwillingness to renegotiate this position with the other eight riparian states. Othieno and Zondi (2006) argue that Egypt's hard-line stance and intransigence can be attributed not only to the fact that the Nile provides a source of its survival, but also to the fact that traditionally Cairo has had the support of the United States as Washington's key ally in the Middle East and North Africa (Hira and Parfitt, 2004; Othieno and Zondi, 2006).

Othieno and Zondi (2006) argue that other Nile states have therefore resented Egypt's control of and dominion over their use of the Nile waters. These authors cite the example of Tanzania's attempt to launch a project in 2004 that involved watering the Shinyanga region, 160 km from Lake Victoria, which was funded by the Chinese at a cost of US$27 million (ibid.). The Egyptian response was to veto the project on the basis of its 'right' to do so as interpreted from the 1929 agreement as it would affect the Nile's water supply downstream (ibid.). In the past, Ethiopia too, has been prohibited from building any major dams that would reduce the flow of the Blue Nile's waters into the greater Nile River. Similarly, Kenya has, in the past, threatened to withdraw from the 1929 agreement so that it could use the Nile's waters for the irrigation of some of the driest parts of its territory. In response, Egypt stated that withdrawing from the treaty would be tantamount to a declaration of war (ibid.).

The Nile Basin has therefore been a global hotspot for potential conflict over water resources for several decades now and many a multilateral initiative aimed at cooperation has failed or has been nullified by riparian states. Added to this, there has been a range of broader political disputes, both inter and intrastate, that have touched on transboundary water issues further complicating the situation, a lack of trust between states due to historical ethnic/religious/cultural cleavages being a key obstacle (Brunnée and Toope, 2002; Spiegel, 2005).

Institutional and legislative development since the 1990s

While the waters of the Nile have historically created or deepened tension among Nile riparian states, opportunities for cooperation have also been evident, and are increasing as a result of increased institutional and legislative development. The 1990s saw several developments made in multilateral management of the Nile Basin that indicate an emerging spirit of cooperation. As a result of burgeoning multilateral institutions, initiatives such as the Nile Basin Initiative (NBI) formed in 1999 and task groups/committees such as an intergovernmental Technical Cooperation Committee for the Promotion of Development and Environmental Protection on the Nile (TECCONILE), external transboundary cooperation norms have emerged in the region, however, with slightly less ease of socialization than they have in southern Africa. This is partly due to the fact that the interest in the Nile at the political level differs greatly among the Nile riparians, as national water plans tend to be designed in isolation, accompanied by a significant level of political distrust and a lack of information sharing (Brunnée and Toope, 2002; Spiegel, 2005).

Moreover, due to the concerted effort towards developing and sustaining a cooperative milieu in the form of basin-wide schemes involving the production of hydroelectric power and upstream water storage, international donors such as the World Bank have provided funding with few but nonetheless strings attached. In other words, the less tangible and often vague global norm set of transboundary cooperation seems to be at times in conflict with the tangible and highly prioritized values of economic development in the region.

International context

One of the major legal problems in the Nile case has been the inability to strike a balance between the principle of equitable utilization and the no harm doctrine. To date, the riparian states have been unable to ratify a comprehensive legal framework. As such, the UN Convention on the Law of the Non-Navigational Uses of International Watercourses is applicable as the only global Convention that governs the utilization, management and development of shared water resources for non-navigational purposes. However, the difficulty transboundary cooperation norms have had at regional acceptance in the Nile is also evident in the unwillingness by some riparian states to ratify the UN Convention on the Law of the Non-Navigational Uses of International Watercourses (Spiegel, 2005). According to a UN press release, Sudan and Kenya voted for the UN Convention; Egypt, Ethiopia, Rwanda and Tanzania abstained; Burundi voted against; and Uganda, Eritrea and the DRC were absent (UN, 1997b).

Spiegel summarizes each riparian's decision aptly:

> Ethiopia protested that giving priority to the no harm doctrine would override the right to equitable and reasonable utilisation. On the opposing side, Egypt continued to claim that the no harm rule was the foundation of international watercourse law and that it should not be given the same weight as equitable utilisation. It has been suggested that the [UN] Convention's success at balancing the interests of upper and lower Nile riparians was in fact the reason for its lack of success on the ballot. Indeed, it was surprising that Egypt abstained from the vote, considering the view that the [UN] Convention was biased towards lower developed riparians. It is important to note that none of the Nile riparians have since ratified or signed the [UN] Convention, perhaps challenging its probable status as customary international law in the region. (Spiegel, 2005: 356)

The UN Convention therefore, acts as a useful, albeit incomplete, tool and offers some value as a framework, but is once again, less effective as an indicator for the acceptance and impact of transboundary cooperation at a national level in terms of compliance, implementation and translation of global cooperative governance norms to the local level. According to Spiegel, one of its assets is its focus on cooperation largely devoid of political influence (Spiegel, 2005). Spiegel further argues that since the Nile Basin suffers from a large inequality of political and economic power among its members, by creating a community of interest, the UN Convention focuses on the Nile River itself and its outreach into its communities rather than on the diverse political players who divide and control the distribution of its waters (ibid.). However, as previously mentioned, the Convention does not distinguish between actual compliance and rhetoric. As such, it does little to uncover inconsistencies between norm socialization at a state/elite level and norm socialization at a sub-national level or norm contestation/dynamism between global principles and pre-existing domestic norms. It is therefore not sufficient to merely evaluate norm effects by looking at the existence of a treaty/convention and how many signatories it has in a particular basin. It is for this reason that an investigation of domestic configurations is vital to determine whether the socialization of global norms occurs at the local and regional levels in terms of compliance to legal principles and the implementation thereof.

State sovereignty norms in the Nile

In its most simplistic sense, the issue of sovereignty, as it relates to hydropolitics involves the debate between sovereignty and equitable distribution of shared water resources. Underlying this is the contradiction between the compartmentalization of states who claim sovereignty rights over resources in their territory versus the indivisible and uninterrupted continuum of water (Westcoat, 1992). The question here is simple: *can a country use its water as it pleases*? This question ultimately results in a clash of two global norms, that is sovereign ownership and exclusive rights over one's resources versus the principle of shared ownership and equitable utilization of an international river. According to Spiegel, this debate has stemmed largely from four doctrines adopted from US riparian law: absolute territorial sovereignty, absolute territorial integrity, limited territorial sovereignty and community of interests (Spiegel, 2005).

Absolute territorial sovereignty, otherwise referred to as the Harmon Doctrine of 1895, is strictly in favour of upstream riparians, but has never been put into practice officially (ibid.). Absolute territorial integrity falls on the opposite end of the spectrum and reflects the notion that upstream riparians are prohibited from doing anything that may affect the natural flow of the water into the downstream state (ibid.). This principle is naturally in favour of downstream states, and may even have a debilitating effect on 'slow-to-develop' upstream riparians, such as Ethiopia for example. This is also the origin of the no harm doctrine, prohibiting any harm done to a state's watercourses that might affect natural flow. Similar to the absolute territorial sovereignty principle, absolute territorial integrity is rarely used in practice, because it denies the needs and reliance of other riparians on a transboundary river (ibid.).

Limited territorial sovereignty acts as the middle ground between the two principles discussed previously, and is subsequently, the prevailing theory of international watercourse rights and duties today (ibid.). This principle translates into respecting the rights of other riparians as they all have an equality of right. This has evolved into the principle of equitable utilization. Finally, the fourth principle, community of interests is also not widely accepted (in part because it so closely resembles the principle of equitable utilization) and is based on a community of interests created by the natural, physical unity of a watercourse, such as the present and prospective uses of the watercourses and the health of the ecosystem (ibid.).

While the principles of equitable utilization and no harm, have been codified increasingly in international water law, it remains to be fully acknowledged, given local meaning, and implemented in practice, at regional and domestic levels. The fact that the 1997 UN Convention is yet to enter into force can largely be explained by the reluctance of certain states to sign away their various hard-line stances. The official abandonment of the doctrines which deny other riparians access to water in favour of doctrines which promote sharing, cooperation and interdependence, is a long process and involves the complex task of analysing the different needs of the water users in each riparian state and how they can be amicably met.

In addition to the evolution of sovereignty norms as it relates to water law, a second dimension of sovereignty particularly relevant for the African landscape is the challenge of sovereignty for African states (Turton, 1999b). Among a list of internal (or subnational) threats and external threats, Turton argues that (1) Many quasi-states in Africa have failed to pass the test for internal sovereignty in terms of the capacity to be self-governing, for example lack in service delivery of which water and sanitation is pertinent; (2) Concerns about the Western notion of standards of civilization, particularly under the banner of human rights and advocated by powerful international NGOs; (3) The core-periphery structure of the post-Cold War international system gives both power and international legitimacy to the core to re-impose a degree of unequal political relations on the periphery. For example, the UN as an embodiment of the principle of sovereign equality, has imposed sanctions on states such as Somalia, Angola, Burundi, Libya, Liberia and Mozambique, hereby degrading their status as sovereign equals (Turton, 1999). These challenges to African states' sovereignty create both drivers and obstacles for effective transboundary water resource management in Africa. On the one hand, interstate cooperation is becoming increasingly common as Cold War perceptions of sovereignty (absolute territorial sovereignty/integrity) are making way for newer interdependent regional and multilateral collaborations. On the other hand, the challenges African states face regarding both internal and external threats to sovereignty make them both more susceptible to the socialization of global norms and also create unique domestic configurations with localized norm sets that run contrary to Western principles, allowing for either norm distortion, localization or norm contestation.

Basin-level context

At the basin level, various organizations have been created in an attempt to stimulate sustainable development and cooperation in the greater Nile River basin. While some initiatives have failed due to financial and political obstacles, in recent times, Nile riparian states have begun to recognize the potential gains from cooperation within and beyond the basin. Indeed, bilateral and sub-basin agreements concluded since the 1970s indicate an increasing trend towards cooperation based on the mutually beneficial use of the shared water resources (Granit et al., 2010). As such, tremendous resources have been pooled to create institutions or strengthen existing ones through capacity and trust building initiatives, policy harmonization plans, and basin-wide communication and information exchange programmes. These initiatives have created regional norms of economic development and communication which have received basin-wide support and as such have been socialized. In many respects, these processes have been easier to implement due to institutional tiers at all levels of scale but have also suffered several structural weaknesses. A series of such institutional developments are highlighted below.

Undugu Commission (1983–93)

The word *Undugu* is derived from the Swahili word, *Ndugu* meaning 'Brotherhood'. It was formed in accordance with the 16th OAU Summit of July 1979, which called for self-reliance of African states as well as inter-dependence (Ahmad, 1994). It was also further inspired by the African Summit (1980) Lagos Plan of Action that called for an African commitment to strengthen the existing regional economic communities and the establishment of joint river and lake basin organizations to promote intergovernmental cooperation in the development of shared water resources (ibid.). Undugu was therefore created in 1983, and operated as an unofficial grouping (Ahmad, 1994; Tadesse, 2008). Its broadly defined objectives included consultation on infrastructure, culture, environment, telecommunications, energy, trade and water resources (Arsano and Tamrat, 2005).

Its members comprised of Egypt, Sudan, Uganda, the DRC and the Central African Republic (even though the latter is not a Nile riparian) (ibid.). Burundi, Tanzania, Kenya and Ethiopia participated later but only as observers, and Eritrea never joined the group (ibid.). It has been argued that the lack of complete support by all riparian states from the onset was regarded as an impediment to the implementation of principles developed at meetings of the Ministerial Council (Ahmad, 1994). The group held 66 meetings at the technical and ministerial level between 1977 and 1992, but produced few results (Ahmad, 1994; Mohamoda, 2003).

The TECCONILE Initiative (1993–8)

The TECCONILE[3] was created in 1993 and was the first attempt to focus on formulating a long-term development agenda for the Nile River basin (Tadesse, 2008). TECCONILE initiated a series of ten Nile conferences in 1993, with the aim of providing an informal forum for dialogue among Nile riparian states and with the international community. This series resulted in the development of a Nile River Basin Action Plan adopted in 1995 with financial support from the Canadian International Development Agency (CIDA) (Arsano and Tamrat, 2005; NBI, 2001; Tadesse, 2008). Original members of this community included Egypt, Rwanda, Sudan, Tanzania, Uganda and the DRC, while Burundi, Ethiopia Kenya and later Eritrea, maintained observer status (Tadesse, 2008).

The plan outlined 21 projects at a cost of US$100 million, and in 1997 (ibid.), the World Bank agreed to a request by the Nile Council of Ministers of Water Affairs to lead and coordinate donor support for its activities (NBI, 2001). Ethiopia submitted reservations about the Nile Basin Action Plan proposing that the project be undertaken by a multi-disciplinary panel of experts (POE) (Tadesse, 2008). The TECCONILE accepted Ethiopia's proposal to form a POE with the mandate for the development and recommendation of a permanent Nile Basin Cooperative Framework Agreement (CFA) (ibid.).

The POE comprised of three delegates from each Nile riparian state including lawyers, water resource specialists and senior government officials. In 2000, they produced the draft text for the CFA, encompassing general principles, rights and obligations and institutional structure (NBI, 2001). The draft framework document has made tremendous strides in getting riparian states closer to reaching a basin-wide treaty however key issues remain to be resolved. To date, negotiations on the treaty have been concluded at the ministerial level, which started with the POE but later, moved to a negotiation committee.

The Nile Basin Initiative (NBI)

The next major institutional development came in the form of the NBI, which was launched in 1999 as a transitional and temporary institutional mechanism to be replaced by a river basin commission at a later stage. Due to the delay in the development of a fully fledged commission, the NBI still operates as the umbrella institution presiding over transboundary water governance matters in the basin. Additionally, it was the first multilateral arrangement to include *all* Nile riparian countries in a regional partnership to catalyse economic development and regional integration, to fight poverty and promote stability in the region.

The NBI's shared vision agreed upon by member states is, 'To achieve sustainable socio-economic development through equitable utilisation of, and benefit from, the common Nile Basin Water resources' (Waako, 2008: 3). The NBI organizational structure (see Figure 4.1) is made up of the Council of Ministers of Water Affairs of the Nile Basin States (Nile-COM), which serves as the highest decision-making body of the NBI. Its chair rotates annually, and it is subsequently divided into the Eastern Nile Council of Ministers (EN-COM) presiding over issues pertaining to the Blue Nile, and the Nile Equatorial Lakes Council of Ministers (NEL-COM).

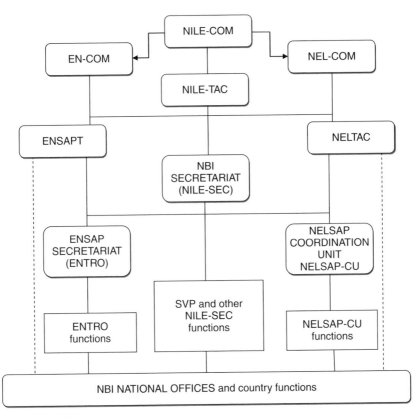

Figure 4.1 NBI operational structure

Institutional designs that help or hinder
norm convergence at the basin level

While EN-COM is supported by the Eastern Nile Subsidiary Action Programme Technical Team (ENSAPT), NEL-COM is supported by the Nile Equatorial Lakes Technical Advisory Committee (NELTAC) (ibid.). The NBI also comprises of the Technical Advisory Committee (Nile-TAC), which comprises of technical representatives from the member states who report to Nile-COM, and is charged with technical guidance of the NBI (NBI, 2001). Nile-TAC is composed of two senior officials from each member country (ibid.). Finally, a Secretariat (Nile-Sec) is based in Entebbe, Uganda. The Nile-Sec is divided into two investment-oriented Subsidiary Action Programmes that is the Eastern Nile Subsidiary Action Programme (ENSAP) comprising of Egypt, Sudan and Ethiopia; and the Nile Equatorial Lakes Subsidiary Action Programme (NELSAP) comprising of Burundi, DRC, Kenya, Rwanda, Tanzania and Uganda as well as Sudan and Egypt.[4] These programmes manage investment projects and ensure that they remain within budget and on schedule (NBI, 2001; Waako, 2008).

The mere existence of multilateral cooperative arrangements is not the only way in which norm convergence is promoted at the basin level. The very institutional design of multilateral arrangements also helps or hinders the way in which actors behave as a collective. The NBI as well as the CFA have both contributed to norm convergence at the basin level.

The NBI and orchestrated norm convergence

By way of its institutional design, the NBI has committed itself to building trust among the riparian countries and promoting cooperative multi-purpose investments in the area of energy and power trade, agriculture, watershed management, information sharing, monitoring and the environment (Waako, 2008). One could also make the argument that the NBI has orchestrated the socialization of specific norms around issue clusters through its Strategic Action Programme (SAP). The SAP has a two-tiered objective: (1) To achieve a shared vision in order to provide a framework for (2) Activities on the ground (NBI, 2001). These ideas/norms are translated into actions through two complementary sub-programmes: (1) Shared Vision Programmes (SVPs), which aim to create a coordination mechanism and 'enabling environment' for cooperation action; and (2) Subsidiary Action Programmes that plan and implement action on the ground at the lowest appropriate level (NBI, 2001). While the Subsidiary Action Programmes deal with the implementation of investment activities on the ground, which help to realize the shared vision, the SVP relates to ideational and norm convergence at the basin level in order to achieve implementation. Extensive resources have also been put into this process to facilitate collaborative action, exchanges of experiences, trust and capacity building, designed to build a strong foundation for regional cooperation, and thereby defining the type of regional cooperation (through the establishment of agreed upon rules, norms and ideas).

The SVP includes seven thematic projects and one SVP Coordination Project managed by the Nile-Sec. These include projects on water resources, the environment, power trade, agriculture, applied training, communications and stakeholder involvement (NBI, 2001; Waako, 2008). The SVP Coordination Project was created to strengthen the capacity of the NBI institutions. The unique way in which the SVPs are structured has also contributed substantially to creating national ownership of these SVPs by (1) having each thematic project housed in a different riparian country, and (2) by redistributing leadership, that is by delegating project managers to offices in other riparian countries and not in their country of origin.[5] As Wondimu notes, 'We have an Ethiopian in Sudan, we have a Rwandese in Egypt, we have an Egyptian in Ethiopia, we have a Ugandan in Tanzania, this type of arrangement, Kenyan in Uganda. So you don't see any leader of that project sitting within his country, because it also creates a sense of ownership for the other countries whereby they see it as giving benefits to their countries as well.'[6] This approach has facilitated trust and created ownership by all riparians and local communities.

Collectively, SVP activities have helped to promote a common understanding of the interaction between national policies, regional needs and cooperative development, forming a more effective basis for cooperation at the regional and sub-regional levels (Waako, 2008). Basin-wide, sub-regional and national information exchange under the SVPs are active and are being used to facilitate dialogue (ibid.). Capacity building is another objective, although this is a challenging feat with riparian countries operating at vastly different capacity levels (ibid.). Stakeholder consultation is currently underway at regional, sub-regional, national levels of scale including investment consultations and socioeconomic development and benefit-sharing activities (ibid.). Protocols for transboundary data-sharing and other related protocols are being developed (ibid.). Moreover, significant progress has been made in terms of policy alignment and harmonization between national water policies and transboundary water strategies (ibid.). These achievements all point to the conclusion that the SVP has contributed substantially, and was in fact designed, to build a Nile basin community of interest; to facilitate lateral norm convergence from state to state, as well as from state level to the basin level. As Waako (2008) concludes, these achievements have helped to build a technical foundation for water management in the basin; and establish and promote the NBI as a trusted institution at all levels.

Cooperation despite a stalemate on the Cooperative Framework (CFA)

The Agreement on the Nile River Basin CFA is ongoing but as yet, has not achieved an overall eleven-country compact (Granit et al., 2010). It was designed to be the guiding framework for cooperative management in the basin, and therefore contains general principles with respect to protection, utilization, subsidiarity, equitable and reasonable, prevention of significant harm, community of interest, data and information exchange, peaceful resolution of disputes, conservation and sustainable development of the basin at large to mention a few (NBI, 2000: Article 3). The agreement envisages the establishment of a permanent river commission beyond the NBI's temporary structure (ibid.: Article 15), which 'shall succeed to all rights, obligations and assets of the Nile Basin Initiative at entry into force of the CFA' (ibid.: Article 30).

Only one article, the phrasing of Article 14(b) on water security, remains to be resolved (NBI, 2009a). It stated that '. . . the Nile Basin States therefore agree, in a spirit of cooperation, to work together to ensure that all states achieve and sustain water security and not to significantly affect the water security of any other Nile Basin States' (NBI, 2000: Article 14(b)). Drafted in an attempt to harmonize divergent claims of upstream and downstream riparian states, Article 14(b) was deliberately vague in order to diffuse conflictive positions and avoid a stalemate (Erdogan, 2009). However, Egypt and Sudan objected to this, arguing instead, that the wording be changed to: '. . . the Nile Basin States therefore agree, in a spirit of cooperation, to work together to ensure that all states achieve and sustain water security and not to adversely affect the water security and current uses and rights of any other Nile Basin State' (ibid.). According to the former Executive Director of the NBI, Mr Audace Ndayizeye, 'the ministers decided to refer the impending issue to the heads of states. And we hope that the heads of states can take a decision. Otherwise 39 articles have been agreed upon except that one'.[7] Concluding this process and adopting a CFA would establish a permanent river basin commission, and may facilitate incremental basin-wide socialization and internationalization of agreed upon norms, both global and regional. The 'security' article stipulates that it will be the responsibility of the Nile River Basin Commission to resolve the text of the provision within six months after its establishment (Granit et al., 2010).

The CFA was opened for signature on 14 May 2010 for a period of one year until 13 May 2011 (NBI, 2010). To date, only five states: Ethiopia, Kenya, Uganda, Tanzania and Rwanda have signed the agreement (Menya, 2010). The CFA will only enter into force after six states have ratified the agreement on the sixtieth day following the date of deposit of the sixth instrument of ratification[8] or accession with the African Union (AU) (NBI, 2000: Article 42). The AU is therefore the designated depository of the treaty (Granit et al., 2010). With entry into force of the agreement, the Nile River Basin Commission will be a legal entity that succeeds to all rights, obligations and assets of the NBI (NBI, 2000: Articles 15 and 30).

Sub-basin level and sub-regional contexts

Due to its biophysical magnitude, the Nile River basin is institutionally sub-divided into two river systems or sub-basins, the Eastern/Blue Nile and the Nile Equatorial Lakes Sub-Basin (NELSB) or White Nile. However, this division of the basin into two parts is largely based on economic and political sub-groupings. The World Bank's role in investment projects also helped define the cooperative parameters. Instead of sticking to Operational Directive 7.70 which prohibits it from lending to one riparian if any other riparian objects to the proposed project, another approach was adopted – subsidiarity (Nicol, 2003a). This enabled the sub-division of the basin into two key areas, and thus, facilitated continued cooperation through a reduction in transaction costs and increased linkage of benefits to riparian countries (ibid.). In accordance with these groupings, sub-regional economic institutions are similarly structured in alignment with the NBI's sub-basin organs.

The NELSB comprises of those countries on the White Nile that are riparian to the Nile namely: Burundi, DRC, Tanzania, Kenya, Uganda and Rwanda, but excluding the Sudans and Egypt. Several of these countries are also united by their riparian status to Lake Victoria, which is a significant economic resource. Several institutions and initiatives exist in this region, most notably the Lake Victoria Environmental Management Project (LVEMP), the Lake Victoria Basin Commission (LVBC) formed as a branch of the East African Community (EAC) as well as the Lake Victoria Fisheries Organization (LVFO). Several White Nile states are also linked with other regional economic communities, such as SADC, as well as the Common Market for Eastern and Southern Africa (COMESA), the Economic Community of Central African States (ECCAS) and the League of Arab States. Additionally, some White Nile states have enjoyed a history of cooperative arrangements with each other. Kenya, Tanzania and Uganda particularly, have had a long history of cooperation under several regional integration arrangements. These have included the Customs Union between Kenya and Uganda in 1917, which the then Tanganyika (present-day Tanzania) joined in 1927, the East African High Commission between 1948 and 1961, the East African Common Services Organization (1961–7), the Permanent Tripartite Commission for East African Cooperation (1967–77) and the Permanent Tripartite Commission (1993–2000).

Lake Victoria Environmental Management Project (LVEMP)

The LVEMP started in 1997 and its aim was to restore the degraded lake ecosystem (NBI, 2001). This agreement between Kenya, Tanzania and Uganda, is laying the foundation for a long-term programme on investments to help sustain the many activities in the lake and its catchment areas. As part of a complementary long-term process, the governments of Kenya, Tanzania and Uganda have formalized cooperation through the EAC (EAC, 2007, 2011a, 2011b).

The East African Community (EAC)

Following the dissolution of the Permanent Tripartite Commission for East African Cooperation in 1977, Kenya, Tanzania and Uganda also negotiated and signed a Mediation Agreement for the Division of Assets and Liabilities in 1984 (ibid.). This led to the signing of the Agreement for the Establishment of the Permanent Tripartite Commission for East Africa Cooperation in November 1993 (ibid.). Following the establishment of a Secretariat in 1996 in Arusha, Tanzania, the Agreement establishing the Permanent Tripartite Commission was upgraded, and a treaty-making process was initiated (ibid.). The conclusion of this process and the signing of the Treaty for the Establishment of the East African Community in November 1999, led to the establishment of the East African Community in July 2000 (ibid.). Burundi and Rwanda joined the organization in 2006 (Cascao, 2009). The treaty was subsequently amended in 2007 to put in place processes to establish an East African Customs Union, a Common Market, and ultimately, a Political Federation (EAC, 2007).

The EAC promotes the establishment of a range of regional development, economic policy cooperation, trade and political co-ordination initiatives and entities. Personalized politics and alliances have, in the past, impacted on the effectiveness of sub-basin organizations (the Kagera Basin Organization (KBO) being a case in point), however, this has to a large extent, been circumvented in recent EAC operations.

Despite initial caution expressed by Uganda and Tanzania of Kenya's economic hegemony and therefore its influence in the EAC, all countries have benefited from membership. Similarly, new member state, Burundi has seen the mushrooming of transport companies as well as increased movement of peoples for business purposes to Kigali, Kampala, Nairobi and Dar es Salaam (East African Business Week, 2010). Regular flights have been facilitated by the removal of visa fees by Tanzania for example, and the removal of vehicle crossing tariffs at border entry points (ibid.). Additionally, Burundi has seen its financial and telecommunication sectors grow, with the movement of services in terms of cross-border investment and the proliferation of mobile telephone companies (ibid.).

The Lake Victory Basin Commission

As an organ of the EAC, the LVBC coordinates the various interventions on Lake Victoria and its basin and therefore serves as a centre for promotion of investments and information sharing among various stakeholders (EAC, 2011b). The EAC, seeing the need to develop Lake Victoria into a 'regional economic growth zone', established this programme in 2001 to focus on the harmonization of policies and laws on the management of the environment in the catchment area, to manage the eradication of alien species such as the water hyacinth, to manage the conservation of aquatic resources including fisheries, and to oversee economic activities (fishing, industry, agriculture, tourism), as well as to focus on the development of hydraulic infrastructure such as irrigated agriculture and hydropower energy in the Lake Victoria Basin (ibid.).

Lake Victory Fisheries Organization (LVFO)

The LVFO is also noteworthy since it too is an organ of the EAC with a specific mandate to manage the fishery stock of Lake Victoria. Moreover, the LVFO is an overlay institution made up of partner agencies such as fisheries departments/ministries, fisheries research institutes, committees and working groups. The LVFO's core functions are also to manage fisheries and the control of alien species (both fauna and flora) pertaining to the Lake, in addition to the development of aquaculture, fisheries research, post-harvest development and policy and legislation development (Nyeko, 2008).

Kagera Basin Organization (KBO)

Another sub-basin that exists on the White Nile is the Kagera River sub-basin. This sub-basin is significant for its role in cooperative institutional arrangements involving some of the White Nile riparians: Burundi, Rwanda, Tanzania and Uganda. The KBO was established in 1977 in an attempt to facilitate basin-wide development and cooperation on the Kagera (Mbaziira et al., nd.). This agreement was signed by Burundi, Rwanda and Tanzania, and in 1981, Uganda acceded to it. However, the KBO became defunct and the formal dissolution occurred in July 2004 following a decision by the Kagera Council of Ministers that all KBO activities be transferred to the EAC upon its reactivation (ibid.). Scholars have attributed the KBO's dissolution to its failure to deploy appropriate social resources to engender a culture that would enable the riparian states to sacrifice constituency interests and focus on the goal of fighting poverty (ibid.). In essence, they failed to achieve internal cohesion, commitment and ultimately norm convergence. The experiences from the KBO do however, offer several lessons for institutional development in the NELSB in terms of the effects of political stability, individual commitment, financial resources mobilization and importantly, the strengthening of social resources to identify, define and deploy the appropriate development, reform and adaptation mechanisms for strengthening institutional capacity (ibid.).

Intergovernmental Authority on Development (IGAD)

Originally established as the Intergovernmental Authority on Drought and Development (IGADD) in 1986 with a very narrow mandate around the issues of drought and desertification, the IGAD in Eastern Africa was created in 1996 to supersede its predecessor (IGAD, 2010). Member states: Djibouti, Ethiopia, Kenya, Somalia, Sudan and Uganda, decided to expand the mandate to address broader political and socioeconomic issues in a regional context. The State of Eritrea was admitted as the seventh member of the Authority at the 4th Summit of Heads of State and Government in Addis Ababa, September 1993 (ibid.).

IGAD's priority areas of cooperation include, conflict prevention, management and resolution and humanitarian affairs; and infrastructure development (Transport and Communications). Much of IGAD's attention is also directed at peace efforts in Somalia and the Sudan. Additionally, IGAD places an emphasis on capacity-building and awareness creation, as well as on the early warning of conflicts (ibid.). Other issues of importance include food security and developing appropriate modalities for regional peacekeeping.

IGAD's interventions in the NELSB are by virtue of its supportive role to Sudan, particularly given the recent secession of South Sudan from Sudan in 2010. In June 2008, IGAD established an office for its Special Envoy to Sudan on the Comprehensive Peace Agreement (IGAD, 2009). Since January 2009, IGAD has been working closely with the Assessment and Evaluation Commission (AEC), as well as the Sudanese Government of National Unity (GNU) and the Government of South Sudan (GoSS), to ensure the timely implementation of critical Comprehensive Peace Agreement (CPA) provisions (Helly, 2009).

League of Arab States

The League of Arab States, or Arab League, is another voluntary association with linkages to the NELSB. It comprises of countries whose peoples are mainly Arabic speaking. It has 22 member states, and aims to strengthen ties among them, coordinate their policies and direct them towards the common good (BBC, 2011). The League's involvement in the Nile occurs by virtue of Egypt and Sudan's membership status to the League. The decision to establish the Arab Water Council in 2004 and the Arab Water Ministers Council in 2004 reflects the agreement of Arab States to join a coordinated effort towards achieving water security at the regional and state level and to face the water scarcity challenges facing Arab countries (Arab Water Council, 2009). Member states such as Egypt and Sudan have looked to the Council for advice on strategies for negotiation on the Nile. And in this regard, the League of Arab States has acted as a norm entrepreneur in and of itself, influencing the appropriateness of Egyptian and Sudanese water diplomacy. With reference to the signing and ratification of the CFA, the Chairman of the Arab Water Council and Egypt's former minister of irrigation and water resources, Mahmoud Abu Zeid, claimed that 'The Arab Water Council can offer advice to the Nile Basin countries on how to reach an agreement' (Egypt News, 2010).

Economic Community of Central African States (ECCAS)

The ECCAS is another regional economic community established in 1985 although inactive for several years due to financial difficulties and the conflict in the Great Lakes region. In terms of water management, ECCAS promotes integrated water resources management, and recently adopted a regional water policy. The involvement of ECCAS in the Nile occurs by virtue of Rwanda, Burundi and the DRC's membership status to ECCAS.

The complexity of institutional arrangements

These institutional arrangements, however entrenched or superficial, point to a complex institutional structure in the NELSB and epitomize the interconnectedness of transboundary water governance. First, the sub-basin's water resources include one of the world's great complexes of lakes, wetlands and rivers resulting in biophysical complexity. There are strong hydrological and environmental interactions between individual hydrological units as well as with humans, organizations and governments. The NELSB therefore comprises of multiple heterogeneous elements and agents that interact with one another in non-linear ways.

Secondly, the sub-systems (EAC, LVBC and LVFO) found in the intricate institutional linkages in the NELSB comprise of some or all NELSB countries (see Figure 6.3). Additionally, several other regional economic communities overlap in the NELSB: the

SADC, the IGAD, the COMESA, the Economic Community of Great Lakes Countries (CEPGL) and the ECCAS. Given the number of distinct agents typically found in these cooperative arrangements, the multiple sub-systems add infinitely more layers of complexity as they influence one another. The 'sub-regionalization' or aggregation of the White Nile into the NELSB by riparian states has therefore contributed in large part to the formation of patterns of sub-basin solidarity and the creation of a sub-regional voice within Nile hydropolitics. The sub-basin itself has also obtained significantly more leverage, and has articulated and developed a unique sub-basin voice.

The non-linear evolution of institutional development is also significant for it fosters a community of interests through policy coordination and formation of joint legal agreements and programmes. Countries have established various interstate organizations to which all or some White Nile states are party, and follow non-linear basin-wide institutional development. The sub-basin exhibits patterns of adaptation by its increased negotiating leverage and greater political economy stability. The emergence of such patterns has occurred from low-level rules and events that might not have been initially anticipated, and not through the establishment of a basin-wide cooperative agreement or opposition to Egypt's monopoly over the Nile. This emergent behaviour is therefore useful in developing management strategies to cope with sociopolitical, socioeconomic and institutional change in the basin.

As a result of this complexity, the regional integration agenda is strong and provides a forum for cooperation in many aspects including peace and security, trade, transport, natural resources management and immigration (Granit et al., 2010). On the other hand, this sub-basin could also be interpreted as being institutionally overburdened. By way of example, Nyeko has argued that the LVFO's relationship with the LVBC is unclear due to the ambiguous demarcation of roles and responsibilities (Nyeko, 2008). He argues that the scope for cooperation and communication requires resolution to prevent duplication or conflicting agendas (ibid.). In terms of the extent of coordination and synergy or the overlap of responsibilities and functions, the EAC pointed to the institutional complexity due to the need to define and consolidate different interests in different fora.[9] According to Tom Okurut, head of the LVBC, the LVBC helps to articulate the interests of the East African people in NBI processes involving East African states but also non-East African states.[10] 'And that's why the LVBC is here, to better define our interests. So that when we are negotiating in the NBI process, ours are well-defined as a region.'[11] Indeed, the relevance of the existing institutional complexity presents challenges but also opportunities for sectors that are directly or indirectly involved with water issues to increasingly integrate in terms of decision-making in agriculture, energy, industry and urban development in particular.

National context

In terms of the national context, upstream countries have been mainly characterized by (British or Belgian) colonial rule, economic underdevelopment, internal conflict, political instability, lack of financial support and capacity, lack of water policies or strong governance structures such as institutions and weak bargaining strategies. As a result, the waters of the White Nile have remained mostly under-utilized (Cascao,

2009). Several scholars have alluded to the winds of change in the basin as a whole, brought on by increasing economic and political stability of upstream countries as well as increased integration (ibid.). Upstream riparians are becoming more willing and able to develop their water resources to meet national development needs (ibid.). They have more financial support, both in terms of their own resources, but also access to external donors such as the World Bank and China, support which was not available a decade ago (ibid.).

Politically, the years 2006–12 marked a period of eventful electoral and political activity for the sub-basin, which had a significant effect on regional integration efforts and institutional development (see Figure 4.2). These political and economic changes in the NELSB have contributed to changes in the basin's balance of power. However, recent electoral processes have also halted the EAC's regional integration processes. Additionally, the retention of old leadership ensures that existing cooperative norms will remain prioritized but may also leave norm entrepreneurs to use coercive mechanisms of norm convergence such as social sanctioning/influence if the critical mass, that is the national population, become disillusioned and aggressively resist national norms. As Flockhart (2006) notes, social influence elicits norm-conforming behaviour through the distribution of social rewards and punishments. This trend is evident in countries throughout the region such as the DRC, Libya, Tunisia and Egypt, where a wave of wide-spread political activism and opposition to and disillusion with meritocracy has led to critical masses detaching themselves from the former collective identity with the state.

A few highlights include the re-election of Paul Kagame of the Rwandan Patriotic Front (RPF) in Rwanda's presidential elections that took place on 9 August 2010. While opposition and human rights groups criticized the election for being repressive, and lacking in credible competition, both the UN and the EU expressed concerns about the deteriorating human rights situation in Rwanda ahead of the election (Granit et al., 2010). Similarly, the BBC and Amnesty International also condemned the attacks (Amnesty International, 2010).

The withdrawal of the opposition parties from Burundi's national presidential elections in June 2010, in protest over what they considered to be an unfair electoral process, resulted in a similar overwhelming majority vote for President Pierre Nkurunziza, who was re-elected for another five-year term (Granit et al., 2010). This resulted in Nkurunziza's party, the CNDD-FDD, winning a two-thirds majority in parliament, changing Burundi's political system from multiparty into single party dominance (WER, 2010). Burundi's pre-election period was also rife with civil unrest, with grenade and arson attacks being carried out on the offices of the CNDD–FDD, resulting in the death of several activists (ibid.).

Along with Kenya's referendum on a new constitution and promulgation thereof, which has called for radical changes in the political structure of the country towards a decentralized system of governance, these political events were praised for reinforcing stability in an economically promising region. Tanzania too, conducted parliamentary and presidential elections on 31 October 2010, which saw Jakaya Kikwete re-elected for another five-year term on 6 November 2010 (Granit et al., 2010). The election trend was followed by Uganda's presidential elections in February 2011, where a familiar

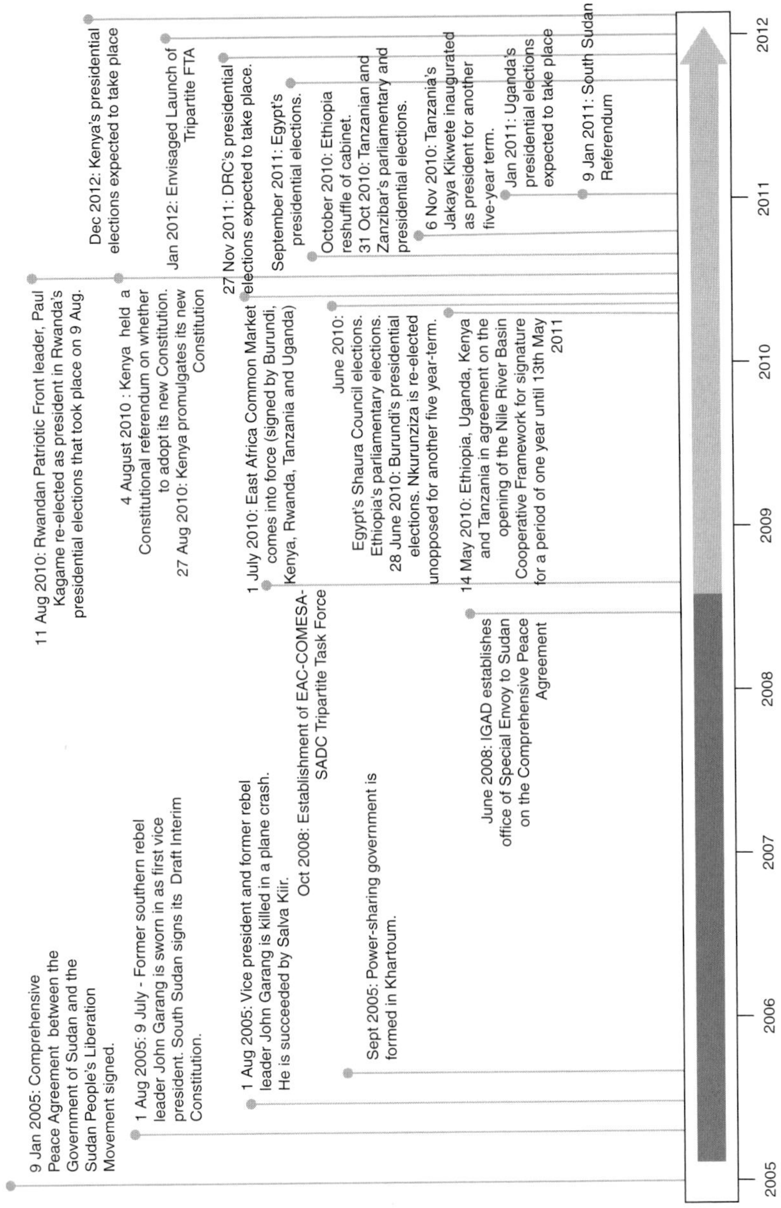

Figure 4.2 Timeline of political events in the NELSB region (adapted from Granit et al., 2010)

face, that of President Yoweri Museveni was re-elected for another five-year term. While the retention of old leadership does have positive implications for institutional development on the Nile in terms of continuity, electoral processes have had a stalling effect on the EAC's calendar of statutory meetings, where meetings have been postponed to accommodate for national elections (The Citizen, 2010). The DRC also conducted its presidential elections on 27 November 2011 and although the results were heavily disputed, President Joseph Kabila was declared the winner and was subsequently re-elected for another term. Kenya's elections are expected to take place in December 2012 (Granit et al., 2010). Brief country-specific summaries also reflect the degree of political and institutional change that has occurred in recent years.

Tanzania

First, Tanzania is blessed with more transboundary waters than any other African country (Mutayoba, 2008), and shares 12 international rivers and lakes with other nations.[12] The institutional framework guiding water management, supply and sanitation in Tanzania is the National Water Policy (NAWAPO) of July 2002 as well the Water Supply and Sanitation Act Nr. 12 enacted in May 2009. Tanzania is however in the process of reviewing its policies particularly as it relates to current and future transboundary challenges, most notably the falling levels of Lake Victoria (Granit et al., 2010). A new national water resources management policy is also being developed that emphasizes the treatment of water as an economic good, combined with environmental protection, greater participation of stakeholders and legal and institutional systems.

In terms of water-sharing strategies of the Nile waters, Tanzania has articulated its needs as wanting to exercise its riparian rights on Lake Victoria, having great interest in developing and conserving the resources of the Lake Victoria sub-basin and having an interest in developing tourism and agriculture (Tadesse, 2008). Since it poses a relatively smaller threat to the quantity and the quality of the Nile River, Tanzania would benefit from basin-wide cooperation (ibid.).

Tanzanian international water law has also been greatly influenced by the Nyerere Doctrine, which is based on the selective succession to treaties. Following independence in 1961, Julius Nyerere, the first president of independent Tanganyika, invoked an optional doctrine which stated that international agreements dating back to colonial times could be renegotiated or repudiated when a state becomes independent. This was based on the notion that newly independent nations could not be bound to laws that the state was not in a sovereign position to agree to or change at the time (Collins, 1994; Makonnen, 1984; Okidi, 1990). The doctrine therefore enabled newly independent states to review all international treaties that it stood to inherit and choose which of those agreements it would accept or not, following a probation period of two years (Waldock, 1972). Shortly after independence in 1962, the government of Tanzania, therefore rejected the 1929 Nile Waters Agreement and all other agreements signed by Britain on its behalf, citing the Nyerere Doctrine (Kalpakian, 2004). The Nyerere Doctrine is therefore significant for the role it has played in codifying norm resistance to externally imposed norms, and giving a certain degree of agency back to NELSB countries.

Today, Tanzania is a stable regional actor. There has been a gradual increase in political pluralism, but a dominant party system still resides with the ruling party, Charma Cha Mapinduzi (CCM) still in power. In the 2010 presidential elections opposition parties were widely considered to have no real chance of gaining power. Tanzania's GDP growth rate is also increasing incrementally (estimated at 6.4% in 2010 and 7.1% in 2011 by the Economist Intelligence Unit) and has a low and stable inflation rate (Dagne, 2010). Tanzania is a member of the EAC, along with Kenya and Uganda. It is also a SADC member state, and cooperates with its southern neighbours on regional economic development projects, particularly transport. Tanzania has also helped to facilitate an end to the conflict in Burundi.

Kenya

Kenya gained independence in 1963 and followed Tanzania's example by invoking the Nyerere Doctrine, and rejecting the 1929 Agreement. Tadesse (2008) argues that while Kenya has no significant claim to Nile water allocation, it has interests in developing its part of the basin, particularly because a lack of access to adequate water resources is one of the most critical hindrances to socioeconomic development in the country. Additionally, while it is not directly affected by the status quo, Kenya expects its riparian rights to be respected and upheld, hopes to gain from basin-wide cooperation and supports new Nile water agreements (ibid.).

In terms of basin-wide relations, Waterbury argues that Kenya has always seen itself as a 'broker' in the Nile basin and has never exhibited much interest in any binding agreements on water use (Waterbury, 2002). However, Kenya does have major economic interest in Lake Victoria, as is evident by its membership status in all regional cooperative arrangements regarding the lake itself.

In terms of policy reform, in 1999, Kenya adopted a new National Water Policy, which articulated the government's role in water services provision as a regulator and provider of an enabling environment (NBI, 2012a). This policy document as well as the subsequent New Water Act of 2002 advocates for a decentralized water management framework and prioritizes both communities and the private sector. Water is treated as an economic and social good through the 'polluter pays' principle, while integrated approaches, community participation and institutional development are also prioritized (ibid.).

In August 2010, Kenya also adopted a new constitution that declares that, 'Every person has the right to a clean and healthy environment, which includes the right – a) to have the environment protected for the benefit of present and future generations through legislative and other measures' (Republic of Kenya, 2010). Article 69 also holds the state responsible for maintaining tree cover over at least 10% of the nation's land; for encouraging public participation in protecting and managing the environment; protecting indigenous knowledge of biodiversity; and establishing systems of environmental impact assessment (ibid.).

According to Granit et al. (2010), the new constitution is a key development in political reforms aimed at preventing a repeat of the 2008 post-election violence that negatively affected regional trade with countries like Rwanda who depend on the stability of its neighbours for the safe passage of its goods along East Africa's main truck routes (Granit et al., 2010). For instance, all of Kenya's petrol, diesel and heavy oil supplies, which fuel Rwanda's electricity generators, must be transported by road from the coastal cities of Mombasa in Kenya and Dar es Salaam in Tanzania (ibid.). The 2008 post-election violence effectively blocked transport flows of these goods to the coastal cities.

Uganda

Uganda is another very important riparian among the NELSB states as a result of its water contribution (Tadesse, 2004). Owing to the abundance of rainfall, and the characteristics of hydrology of the Sudd, its consumptive demands are not a serious threat to downstream users. Uganda does, however, have a great deal of interest in ensuring its entitlement in future Nile water agreements, and also expects to benefit from basin-wide cooperation programmes, particularly in agriculture and hydro-power development (ibid.). The 250 MW Bujagali Hydropower scheme (Independent Power Project) located upstream on the White Nile near Jinja, Uganda, was developed with no objection from the NBI partners (Granit et al., 2010).

Over the past decade, Uganda has taken considerable steps to rationalize water resources management and development by instituting a range of statutes, policies and action plans on environment and water (NBI, 2012b; see Figure 4.3). These provide the framework for the sustainable management and use of water, the provision of clean water for domestic purposes to all citizens, the orderly development and use of water for purposes other than domestic use and the control of pollution (ibid.). As stated in Uganda's National Water Policy of 1999, 'it is in Uganda's interest to ensure that the good water quality in the water bodies within the national boundaries is maintained for sustainable use' (Republic of Uganda, 1999). Based on Uganda's overall policy objectives of good neighbourliness and promotion of regional cooperation for optimal use, Uganda's policy principles therefore adhere to the various accepted principles of international law, regional and basin-wide bodies of cooperation such as TECCONILE, IGAD, the KBO and LVFO (ibid.).

Burundi, Rwanda and the DRC

Burundi, the DRC and Rwanda, initially regarded as secondary players in the Nile River basin as a whole, have begun to articulate their interests by virtue of specific interests in various sub-basins. Burundi's interest in the Nile is by virtue of its dependence on the Kagera River (Tadesse, 2008), particularly for hydropower generation. While its consumptive water demand is relatively low, and while it does not expect water allocation from the Nile, it does claim riparian rights on the Kagera River. It also has strategic interests in the Lake Victoria Basin and could benefit from regional cooperation (Waterbury, 2002). Burundi has also been constrained by political instability and internal violence, contributing factors to its lack of capacity. In this regard, it has sought out the assistance of the NBI to help develop its capacity in an attempt to level the playing field at basin-wide negotiations (Granit et al., 2010).

In terms of Burundi's water policy framework, several national ministries have a stake in water management, leading to the overlap of responsibilities, with little compatibility in the skills available (NBI, 2012c). This is further complicated by the fact that the 1992 legal framework has many gaps, and currently lacks a means of implementation (ibid.). As a result, the planning and utilization of water resources due to poor coordination of activities between the various actors in the government is a major constraint in Burundi's national water management landscape (ibid.)

Rwanda has similar interests to Burundi in that it is also blessed with high and regular rainfall and is mainly interested in strengthening its hydropower capabilities (Tadesse, 2008). The Kagera River inflow is therefore also critically important to the water balance of Lake Victoria, in which Rwanda is a key riparian player. Moreover, it expects to gain from regional cooperation and this is evident in its bid to join the EAC. It is also in support of a new basin-wide agreement (ibid.).

The DRC is an interesting case, because only recently, has it expressed any interest in the Nile (Waterbury, 2002), because its main focus has typically been on the Congo River basin, the world's second largest river in terms of discharge (NBI, 2012d). Its dependence on the White Nile for its development is therefore minimal, and as such its consumptive demands in the basin are relatively low (ibid.). However, Waterbury argues that when Mobuto Sese Seko was president, he entertained an Egyptian proposal to build a power grid leading from the Great Inga hydropower station to the Nile basin, which would eventually lead all the way to Europe (Granit et al., 2010). The Inga Dams also served a political objective. They enabled Kinshasa to control the energy supply of the sometimes rebellious Shaba province. Currently, the two hydroelectric dams, Inga I and Inga II, operate at low output, and are commonly regarded as white elephants although rehabilitation plans are underway.

The DRC contributes significantly to Lake Victoria and Lake Albert, and as such, it has expressed interest in ascertaining its riparian rights, promoting tourism as well as its fishing and shipping rights on and in Lake Albert (Tadesse, 2008; Waterbury, 2002). It also has expressed a newfound interest in cooperating in mutually beneficial basin management programmes, evident in the fact that the former Executive Director of the NBI was Congolese. In this regard, it also supports the formation of a future basin-wide agreement (Tadesse, 2008).

In terms of the DRC's national policy framework, there is no overall national strategy guiding the sector although the development of a national water law is underway (NBI, 2012d; see Figure 4.3). While water supply and sanitation development plans have been developed, they have not as yet been implemented (ibid.).

Egypt, Ethiopia and the Sudans

While Egypt, Ethiopia and the Sudans are not part of the NELSB, a brief overview of their national contexts is noteworthy because they have direct bearing on water governance issues in the sub-basin particularly given the Arab Spring, 2011 Egyptian Revolution and the ousting of President Hosni Mubarak, South Sudan's secession, and Ethiopia's unilateral dam development plans. These recent events could act as both drivers and barriers to norm convergence in the NELSB by either promoting cooperative strategies or exacerbating existing conflicts.

A review of newspapers and other regional popular press reveals a swarm of articles describing the political activity in 2011 and its effect on transboundary water management in the Nile Basin (Femia and Werrel, 2011; The Guardian, 2011). First, political change in Egypt and Sudan has created an opportunity to reconsider their water-sharing arrangements with the other basin states. Both Sudan and Egypt have traditionally expressed renegotiation as a threat to their access and control of the waters (Femia and Werrell, 2011). However, political change associated with a post-Mubarak Egypt and South Sudan's secession may indeed see a re-shifting of political alliances, new norm emergence in particular areas and a re-positioning of existing riparian interests.

Secondly, the instability of the revolution has notably softened Egypt's hegemony, regional presence and diplomatic strength in re-asserting its historic rights to the river (The Guardian, 2011). The Mubarak regime also had significant support from the United States, which gave Egypt both a diplomatic and military advantage over the less powerful upstream states (ibid.). On several occasions, Egypt pressurized the Arab League not to supply loans to Ethiopia for Nile water development (ibid.).

Thirdly, South Sudan's recent independence is also likely to have an influence on regional and NELSB dynamics. As a result of the 9 January 2011 Referendum, South Sudan gained independence on 9 July 2011 and became the 193rd member of the global family of nations, and the 54th African state.

South Sudan's independence was the culmination of the peace process that was concluded on 9 January 2005, when the CPA was signed between the government of the Sudan and the Sudan People's Liberation Movement/Army (SPLM/A) (Comprehensive Peace Agreement, 2005). The CPA, signed in Naivasha, Kenya, consisted of six protocols and agreements dealing with a wide range of issues including: the right of self-determination for the people of Southern Sudan (stipulated and elaborated in the Machakos Protocol); power sharing; wealth sharing; security arrangements; resolution of the Abyei conflict; and resolution of the conflict in the two states of Southern Kordofan and Blue Nile.

The main provisions of the CPA were reflected in the Interim National Constitution of the Republic of the Sudan issued in July 2005. The Constitution set forth detailed governance principles and institutions for the six-year interim period that started on 9 July 2005, six months after the conclusion of the CPA on 9 January 2005, and ended on 8 July 2011, six months after the undertaking of the referendum on self-determination on 9 January 2011.

In terms of South Sudan's position regarding the waters of the Nile, South Sudan's interest is largely due to its plans to expand its agricultural sector. While Sudan is relatively less dependent on the waters of the Nile than Egypt as it has extensive rain-fed areas within its borders, it has a large potential for irrigated agriculture drawing water from the Nile (Waterbury, 2002). Both the North and the South claim to have agreed on continued cooperation on water sharing governed by the agreed quotas in the NBI (Granit et al., 2010). However, South Sudan has also expressed its development needs, for example in its plan to build a dam in Wau, on a tributary of the White Nile (The Guardian, 2011).

Fourthly, the construction of new dams by upstream countries is yet another national issue that is bound to influence NELSB dynamics and norm convergence. This sentiment was reflected in a statement made by Ethiopian Prime Minister, Meles Zenawi's confirming the construction of the Grand Ethiopian Renaissance dam just one month after Mubarak was ousted from power (ibid.). The proposed dam will be the largest in Africa, and is forecast to generate 5,250 megawatts of hydroelectric power (ibid.). Moreover, external support for dam building, particularly with Chinese finance and expertise, as was the case with the Tekeze dam in Ethiopia, is a further important dimension leveraging unilateral dam construction (ibid.).

Finally, national food security also plays a pivotal role in sub-basin relations as water demand for agriculture makes up a considerable portion of total water demand in the basin (Femia and Werrell, 2011). East Africa is currently experiencing the worst drought in 60 years causing many Somalis to flee to nearby Kenya or Ethiopia (The Guardian, 2011). In addition, shortages of food production such as crop failure of wheat in China, Saudi Arabia and South Korea, has led these countries to lease land abroad, in places such as Ethiopia and Sudan (ibid.). This has resulted in a high demand for agricultural land in these countries to produce crops for export, a phenomenon described as 'land grabbing' (Granit et al., 2010). Since water rights are often incorporated into land deals or leases, which do not fall within the confines of traditional water use patterns, land grabbing may contribute to the ultimate reduction of water available for other basin needs (Femia and Werrell, 2011). This may lead to the export of 'virtual water', or the flow of water embedded in crops out of the region to the water-poor countries abroad (ibid.).

Regional peace and democratization, with its high potential for social and economic change and its typical expansion of state capacity therefore increases the demand for land and may also increase the likelihood of disputes over land and natural resources in South Sudan (Granit et al., 2010). For example, in the three contested areas of Southern Blue Nile and Southern Kordofan (Nuba Mountains and Abyei), land grabbing by merchants and foreign investors combined with intensified disputes over rights to grazing and farming land is one example of how a context of peace-building and economic development could increase or perpetuate localized conflicts of this nature (ibid.). Because of its spill over effects, national insecurity issues as a result of natural resource constraints therefore threaten regional peace-building and subsequently the formation of a community of interest affecting all states in the NELSB.

Summary of legislative and institutional framework

In summary, the legislative and institutional framework of the Nile has been historically characterized by unilateral development as a result of colonial agreements. This has resulted in the lack of multilateral treaty agreements governing the entire Nile River basin. Trust-building is of paramount importance to rebuild riparian relationships.

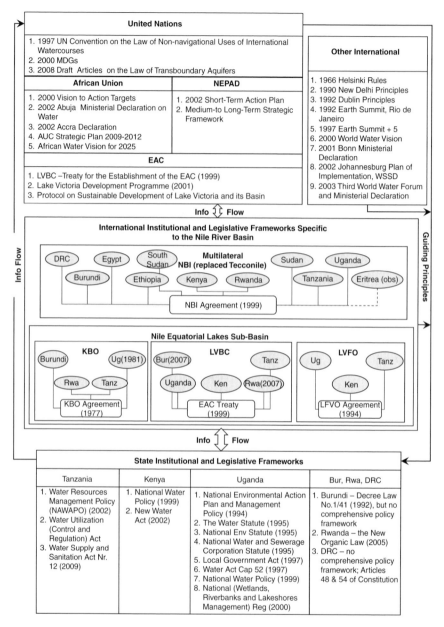

Figure 4.3 The current institutional framework of the Nile Equatorial Lake Sub-Basin

Historically, a central legalistic challenge in the Nile has been the inability to strike a balance between the principle of equitable utilization and the no harm doctrine, with downstream countries invoking historic rights to water and the no harm doctrine, and upstream countries citing equitable use. As such, the UN Convention has added little value in terms of clarifying these misunderstandings. If anything, the Nile River basin displays a typical case example of norm resistance to global normative principles.

However, the past decade has seen major developments made towards multilateral cooperation, peace-building, democratization and economic stability (see Figure 4.3). Some institutions have displayed behaviour that resembles an attempt to orchestrate norm convergence, however, due to the Nile's unique sociopolitical and historical context, this has not always produced intended results.

Change in power asymmetries

As previously noted, the Nile River basin has undergone several political and economic changes over the past decade that are expected to promote shifts in the current balance of power in the basin and thus affect hydropolitical dynamics between Egypt and the NELSB. The NELSB states have seen an increase in economic and political stability and have become more vocal in articulating their interests in basin-wide arrangements. Indeed, the sub-basin itself has obtained significantly more leverage, and while it still pales in comparison to the Eastern Nile in terms of strategic importance and contribution to streamflow, it has articulated and developed a unique sub-basin voice in many respects. In parallel, Egypt has just survived a revolution and the fall of former president, Hosni Mubarak. And even though it is still the economic and military hegemon and has the capacity to project and sustain this might (Cordesman, 2004), Egypt's ideational and discursive hydrohegemonic position may be changing. This is arguably due to a shift in bargaining power evident in the 2010 decision taken by Ethiopia, Uganda, Tanzania, Kenya and Rwanda to sign the CFA without Egypt and Sudan (Warner, 2012). The playing field is changing with Egypt no longer able to maintain complete control over the agenda of Nile hydropolitics by sanctioning issues and keeping NELSB states out of the political process (Lukes, 1974).

Historically, through the use of discursive and bargaining tools and threats, Egypt has been able to influence the basin's overall hydropolitical agenda in both multilateral and bilateral arrangements. By citing its 'historic and acquired rights', as well as the 1959 Agreement, it has been able to steer negotiations in its favour, something which other riparians have not been able to do historically as a result of weaker or no bargaining tools (Cascao, 2009: 248). The latter dynamic has, however, changed in recent times, with upstream countries acquiring more political and economic stability, but also very importantly, a Chinese 'big brother' that has given upstream countries more countervailing power vis-à-vis Egypt (Cascao, 2009; Warner, 2012).

In ideational terms, Egypt has also been the strongest state in the basin. According to Allan, Egypt has been able to sanction particular favoured discourses in the basin (Allan, 1999a). By citing its 'historic rights' and linking its national security to water security, Egyptian norm entrepreneurs have traditionally framed the debate in a highly securitized manner. Several authors have argued that, throughout history, Egypt has employed the 'securitization' tactic (water as security priority or even top national priority) to reinforce its hegemony in the basin, and justify certain actions ('hydraulic mission' and 'resource capture') over the Nile waters. However, as several authors argue, since the 1980s, an ideational shift is taking place in which Egyptian primacy is changing in its approach from revolutionary conquest or militant intimidation to moderation and consensus-building (Rubin, 1998; Warner, 2012).

Additionally, the NELSB riparian states have begun to consolidate their interests into sub-basin cooperative agendas. They are economically and politically stronger than what they were a decade ago. They have developed stronger bargaining tactics and are more vocal in their claims for renegotiation of the basin's volumetric water allocations (Cascao, 2009). And they have shown great determination to develop their water resources. With the help of their new external funding partner, China, they have begun to achieve this.

The role of external actors: enter China

Enter China. External non-state or supra-state actors have played a critically important role in shaping the normative landscape of transboundary water governance in the Nile. Organizations such as the World Bank and the United Nations Development Programme (UNDP) have had a long history of involvement in financing basin-wide activities. Waterbury argues that they have in fact become 'entrepreneurs of cooperation' (Waterbury, 2002: 80). But arguably the most 'economically liberating' development for NELSB countries has been the involvement of China in financing water development projects since 2000, a fact that represents 'an emblematic shift in terms of access to funding and construction contracts for hydraulic infrastructure in the basin' (Cascao, 2009: 260). However, referring to 'China' may make sense heuristically, but ontologically, it is becoming increasingly problematic to speak of it as a monolithic entity (Brown, 2007; Taylor, 2009). In the era of globalization particularly, China's foreign-economic policies are influenced and shaped by a wide range of actors, who in turn, are pressured by a variety of interest groups and demands (Taylor, 2009; Zhang-Yongjin, 2005). Indeed, the involvement of 'China' in infrastructural development projects in Africa is largely run by Chinese-led multinational corporations.

Prior to Chinese involvement, the lack of external support for hydraulic infrastructure projects had been a major constraint to the development of upstream infrastructure, and consequently, maintained the status quo of power relations in the Nile (Cascao, 2009). Traditionally, there has also been reluctance on the part of international and regional financial institutions as well as bilateral donors, to support projects in Ethiopia and the NELSB countries. This reluctance can be attributed to a lack of political stability needed to secure investment in these countries but also unwillingness on the part of donors to fund controversial projects that could potentially affect the water availability to other countries (ibid.). The World Bank, for example, has declined to fund projects in upstream riparian states because the Bank's Operational Directives stipulate that all downstream riparians have to concede to it for any project to be financed (World Bank, 1994). This policy is not unique to the World Bank, with the African Development Bank adopting similar directives. As Waterbury (2002) argues, these directives have granted Egypt 'veto power' which has been used to prevent project development in the upstream catchments.

According to the INGO, International Rivers, in 2008, Chinese companies were involved in several hydraulic infrastructure projects in the Nile Basin countries: six projects in Sudan, three in Ethiopia, and three in Uganda, Burundi and the DRC with several new projects being negotiated currently (Brewer, 2008). Although some of the seven ongoing projects in the region are located in river basins other than the Nile, China's recent presence in the region is clearly substantial (see Map 4.2).

The introduction of China as Africa's new hydraulic infrastructure financier has brought not only new opportunities for dam construction, but also new challenges for hydropolitical dynamics in the region. Chinese involvement, armed with favourable financial contracts, has given NELSB countries the financial freedom to move ahead with unilateral developments without requiring consultation or approval from downstream riparians (Cascao, 2009). In essence, China has taken away Egypt's veto right to halt or stop hydraulic developments upstream.

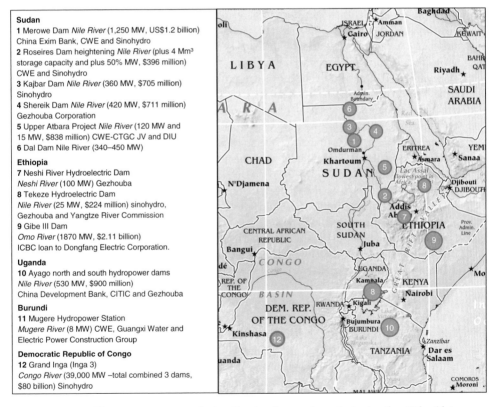

Map 4.2 Chinese support to hydraulic development projects in the Nile (data superimposed on map from The World Factbook, 2009)

China therefore provides more attractive contracts and speedier delivery of projects than its Western competitors due to having regional offices already in place in the basin. Additionally, China has different conceptions of good governance or human rights than the West, and NELSB countries may choose Chinese development projects over Western ones. Equally significant, Chinese and African elites share similar norms and interests of economic prosperity. As such, the normative influence China will exert in terms of transboundary water governance, still remains to be seen, but will almost certainly, continue to grow.

Top-down norm diffusion

Top-down norm diffusion of the global transboundary norm set has not been a smooth process and some might argue that it has in fact not occurred in the NELSB region. If one examines the repudiation of colonial treaties by independent states and the influence the Nyerere Doctrine has had on opposing pre-existing colonial treaties based on historic rights and territorial sovereignty, as well as the unwillingness of Nile riparian states to sign and ratify the UN Convention, there is a clear distrust of external normative frameworks in this basin. Indeed, a normative clash is evident between the principles of equitable utilization and no harm on the one hand favoured by upstream states; and absolute territorial sovereignty and acquired and historic rights on the other hand, favoured by downstream states. Given the fact that most Nile riparian states present at the adoption of the UN Convention abstained during the voting process, the contested principles in the UN Convention have not been able to be socialized by a critical mass. This is in many respects a function of the UN Convention and its inability to maintain equilibrium between the two principles despite the Convention's attempts to neutralize them in Articles 5 and 7. According to Brunnée and Toope (2002), the explanation for the voting pattern by Nile riparians (i.e. Ethiopia, Egypt, Rwanda, Tanzania abstaining; Burundi voting against; Eritrea, Uganda and the DRC absent; and only Kenya and Sudan voting in favour) lies in the deduction that if neither lower riparians nor upper riparians believed that the Convention adequately protected their divergent claims, the Convention may have been ratified by all riparians. Neither side was left with any assurance that the Convention would uphold the legal priority of their respective positions.

That said however, the UN Convention represents a milestone in the development of international water law and does have a significant impact even if it does not enter into force (McCaffrey, 2001b). Its influence is likely to draw from its status as the most authoritative framework of general normative principles and rules governing non-navigational uses of shared watercourses (ibid.). In the Nile Basin, its influence can be seen in the language used in NBI documents, which tries to reconcile the equitable utilization and no harm principles (Brunnée and Toope, 2002). A review of the policy guidelines for the Nile Basin Strategic Action Programme reveals that the foundations of the Shared Vision as well as the Subsidiary Action Programmes are in fact principles of equitable utilization, no significant harm, cooperation in the management and development of the water of the Nile and its sustainable utilization (NBI, 2009b). Another example of the institutionalization of global principles, and therefore, the influence of the UN Convention in the Nile Basin, is to be found in the works undertaken on the formation of the Cooperative Framework (Project D3) of the NBI. The panel of experts (POE), in initiating this process, conducted a series of discussions for the Framework Agreement on the basis of the UN Convention. This elevates the UN Convention to strategic importance as an aid to help formulate future agreements, and has led scholars to predict that once drafted, the CFA would most likely embrace general principles as contained within the UN Convention (Wiebe, 2001).

A similar process of indirect top-down norm diffusion as is occurring in the Orange-Senqu River basin is therefore at play: despite the fact that top-down norm diffusion from the global to regional and state levels has not occurred in the conventional manner, that is when states ratify an international agreement and then implement it, indirect diffusion has occurred where normative principles are altered, or localized to reach broad consensus and to bypass the battle of norms evident in the UN Convention. The NBI has essentially taken what it likes from this framework and incorporated it into its regional normative framework.

Regional norm convergence

As previously noted, the balance of power in the Nile River basin has undergone a significant shift. According to Cascao, the NELSB riparians are currently more determined, organized and integrated than they have ever been (Cascao, 2009). The EAC is considered to be a key element in this unification and convergence process as they have enabled the East African countries to articulate their interests in, for example, Lake Victoria. This forum has given NELSB states greater bargaining power in basin-wide arrangements by allowing them the opportunity to define their sub-basin agenda first. Since the EAC's formation, the NELSB riparians have been able to affirm their rights to utilizing the waters of the Nile (Cascao, 2009; Kagwanja, 2007). Additionally, while the White Nile (to which the Kagera River and Lake Victoria belong) only contributes 14% to the streamflow of the greater Nile, the potential for development upstream is a challenge for the regional hydraulic configuration and Egypt's position[ality] in the Nile (Cascao, 2009). While abstraction will only be minimal (as compared to that projected for the Eastern Nile), the foundation for a new, stronger player is evident – the NELSB riparians are now ready to create and develop their own hydraulic missions (ibid.).

Norm convergence in the NELSB is also evident by the way in which upstream riparians have collectively solidified their longstanding objections to colonial-era water treaties such as the 1929 and 1959 Agreements. These countries have not only stated their opposition to be bound to colonial treaties, but water authorities from this sub-basin have been the most vocal in expressing their interest in the ratification of the new Nile CFA (TNV, 2008: 9 November), which if finalized and ratified, would be the first treaty to comprise all Nile riparian states, and would eventually lead to the Nile Basin Commission.

To summarize, political and economic changes in the NELSB have, to a certain degree, contributed to changes in the basin-wide balance of power (Cascao, 2009). This development has ultimately facilitated norm convergence at the sub-basin level with upstream NELSB riparians redefining their national agendas in a more collective manner than before. This has strengthened their bargaining power as they have become influential players in multilateral negotiations, and have some ability to influence the regional agenda 'and even to pressurise downstream riparians over the legal issues' (ibid.: 253). This can be viewed as a tremendous advancement particularly since the White Nile has always been regarded as less strategically important than the Eastern (Blue) Nile, and as such, its riparians and their agendas played second fiddle. Indeed, the fact that the NBI Secretariat is housed in Uganda is also indicative of the increasing strategic importance the White Nile riparians have in multilateral arrangements.

NELSB positions on the signing of the CFA

On the 14th of May 2010, all NELSB countries with the exception of DRC and Burundi were in agreement on the opening of the Nile River Basin CFA for signature for a period of one year until 13 May 2011. Representatives of Ethiopia, Uganda, Kenya and Tanzania signed the Agreement immediately after the opening. According to the NBI's account of the process, Uganda's Minister Hon. Isaac Musumba said that 'considering that all the principles and articles of the draft Cooperative Framework were discussed by the countries and consensus reached on all except for one clause under Article 14b on Water Security it is appropriate that this document is opened for signature to pave way for establishment of the Nile River Basin Commission' (NBI, 2010). Rwanda's Minister, Ambassador Kamanzi cited a boost in development for the Rwandan population, while Kenya, represented by its High Commissioner to Uganda, H. E. Maj. General Geoffrey L. Okanga, reaffirmed its solidarity in the signing of the Agreement (ibid.). While Kenya did not sign the agreement as its minister could not attend, Kenya's Minister of Water and Irrigation, Hon. Charity Kaluki Ngilu, 'signaled her readiness to sign this agreement as soon as possible because Kenya's position on this matter has not changed and remains the same' (ibid.) Burundi and the DRC, also sent official representatives to the meeting in Entebbe. This multilateral activity suggests that although a stalemate currently exists in terms of the ratification of the CFA, NELSB states are involved in intensive diplomatic engagement. Recent political activity such as the Egyptian revolution and South Sudan's secession has also reinvigorated interstate engagement regarding interstate trade, hydropower and regional power markets.

Drivers and barriers to norm convergence in the NELSB

Despite the myriad drivers of norm convergence that facilitate regional integration efforts, challenges to state-to-state norm convergence at the sub-basin level do however present barriers to norm convergence processes.

Barriers

Capacity constraints

The issue of capacity proves to be a barrier to norm convergence in the sub-basin for two reasons. First, the lack of capacity in the NELSB riparians has been a serious impediment to cooperative growth and development. Seven of the eleven Nile riparian states have undergone severe civil strife, which has resulted in a backlog of water-related investments, inadequate infrastructure management and an institutional and human capacity vacuum (NBCBN-RE, 2011). Moreover, technical and resource capacities to address water quality and other transboundary (as well as national water) issues vary considerably between NELSB riparians. The number of senior water professionals, for example, varies from not more than ten in one riparian state (e.g. Rwanda), to over one hundred in another (e.g. Egypt) (ibid.). Water coordination between sectors of water use is still not integrated (ibid.). As noted in Chapter 4, the lack of capacity obstructs institutional capacity and tests institutional trust/confidence. Allan (1999a) has argued that the unequal distribution of capacity in the basin has exacerbated the historical power asymmetries, where downstream countries such as Egypt, have indeed enjoyed decades of water security as a result of upstream countries' incapacity to control and dam their tributaries.

Capacity-building has therefore been widely accepted as a key ingredient for sustainable development. Investment in human capital is critical, and up until recently, was limited in the Nile Basin. However, the NBI, in an attempt to promote capacity-building in basin states, have identified three primary challenges regarding capacity: (1) lack of capacity on integrated water resources management; (2) uneven distribution of capacity between basin countries; and (3) little interaction among water professionals within the basin. If not addressed, these three challenges could impede norm convergence by obstructing social learning processes, preventing the levelling of the playing field and thereby perpetuating an imposition of norms by a discursive, economic or political elite, and prevent information exchange. The NBI, through one of its SVPs, the Applied Training Project (ATP), has sought to address these challenges by assisting in the development of human resources and institutional capacity, however, it is perhaps too soon to evaluate what the successes are of this project in terms of bringing about norm convergence.

However, the increase in sub-basin stability and recent donor-funded project trends focusing on capacity-building could also be viewed as a barrier to normative convergence in the sub-basin. The growing awareness of the need for capacity building may exacerbate unilateral action by states that slowly become more capacitated to act in this way.

Lack of trust

A lack of trust has also permeated riparian relations in the Nile since the inception of colonial water treaties. This is related to fears and suspicions of unilateral developments, and has contributed to insufficient partnerships between riparian states on development projects. Joint development projects are made more challenging due to limited trade and exchange among riparian countries (NBCBN-RE, 2011). Political, economic, social, cultural and linguistic differences make partnerships all the more difficult (ibid.).

Additionally, the increased political and economic stability of NELSB states have catalysed a recent move towards unilateral development with substantial external financial support (Cascao, 2009). Unilateral trends upstream are becoming all the more apparent, such as the construction of several dams as illustrated in Map 4.2. Two diverging trust processes are therefore, arguably at play: one trust-building process brought about by the increase in basin-wide multilateral cooperation in the form of the NBI and various sub-basin initiatives such as the EAC; and one trust-breaking process brought about by the increase in unilateral developments from non-hegemonic riparian states (ibid.). Current unilateral trends indicate that the Nile riparian states have not completely abandoned their 'hydro-sovereignty' strategy (Wouters, 2000). These trends show that the NBI has in fact failed to materialize a 'shared vision' and build a Nile water community engaged in information exchange, professional interaction and joint problem-solving in the basin (Cascao, 2009; NBCBN-RE, 2011).

Weak institutions

Along with its history of institutional development, water governance on the Nile has had a parallel history of institutional failure. Several institutions, such as the KBO and former versions of the EAC, became defunct as a result of mismanagement, political and economic instability, and the inability of riparian states to 'solve the collective action problem' as quoted by Waterbury (2002: 156), where domestic problems of riparian states ultimately led to its dissolution. A host of factors allude to the KBO's underperformance and eventual dissolution.

First, KBO critiques argue that its mandate was unclear. Its original mandate included overly ambitious activities that extended beyond the river basin. A lack of focus on priority areas reflected a development agenda more suited to a regional development agency, such as the EAC, than an RBO (Mbaziira et al., nd.; Mohamoda, 2003). In this regard, Waterbury has referred to the KBO as 'one of the most ambitious and coherent river organisations in Africa if not the world' (Waterbury, 2002: 155). However, none of its projects were in line with the core functions of a RBO, that is hydrological studies, pollution control, environmental protection or ecological conservation, and instead, included a telecommunications project, acting as a centre for regional economic documentation and a tsetse fly and trypanosomiasis control project (Mbaziira et al., nd.).

Secondly, interstate rivalry, particularly the apprehension by Tanzania of Kenya's hegemonic role in institutions, was brought to the fore in institutional development of the KBO. In order to mitigate Kenya's leadership role, Tanzania championed the KBO in the wake of the EAC's collapse. Moreover, Uganda and Tanzania had long complained of favouritism in the distribution of benefits from the Union (ibid.). Additionally, Tanzania had just invoked the Nyerere Doctrine on State Succession, outlining its policy on the use of the waters of Lake Victoria and its catchment area, which had been adopted by the governments of Uganda, Kenya, Rwanda and Burundi (ibid.). Tanzania therefore hoped to have the KBO act as a replacement for the EAC, and Tanzania would then in turn facilitate trade and transport between landlocked Burundi, Uganda and Rwanda, and the outside world (ibid.).

Thirdly, personalized politics and tensions between riparian states played an important role in constraining activities of the KBO (Kagwanja, 2007). This was most evident when General Idi Amin Dada overthrew Uganda's President Apollo Milton Obote, a personal friend of Mwalimu Julius Nyerere of Tanzania. Nyerere refused to acknowledge Amin's leadership, and despite Uganda and Tanzania sharing a mutual dissatisfaction of Kenya's role in the EAC, Nyerere rejected Amin's nominated delegates to the EAC (Mbaziira et al., nd.). 'Instead, he accused Amin of withdrawing the recognised delegates (nominated by Obote) without prior consultation. He made no secret of his wish to have no dealings with President Amin and, thus, Obote's fall arguably dealt the final blow to the EAC' (Mbaziira et al., nd.: 9).

In retaliation, Amin restricted Uganda's involvement in the KBO to an observer role, and in so doing, undermined the utility of the organization, since studies could only be carried out in three of the four riparian countries (ibid.). Upon Uganda's eventual accession to the treaty, the organization's administrative arrangements had to be restructured to accommodate the Ugandan delegation, which affected coordination activities (ibid.).

Fourthly, the Hutu–Tutsi friction, inherited from the Belgian-constructed microcosm, caused further cleavages in the KBO. Specifically, the tension between two founder members greatly affected organizational processes, resulting in such counterproductive measures as different delegations objecting to projects that seemed to be biased towards the politically dominant group in either country (ibid.). Individual states also refused to send agreed-upon delegations to donor countries and institutions to mobilize resources (ibid.).

Fifthly, Franco-Anglo competition and Cold Water politics also affected the performance of the KBO by damaging internal cohesion. Tanzania's leading role in the KBO exacerbated French and Belgian fears of an Anglo-Saxon erosion of their positionality in the region (ibid.). Tanzania's socialist inclinations in Cold War politics did not help to alleviate these fears. The organization, therefore failed to garner financial support and raise the funds to implement its ambitious project portfolio (Mohamoda, 2003; Waterbury, 1979, 2002).

Sixthly, civil strife, political instability and non-water-related disputes among riparian states led to the lack of political capacity to engage in the KBO (Ncube, 2009; Waterbury, 1979, 2002). The 1990 Rwandese Patriotic Front's (RPF) invasion of Rwanda from Uganda was arguably the primary exacerbating factor to political differences and mistrust between riparian states. Mbaziira et al. aptly summarize this dynamic:

> Since the majority of the invading forces had been members of Uganda's National Resistance Army (NRA), President Juvenial Habyarimana accused his Ugandan counterpart of having aided the invasion, and severed relations between them. With three . . . of the four member states harbouring deep suspicion of each other, the impact on the organisation's activities was such that timely decisions could not be taken on many KBO activities. (Mbaziira et al., nd.: 10)

The invasion also marked the start of the civil war in Rwanda that paved the way for the 1994 genocide. Together with the internal conflicts in Burundi, this meant that it was impossible to continue with project studies and implementation work in about 55% of the KBO's territorial jurisdiction.

Finally, the lack of sustained political will and commitment also contributed to a lack of confidence in the organization's effectiveness and functionality. While the treaty provided for annual meetings between the organization's three institutional organs (the Council of Ministers, the Intergovernmental Commission of Experts, and the Summit), the lack of political commitment was such that prior to its dissolution in 2004, the Summit last met in 1993 while the Council of Ministers only met twice in the same period (Mbaziira et al., nd.; Okidi, 1994). Furthermore, according to Mbaziira et al. (nd.: 10), even these meetings were redundant, because they ended up being mere talk shops, for none of the resolutions taken were ever implemented.

These factors offer many lessons for the institutional strengthening initiatives in the NELSB, particularly the NBI. The NBI launched a US$33 million institutional strengthening project funded by the World Bank in 2008 in an attempt to circumvent the challenges faced by former institutions. However, the absence of a basin-wide cooperative framework to date, and the inability of Nile riparian states to reconcile differences of water security, still pose major challenges to the NBI's sustainability. Institutions' structural weaknesses therefore prevent norm convergence from taking place because they sever institutional trust and political will needed to build resilience that lead to the incremental shift towards a community of interests within institutions. Moreover, once these institutional pathways are negatively affected, the time it takes to rebuild them is often longer than it initially took to create due to the need to do damage control and rebuild trusting relationships.

Drivers

As previously noted, the last decade has seen greater cooperative arrangements of a multilateral nature, particularly at the sub-basin level. These have been facilitated by several key drivers of state-to-state and state-to-sub-basin-to-regional norm convergence and integration.

Trust and confidence-building

There is broad consensus that one of the primary objectives of the NBI's Strategic Action Programmes (SAPs) is confidence-building. Questions therefore, arise as to whether these measures stand a chance at improving the chronic state of mutual mistrust and suspicion that have characterized institutional development on the Nile. Indeed, the NBI's Confidence Building and Stakeholder Involvement (CBSI) Project, is one such project that has increased public awareness and stakeholder involvement in the Nile Basin, expanding understanding and confidence, and fostering basin-wide ownership of the NBI and its programmes.

Policy alignment

Additionally, a harmonized water governance framework enables transboundary cooperative projects to be implemented in a mutually beneficial way for all parties. Harmonization in this sense refers to both the alignment of national, legal and institutional frameworks with that of other riparian states, but also institutional harmonization and integration of policies and procedures within specific organizations such as the NBI and EAC. As part of the recently launched institutional strengthening project, and to help facilitate basin-wide institutional integration and an eventual move towards the establishment of a basin-wide commission, a key priority for the NBI has been the harmonization of NBI policies and procedures across the basin. For instance, the SVP Nile Transboundary Environment Action Project (NTEAP) is enhancing and working towards harmonization of the environment policies of the riparian countries to include transboundary dimensions (NBI, 2008).

The NBI has also encouraged riparian states to align national policies with national policies of neighbouring countries due to the lack of harmonized institutional and regulatory frameworks to effectively manage transboundary watersheds. While many countries have recently enacted new policies for water and environmental management, the degree to which they incorporate transboundary concerns or principles vary. The process of national policy alignment is a long-term endeavour that involves harmonizing water policies with a shared vision of good water management and defined goals for cross-border cooperation through ongoing technical implementation and co-riparian dialogue. This has, up until recently, been non-existent in the Nile Basin.

Norm localization and subsidiarity

Norm localization furthers our understanding of norm congruence and aids in norm convergence by making external norms more acceptable to local contexts by 'giving due agency to local actors' (Acharya, 2004: 269). This allows them to select, borrow and jointly agree on modification in accordance with a pre-existing normative framework to build congruence with emerging global norms. According to Acharya (2004), who coined the term, norm localization goes beyond a mere assessment of the existential fit between domestic and outside identity norms and institutions. The process of norm localization does not only explain 'strictly dichotomous outcomes of acceptance or rejection, localisation describes a complex process and outcome by which norm-takers build congruence between transnational norms (including norms previously institutionalised in a region) and local beliefs and practices' (ibid.: 241).

The principle of subsidiarity is one such principle that has been localized in the Nile Basin. Subsidiarity, as an organizing principle originating in Catholic social theory and EU integration law, is based on the notion that matters ought to be handled by the smallest, lowest or least centralized competent authority (Jordan and Jeppesen, 2000). Subsidiarity is therefore, one of the primary elements of federalism used to allocate powers between different governmental levels (ibid.).

It is presently best known as a fundamental principle of European Union Law and is politically, quite complex. The principle was established in the Treaty of Maastricht signed on 7 February 1992 and entered into force on 1 November 1993 (De Burca, 1998; Jordan and Jeppesen, 2000), and was also contained within the failed Treaty establishing a constitution for Europe. However, at the local level it was already a central principle codified, for example, in the European Charter of Local Self-Government, an instrument of the Council of Europe promulgated in 1985. The present formulation is contained in Article 3b, paragraph 2 of the Maastricht Treaty (formally, the Treaty on the European Union or TEU):

> In areas which do not fall within its exclusive competence, the Community shall take action, in accordance with the principle of subsidiarity, only if and in so far as the objectives of the proposed action cannot be sufficiently achieved by the Member States and can therefore, by reason of the scale or effects of the proposed action, be better achieved by the Community. (EU, 1992: Article 3b.2)

The principle therefore assumes and prioritizes the autonomy and dignity of the individual, and holds that all other levels of society, from the family to the state and the international order, should be in the service of the individual. Subsidiarity also emphasizes the role of small- and medium-sized communities or institutions, such as the family, the church and voluntary associations, as mediating structures which empower individual action and connect the individual with society as a whole.

According to Okurut, organizations such as the EAC, for example, are structured and based on the Treaty (For the Establishment of the East African Community) provisions where they emphasize the principle of subsidiarity.[13] This principle stipulates that action on the ground needs to be planned at the lowest appropriate level. Given the hydrological conditions of the Nile Basin, action on the ground will mainly be planned and implemented at a sub-basin level. Okurut explains that 'You agree what to do regionally, and you implement it nationally. And the regional bodies' task is to ensure they will monitor compliance, [and ensure] the implementation of what was agreed.'

The process of norm localization of the principle of subsidiarity is still an on-going process where 'idea recipients' shape and adjust the content of this 'foreign' idea to make it congruent with local practices (Acharya, 2004: 245). This, according to Acharya is referred to as 'pruning' a foreign idea (ibid.).

The principle of subsidiarity, while being a World Bank condition, has been incorporated into guidelines for the NBI's subsidiary action programmes. According to the Policy Guidelines for the Nile River Basin Strategic Action Program, common understanding has been reached on the following guidelines for the implementation of subsidiary action programmes (NBI, 2009b):

- The appropriate planning level needs to involve all those who will be affected. As such, countries involved will be a function of the location, type and scale of activity, as well as potential upstream and downstream impacts.
- The role of the overall (basin-wide) framework is to ensure appropriate consultation and involvement of those affected on the one hand, and subsidiarity on the other.
- Subsidiary action programmes will build on principles of equitable utilization, no significant harm and cooperation.
- The range of development project options will vary depending on the nature of the needs and opportunities in the different geographical areas.
- Investigations will seek solutions that are beneficial to all involved and distribute benefits, costs and risks equitably as well as use resources efficiently and protect the environment.

These policy guidelines point to the *interpretation and reinterpretation and re-representation* (Acharya, 2004) of the external norm of subsidiarity in an attempt to make it congruent with a constructed local normative order of sub-basin importance. Due to the current trends to include public and stakeholder participation and community involvement in development projects, institutions such as the NBI have gladly borrowed norms, in this instance, subsidiarity, to gain credibility and prestige, from external norm entrepreneurs, such as donors. However, they have also manipulated it to appeal to local constituencies/idea-recipients.

The benefit-sharing paradigm

Finally, there has been a progression towards developing benefit-sharing strategies by NELSB states because of the wide-ranging benefits to states in electricity production, environmental preservation and watershed protection, in addition to helping to minimize the impacts of natural disasters such as droughts or floods. Coordinated development and operation of multipurpose reservoirs among riparians, for example, can facilitate least-cost energy development, and optimize hydropower production, and provide a basis for power trade among countries.

Above and beyond the direct gains of cooperation, cooperation on international rivers also reduces risks of conflict because strong institutional channels are in place through which differences can be negotiated. Joint management, once strengthened with a clearly defined mandate, provides an alternative channel that states can go through other than unilateral development. It also holds them normatively accountable. The benefits from basin-wide cooperation could potentially lead to benefits beyond the basin such as food security and power trade that binds countries together within a framework that promotes peace and stability, thus demonstrating how cooperative water resource management and development could enable economic and political benefits that far exceed those derived directly from the river.

Similarly, regional integration efforts provide an avenue for sharing tangible benefits from transboundary cooperation such as agriculture products and electricity from hydropower generation and intangible benefits such as water quality improvement and flood and drought management (Granit et al., 2010). It has been increasingly recognized among the riparian states that, cooperation on development and management of the Nile water resources can result in major benefits for the welfare of the basin's inhabitants, and as such, the NBI recently drafted its Benefit Sharing Framework (BSF) document, although it is currently undergoing review. Additionally, recent progress in the CFA negotiations indicate that there is growing potential for economic linkages between South Sudan and Uganda and between Burundi, Rwanda and DRC in areas such as power development and trade, agriculture development, transport and technological transfer.

The peace processes are also likely to increase the flow of goods and services, financial and intellectual capital and enhance other beyond the river benefits between the NELSB countries. Regional investment between the southern and northern part of the basin could actively be promoted, creating many economic opportunities that will bring benefits to all involved. Larger markets in Egypt, the DRC, and even beyond the basin could also be served by an increase in production and exchange of agricultural commodities and power trade; while simultaneous access to these markets will be greatly facilitated by inward investments in irrigated agriculture and other technology-intensive projects. Under the management of the NBI's NELSAP, the Nile Equatorial Lakes Countries Electric Grid Interconnection Project is underway and involves the construction and upgrading of 769 km of 110 kV and 220 kV line, as well as the construction and reinforcement of 17 transformer stations that will benefit several NELSB countries. It consists of three main tasks:

1. The Uganda-Rwanda interconnection, which runs from Mbarara substation to Mirama substation in Uganda, then from Mirama substation to the new Birembo station in Rwanda;
2. The Kenya-Uganda interconnection, which runs from Lessos substation in Kenya to Bujagali substation through Tororo substation in Uganda;
3. The upgrading of the Burundi, DRC and Rwanda interconnection.

It is anticipated that these energy developments and interconnectors will have spillover benefits in terms of increased trade and infrastructure development of roads and railways.

While benefit-sharing as a theoretical concept has received much acclaim in recent years, as a practical tool for implementation it has been difficult to operationalize particularly because it may not be congruent with the principle of equitable utilization. It is also difficult to implement in securitized basins, is idealistic in basins with power asymmetries, and it cannot replace water-sharing agreements (Daoudy, 2010; Phillips et al., 2006). Benefit-sharing strategies are highly complex to establish and cannot be implemented without the risk of failing to see the delivery of benefits reaching all stakeholders, at the state and sub-state level (ibid.). Moreover, in order for benefit-sharing processes to be effective, they need to be geographically inclusive and acknowledge threat perceptions held by all parties based on historic, sociopolitical and socioeconomic circumstances (ibid.).

In essence, benefit-sharing implies that states circumvent political influences, and consider the most optimal use of the Nile waters. It could also mean greater involvement by governments who would allow their share of the waters to be used by neighbouring states for the greater regional good. Popular press articles have opined that Ethiopia, with its mountainous terrain, would provide an ideal location for the construction of several small dams to support modest irrigation projects and electricity generation, to help strengthen the industrial base of one of the poorest regions in the world (Hobbs, 2004). However, Hobbs argues that this would involve Ethiopia retaining water that Egyptian officials might argue was theirs, even if the gates of these dams could be opened to release water to Egypt in times of need (ibid.). In 2004, Hobbs indicated with disappointment that it was uncertain whether Egypt, with its long history of contentious relations with Ethiopia, would contemplate a move that could increase its vulnerability, even if this move would improve Ethiopia's economic development and the economic well-being of the region at large (ibid.). Several years later, the uncertainty still remains. What has changed however is the way in which the benefit-sharing paradigm has moved transboundary cooperation strategies beyond the altruistic notion of cooperation as implied by Hobbs – Ethiopia constructing dams, improving its economic development status while Egypt loses out in terms of its volumetric share. The concept of benefit-sharing helps us understand why co-riparians of transboundary river basins would opt for sharing benefits as opposed to simply dividing up the water resources among themselves (Daoudy, 2010). They perceive net benefits as more beneficial than the responsibilities, duties and costs linked to mutual cooperation (ibid.). In this regard, the basket of benefits is much broader to induce states to become more involved (ibid.). This could range from different trade options of flows of water or utilization of water, to capacity-building and information exchange.

Conclusion

This chapter found that a study evaluating present norm convergence in the entire Nile River basin is a constantly changing enterprise. A community of interest is developing in the NELSB but norm convergence is not a static phenomenon. Studies looking at normative frameworks may be limited in their ability to make judgements as to the socialization of norms and norm sets until these norms are in fact internalized and tangible evidence (which is in and of itself difficult to ascertain) exists to justify it. The utility of studies on normative frameworks, however, is in their ability to point out and track normative pathways, and to highlight emerging trends and standards of appropriate behaviour that may otherwise have been masked by state-centric realist analyses. Moreover, they help further our understanding of regional integration processes and the legal, institutional and normative landscape that helps or hinders this.

Additionally, non-linear norm diffusion from the global level is taking place, although some norms are highly contested, and local resistance to them is evident. In the case of the Nile, global norms of no harm and equitable utilization have clashed as a result of upstream-downstream differences. At the sub-basin level, there has been a movement towards norm convergence with NELSB states starting to articulate a joint development agenda for its resources as a result of political stability and economic growth as well as the support of new infrastructure financiers such as China. This is a tremendous achievement given the history of institutional incapacity, lack of trust and varied levels of capacity.

Notes

1   Ethiopia contributes 95% of the streamflow of the Nile in flood period because the White Nile loses a large amount of water to swamp areas near its source and then to evaporation throughout its course over arid terrain (Tadesse, 2008: 3).

2   The no harm doctrine, in this instance, refers to the principle that there may be no harm done to a state's watercourse that might affect its natural flow, thus implying that an upstream state such as Ethiopia may do nothing that might affect the natural flow (quantity and quality) of the water into downstream Egypt.

3   TECCONILE was also the successor of the Hydromet programme launched in 1967, which was a broad-based effort to collect and analyse data on hydro-meteorological aspects of the upper White Nile drainage system.

4   Sudan and Egypt's inclusion in the NELSAP indicates that the strategic interests of these downstream countries also extend to this portion of the basin.

5   Personal Communication with Wondimu, H. (2008) Senior Program Officer, Shared Vision Program, NBI Secretariat, Entebbe, Uganda, Entebbe, Uganda, 30 September 2008.

6   Ibid.

7   Personal Communication with Ndayizeye, A. (2008) Former Executive Director of NBI, Entebbe, Uganda, 30 September 2008.

8   For a glossary of terms relating to Treaty Action see for instance http://actrav.itcilo.org/actravenglish/telearn/global/ilo/law/glossary.htm

9   Personal Communication with Okurut, T. (2008) Head of Lake Victoria Basin Commission (LVBC), East African Community (EAC), Arusha, Tanzania, Entebbe, Uganda, 26 September 2008.

10 Ibid.

11   Ibid.
12   Tanzania's shared rivers and lakes include the three East African Great Lakes (Victoria, Tanganyika and Nyasa), Lakes Chala, Jipe, Natron system; and the Kagera, Mara, Pangani, Umba, Ruvuma and Songwe Rivers. Some wetlands and aquifers are also transboundary (Mutayoba, 2008).
13   Personal Communication with Okurut, T. (2008).

5

Multi-Level Governance in Southern and East Africa

Preceding chapters have described norm development in the Orange-Senqu River basin and the Nile Equatorial Lakes Sub-Basin. This analysis focused on the institutional and legislative landscape within which norms operate, the actors and processes that steer norm development and the drivers and barriers to norm convergence acting as key 'shapers' of standards of behaviour that have determined how water is managed. As a next step, let us now take a look at the relationships between cooperative management norms constructed at different levels of scale in the case-study areas, and the ways in which both norm and context are transformed as a result of the other. The multi-level governance framework of norm development is therefore conceptualized using the four most likely pathways that norms follow to their emergence and socialization in different contexts:

1. Top-down global norm diffusion
2. Lateral norm convergence from state-to-state
3. Bottom-up (local to national) norm convergence
4. Norm dynamism or contestation

Norm convergence in the Orange-Senqu River basin

As is evident from the legal and institutional frameworks influencing the cooperative management of water in the basin, norm convergence in the Orange-Senqu River basin has followed a non-linear path. Most importantly, processes of norm development have been greatly influenced by sociopolitical histories and existing identities.

In the case of top-down global norm diffusion

*What factors determine how the global norm
set is translated in various ways?*

The global norm set of transboundary cooperation as articulated in the 1997 UN Convention has been diffused in a non-linear manner. Although the UN Convention was not ratified by all SADC countries (except South Africa and Namibia), indirect adoption of the global norm set of transboundary cooperation has occurred through the ratification of the Revised SADC Protocol (2000). This alludes to the importance of regional instruments and agents in successful diffusion of global norms, and can be explained by several characteristics.

First, global norm diffusion of the transboundary cooperation norm set occurs largely as a result of norm congruence, or normative fit with domestic and regional dynamics brought about as a result of political change and the water reforms of the 1990s which took place in the region. The successes at which these norms have become incorporated into regional and national legislative and institutional frameworks, are arguably as a result of their legitimating effects of new post-independence and post-apartheid water reform policies, particularly in South Africa and Namibia. The perceived adherence to global principles and standards, in turn, legitimizes political regimes and the sovereignty of states. SADC states that have incorporated global norms of transboundary water governance into their national policies are therefore viewed favourably within the global arena, and adhere to a collective understanding of the most appropriate way for states to act.

Secondly, the manner in which global norms are diffused reveals the importance of context (historical, political, power relations at play) and congruence. As Conca (2006) argues, a non-incremental change in policy in the 1990s in South Africa (but also Lesotho, Namibia and to a lesser extent Botswana) brought about frameworks of national water laws that incorporated norms legitimized in international policy circles. By scratching below superficial analyses, however, one finds that the precursors of norms have their own history of domestic development that predate the norms' arrival at the international level (Conca, 2006). Indeed, South Africa's political transition impacted on its international water diplomacy: it wanted to be regarded as a good neighbour, or at least a better neighbour than was historically the case (ibid.). In this regard, it placed an emphasis on building multilateral cooperative structures to re-build trusting relationships with its neighbours. The desire to rebuild friendly relations with neighbouring states and the world, instigated a wave of outward-looking considerations and deliberately created pathways for norm diffusion.

Conca further argues that water has been an instrument of social control in South Africa, Lesotho Namibia and Botswana, facilitated by the 'hydrology of apartheid' (ibid.: 312) in South Africa, the military government in Lesotho and colonial rule in Namibia and Botswana. The 1990s saw democratization and dramatic, political and constitutional change, particularly in South Africa. This created a window of opportunity for non-incremental reform in water-related law, policy and practice (ibid.). In contrast to the pre-existing legal frameworks (in which riparian rights that accrued to land ownership and the favourable intervention of the state were prioritized – two pillars of the apartheid system, that is racially discriminatory land laws and the intervention of the racially discriminatory state),[1] the new legal frameworks have a much greater emphasis on the international dimension. The 1998 National Water Act of South Africa, for instance, identifies 'meeting international obligations' among its main priorities (ibid.). Additionally, South Africa and Namibia have been active in international water diplomacy, signing and ratifying several bilateral and multilateral accords, endorsing earlier efforts to articulate principles in international water law such as the 1966 Helsinki Rules, and more recently, spear-heading the drafting of the regional SADC Water protocols. The allocation of water licenses, the development of catchment management agencies and the national water strategy are all obliged to take international obligations into consideration (ibid.). This, according to Conca, has created 'a path for the potential influence of international water law principles' (ibid.: 345).

Thirdly, the instrumental role of local actors was also emphasized in terms of their agency in bringing international norms home (Kor, 1998). Local non-governmental groups have been active in South Africa and Lesotho, and have networked with transnational environmental, water and human rights groups, particularly on issues related to the LHWP and the affected local communities that had to be resettled and compensated for the loss of land as a result of the construction of several dams. The INGO, International Rivers, is one such transnational advocacy group that has collaborated with the Transformation Resource Centre (TRC) in Lesotho on issues pertaining to the local impacts of large dams.

How does the global norm set of transboundary cooperation, once constructed internationally, emerge and become socialized in various regional, basin, national and sub-national contexts?

There are also several ways in which global norms influence domestic practices through the action of advocacy coalitions. Local non-state actors have deliberately made themselves amenable to international considerations in an attempt to get their voices heard, and thereby emphasizing the agency of local actors in deliberately encouraging a favourable normative change for them. This logic also emphasizes the agency of local actors in deciding *which* international norms get diffused and *how* this happens. In this regard, domestic actors become proponents of particular global norms allowing for easier socialization while actively resisting others. Local NGOs and community-based organizations (CBOs) have been able to pressurize governments to 'make good on their promise' by inciting particular international norms that best served their interests (Swatuk, 2005a: 878). In a similar vein, marginalized national actors have also turned to international actors such as donors and NGOs because the state failed to serve their interests (Conca, 2006).

Non-state actor networks of experts, or epistemic communities are well connected to their international counterparts (ibid.). Even though apartheid created a pariah state of South Africa, many networks related to water issues felt relatively little impact, owing to the high degree of technical cooperation in the region (ibid.). The South African National Committee on Large Dams (SANCOLD), for instance, remained an active member in the International Committee on Large Dams (ICOLD) throughout the apartheid era. The end of apartheid built on this strong foundation and saw a surge in new national expert networking on other water-related topics.

Why is the global norm set incorporated into regional/basin/national policy and/or behaviour?

Local actors have therefore displayed instrumental commitment to global norms. These state actors have undertaken cost/benefit calculations and publicly committed themselves to a norm only to the extent that it helped them achieve some other more fundamental, and usually, national objective – the desire to be seen as independent (in the case of Namibia), and democratic (in the case of South Africa, Lesotho and Botswana). The precursors of international norms therefore have their own history of domestic development that predates their arrival at the international level (Conca, 2006).

For whom and by whom? is the global norm set created?

Finally, in terms of influential actors, global norms have in large part been created by pioneering, European states, for global coverage. However, the SADC, and specifically, the Orange-Senqu case study, proves that global norms can, and usually are, successful only if there is normative fit with domestic norms and interests. Oftentimes, global norms are manipulated and transformed to push particular agendas. Grafting allows norms to be reframed to suit specific audiences (Acharya, 2004). Ambiguous or vague norms such as equitable utilization may be grafted to other norms such as 'good governance' or reframed to appeal to a wider audience (i.e. 'water as a human right') in order to garner support from national governments, constituencies and also transnational entities such as donors (Swatuk, 2005a). This argument complements the way in which norms and principles are phrased in international legislative frameworks. These principles have become part of the 'language' of protocols and, as such, are meant to be deliberately vague to ensure broad-based support. It is left up to the interpretation of regional institutions and riparian states to articulate what these principles mean for specific basins and nations.

In the case of lateral norm convergence from state-to-state or state-to-basin-to-region

What factors in the regional/basin/sub-basin configuration account for a powerful norm set at these levels of scale?

The degree of lateral norm convergence in the Orange-Senqu River basin is also a result of the near-simultaneous 1990s wave of national institutional and legal transitions in South Africa, Namibia and Lesotho and later Botswana. This helped to facilitate state-to-state policy harmonization and alignment, and regional norm convergence from the state to the basin level. This is not to say that policies are aligned at present, but it alludes to the *potential* for more harmonization between state policies. Indeed, conflicting national interests and institutional inconsistencies still exist in some shared river basins and 'complicate[s] the challenge of reconciling the existing patchwork of international arrangements with the comprehensive vision of the SADC protocol' (Conca, 2006: 365). However, through processes such as the movement towards a paradigm shift from water-sharing to benefit-sharing, river basins such as the Orange-Senqu, and their multilateral coordinating commissions, such as ORASECOM, have begun to help redefine national interests by identifying the development opportunities to be shared from cooperation that go beyond the river and its water resources (these include hydropower trade etc.).

How do norms converge regionally or within a basin?

The significance of regional mechanisms to the facilitation of norm convergence can also not be denied. The SADC Water Division established in 1996, the establishment of the SADC Water Sector Coordinating Unit (SADC-WSCU) and the Water Resources Technical Committee (WRTC) were key drivers in the drafting of the Protocol and the regional institutional infrastructure.

However, the road to regional integration and norm convergence regarding transboundary water governance has certainly not been a smooth one despite good intention. Examples of fragmented cooperative initiatives exist outside of the Orange-Senqu River basin including the lengthy and controversial process of establishing a river basin commission (RBO) on the Zambezi River, the longer than anticipated time it took to establish the tripartite Incomaputo Accord with Mozambique and Swaziland and the difficulties in establishing a Secretariat for the OKACOM. And while multilateral commissions have been formed for several river basins (e.g. the Cunene, Incomati, Limpopo, Orange-Senqu, Okavango, Umbeluzi and Zambezi basins), these commissions remain almost purely advisory in nature. Each country still conducts its normal processes of decision-making for managing the water resources within the boundaries of its sovereign territory (Turton et al., 2005). This could suggest that the countries concerned are reluctant to delegate part of their sovereign responsibility to another party (in this case to an institution for the management of water resources), especially where these resources are critical for their future social and economic development (Turton and Ashton, 2008: 313). Alternatively, as is evident in the Orange-Senqu Basin, it can also be the case that due to pre-existing bilateral regimes, multilateral regimes are slower to develop and their mandates are questioned as a result of project-based bilateral agreements conducting most operational functions such as infrastructural developments.

Barriers to norm convergence, therefore, exist at the basin level, due to constraints shared by all four countries. These include capacity constraints, skills flight and the lack of sustainable knowledge transfer policies. While most evidence points to the gradual development of a community of interests in the Orange-Senqu River basin and a slower progression at the SADC level, multilateral accords such as ORASECOM will be the litmus test along with the newly institutionalized water laws that give priority to international commitments.

Why are regional norms incorporated into regional/basin/state policy and/or behaviour?

While Conca's Maryland School (Conca et al., 2006) argued that cumulative basin-to-basin norm dissemination has not occurred significantly in recent years and therefore shows little evidence of regional norm convergence or basin-to-basin norm spread, the southern African case proves otherwise. The 1990s saw an upsurge in transboundary water diplomacy between SADC states, with a focus shifting to the creation of joint water commissions. Conca argues that this stark increase in regional cooperation predates the rise of the ANC to power in 1994 but was accelerated by this transition (ibid.). One of the ANC's primary objectives, upon obtaining power, was the goal of repairing the damage caused to regional relations during the apartheid era, with a particular focus on shared water resources as one element through which to achieve regional cooperation (ibid.). This stemmed from the increase in national water demand due to industrial and population growth, and the realization that South Africa would need to tap into exogenous water supplies to meet this demand. This facilitated the development of stable and adequate rules for shared water governance (Conca, 2006: 363). Normative fit therefore exists between national incentives to portray a country in a certain way (democratic, independent, good neighbourly), and regional objectives of better integration and coordination. Both have encouraged and even necessitated greater multilateral cooperation and information exchange.

Multilateral basin-wide agreements have therefore been signed in all of the SADC basins that have a significant level of development (Ashton et al., 2005; Turton and Ashton, 2008). Additionally, the wide range of bilateral and basin-wide agreements signed by the individual states within the SADC region, and their accession to important international agreements, suggest that SADC states are committed to strengthening levels of cooperation between states and reducing the potential for disputes and conflicts to occur (Ashton et al., 2005; Turton and Ashton, 2008). The region's shared water resources, has therefore been a driver for cooperative initiatives in the SADC region. Indeed, the SADC Water Division has played a central role in facilitating coordination of such initiatives, and has encouraged the creation of a 'common understanding' between all member states. Larry Swatuk attributes this to an emerging regional vision of sustainable economic development that combines elements of coordinated resource management, ecotourism and external neo-liberal pressures (Conca, 2006; Swatuk, 2002a; Swatuk, 2002b).

Additionally, the strategic importance of the shared waters of the Orange-Senqu has necessitated the solidifying of basin-wide cooperative strategies, and as such, the global norm set has been incorporated into regional, basin and national policy and behaviour. Through the establishment of ORASECOM, commitment to regional norm convergence has become institutionalized, which may raise the costs of norm-breaking behaviour.

There may also be an argument to be made for the South African desire to project its influence outside its borders. According to Conca, at the same time that international water law may be emerging in the South African domestic context, the reverse is also true, in that regional and international agreements represent one way in which the changing character of South African water law, policy and normative codes of conduct can reach outward and influence neighbouring state behaviour (Conca, 2006). For example, the South African Department of Water Affairs' 1997 White Paper emphasized the goal of projecting emerging domestic water principles into regional water relations: 'The objective in relation to our neighbours is the same as it is within South Africa's borders, to ensure that we adjust to the pressures and demands of the future through cooperation, not conflict, in harmony with the needs of our common developmental goals and the protection of our environment' (DWAF, 1997: 5).

For whom and by whom? are regional norms created?

Finally, transboundary water governance in the SADC region plays itself out amidst profound power asymmetries within SADC states (e.g. rural/urban; urban/peri-urban; white/black; male/female), between states (South Africa and 'the rest of SADC'), and between the region and the world (SADC and the United States, and SADC and the EU). While regional mechanisms such as the SADC WD, SADC Parliamentary Forum (SADC PF) have been the main proponents of regional norms, the normative framework has been influenced by a vast number of actors. It is therefore at this, the regional level, where multi-level normative influences are most felt. That said however, the sovereign nation state still reigns supreme as the primary norm creators, determining which norms gain acceptance at the regional level, and why.

The significance of key individuals, acting as norm entrepreneurs, have also given effect to regional norms in multilateral fora and nationally. The politically charged nature of institutional memory loss, particularly in Namibia and South Africa, as a result of experienced individuals retiring or leaving the water sector, has therefore been met with concern. Moreover, inadequate sustainable knowledge transfer policies have been institutionalized to retain this fleeting knowledge.

The hegemonic nature of South Africa's transboundary governance has also greatly influenced the types of norms and principles discussed at the regional level. As Funke and Turton (2008) argue, the nature of South Africa's relations with its fellow riparians post-apartheid, has seen a movement away from *puissance* (i.e. strength or force, particularly as it relates to military might in the case of states) to *pouvoir* (i.e. the power over an outcome as a result of diplomatic interaction, persuasion, engagement and the mobilization of public opinion).

However, norms created and institutionalized at the regional level by the SADC WD, SADC PF, member states, with external donor influences, have been ambiguous or deliberately vague in wording (e.g. policy harmonization and alignment). The onus is once again on member states to give effect to these norms by defining it according to national contexts. For example, a key role of the SADC WD is to monitor the application of the SADC Protocol, the Regional Water Policy (RWP) for SADC and the Regional Water Strategy (RWS), and the facilitation of the harmonization of water law and policies between SADC member states. The SADC WD does not have the mandate to implement and enforce the policy harmonization imperatives in the member states. This obligation falls on the member states, whose national laws must ensure that obligations stemming from international agreements such as the SADC Protocol or basin-wide water management agreements are being met (Malzbender and Earle, 2009).

In the case of bottom-up (local to national) norm convergence

What factors determine the success to which local norms influence state policy and behaviour or their inability to do so?

While still limited, an increasing body of research is providing evidence for the importance of incorporating indigenous knowledge in contemporary legal, institutional and policy frameworks because of its ability to facilitate communication and decision-making from the local level. These indigenous information systems are dynamic, in that they are continually influenced by internal creativity and experimentation as well as by contact with external systems and normative frameworks (Flavier et al., 1995). Mainstream research tends to focus on the ways in which these local normative and knowledge frameworks have been transformed as a result of national or external influences, but less research has been conducted on what these local knowledge systems have to offer and how they may influence behaviour at higher levels of scale.

Despite limited determining factors, the degree to which local actors can articulate their interests in national fora (if those exist) is one way in which they have been able to successfully influence state/national policy. This involves capacity, and local actor awareness of institutional and political processes at other levels of scale. In the case of the LHWP, the TRC and the Survivors of the Lesotho Dams (SOLD) with the help of the INGO, International Rivers, for example, have become extremely active, focusing on social issues such as the resettlement of villagers and problems regarding the delivery of promised compensation, as well as the new social issues created through reallocation and building projects (Kranz et al., 2005a). Meissner (2000b, 2000c, 2004, 2005) in his analyses of the agency exhibited by non-state actors and interest groups on the LHWP and in other southern African basins is a notable exception. But it should be stated that these are isolated cases, and in most other areas in SADC, researchers have reported little or no local awareness/knowledge of the degree to which local norms and interests significantly influence national and regional contexts (Ngana et al., 2003; Nkhoma and Mulwafu, 2004). More specifically, evidence of the degree to which norms have filtered up from the local level to national, regional and global policy frameworks is less apparent than norm convergence from the top down. This is yet another area of norms research that could add tremendous value to cooperative management of water and the policy landscape within which it is embedded.

Moreover, having well-articulated interests and voicing them is sometimes insufficient to have local norms infiltrate state policy and or behaviour. These local actors have to be present at discussions, and their voices incorporated into operational frameworks. Due to the highly technical nature of water management in the region a technically knowledgeable epistemic community usually dominates the production and application of knowledge (Swatuk, 2005b). Their conservationist or technical interests therefore take precedence over that of local actors in that they are present at organizational platforms to convince policymakers to embrace global environmental norms while local actors are not (ibid.). This point emphasizes the power asymmetries at play in norm diffusion advancing the argument made for local agency – indeed, some local actors are privileged with more agency than others.

Additionally, incorporating indigenous and traditional knowledge raises a number of complex issues, such as, land tenure rights, genetic resource ownership, intellectual property rights and benefit sharing that policymakers prefer to sidestep (Ten and Laird, 1999). Even though there are clear benefits to integrating these knowledge systems and normative frameworks into Western policy and practice, indigenous knowledge, norms and understandings of water are still misunderstood and are largely ignored in water projects to date or meaningfully included in water policy and planning processes (RAK, 2008). Moreover, customary access and rights to water are rarely ever recognized by state authorities that have obtained control of indigenous areas and sources of water (ibid.). These areas are now being developed and local actors find themselves impacted by outside forces beyond their control (ibid.).

Another critically important factor determining the degree to which local norms get attention at the national level is the degree to which they help further national agendas. It needs to be recognized that norm entrepreneurs at the national level have displayed instrumental commitment to local norms in attempts to garner public and donor support, under the much used catch phrases of public participation, gender mainstreaming and HIV/AIDS mainstreaming. Public participation, for instance, has been used to legitimize changes already predetermined by central government in collaboration with donors in various parts of Africa (Dungumaro and Madulu, 2003).

How do local (culturally specific) norms affect national-level water governance?

Local norms impact global, regional as well as national level water governance in various ways, which may in turn impact transboundary cooperative frameworks. According to Swatuk (2005a: 874), a range of local actors, 'From landless peasant to NGO operator to national elite – are engaged in a continuous dialogue with national, regional and especially global actors, be they mercenary, missionary or fellow traveller'. Unfortunately, the few cases acknowledged where local, culturally specific or historically based norms affect national-level water governance is when there is a sharp resistance to a national norm that has been forced upon local actors as the example of 'water theft' or illegal abstraction of water for farm use in the Upper Vaal exemplified. However, Thrupp (1989) argues that the incorporation of indigenous knowledge and its accompanying normative frameworks into development projects may contribute to local empowerment and development, increasing self-sufficiency and strengthening self-determination. According to the Orange-Senqu River Awareness Kit, utilizing this knowledge and being aware of local norms during the implementation of projects gives it legitimacy and credibility by local as well as outside actors; and this increases the sense of ownership by providing incentives to solve problems with local ingenuity and resources (RAK, 2008).

While the instrumental adoption of local norms may help to legitimize decisions made at the national level, local norms may also be packaged in ways that appeal to or further national interests. In this regard, local norms may be reframed (e.g. water as a basic human right or the injustice of resettlement as a result of damming) to appeal to a wider national audience in order to force government's hand and also attract interest from influential donors (Swatuk, 2005a).

Why do external norms face local resistance?

External norms may also face local resistance due to longstanding domestic norms. The issue of 'water theft', unlawful farm use or illegal abstraction aptly depicts the resistance of new externally induced, legal and normative principles constructed at the national level, by local historically constructed normative frameworks. This has been the result of poor implementation of the new water law in some areas where the requirement to obtain permits and its impact on farming practices was not adequately communicated to farmers, or properly enforced by authorities. Illegal water abstraction for farm use has become a critical management dilemma for South African water managers, who regard this as stealing from paid users.

The main problem is a normative dispute between pre-existing land rights and newly institutionalized principles of water privatization and equitable utilization. Farmers argue that they are merely abstracting water which would have been available to them through the natural flow in the river. They have invoked historic land rights and therefore riparian rights to water. This problem remains unresolved, and while it is predominantly a purely national concern, it could indirectly impact on transboundary cooperative agendas, particularly, because the water being transferred comes from Lesotho, and for which the Government of South Africa pays royalties. The specifics of IBT schemes could potentially be reviewed to prevent this from occurring in the future, and this may affect how and where water is transferred.

Additionally, scholars researching the challenges to water reform processes (Tapela, 2002) have pointed out the difficulties in overlaying a new institution on top of a variety of other existing institutions with different jurisdictional boundaries (e.g. Rural Development Council, Provincial Government, District Council etc.). Swatuk (2005) further argues that new institutions have undermined existing forms of cooperation and conflict resolution. Evidence therefore shows that southern African governments have been reluctant to entrust stakeholders with too much power, rural dwellers have been generally suspicious of the motives behind reform, and empowered actors have used the language of local norms to tout broad-based participation. This provides a suitable breeding ground for norm resistance. In this regard, local actors display resistance to norms that challenge longstanding (and entrenched) practices of how things are done.

For whom and by whom? are local norms created?

Local norms have a variety of sources. In the Orange-Senqu River basin, these may include sociocultural beliefs, pre-existing historical practices based on apartheid or colonial legacies. A wide range of actors have therefore also contributed to the creation of local norms that are context-specific. A more pertinent question however, relates to whose interests are accepted and whose are redefined when norm dynamism and/or contestation occurs.

In the case of norm dynamism or contestation

What are the relationships between various levels of norms?
Are they antagonistic and competitive or can they coexist in a
harmonious way? What are the asymmetric power relations at play?

The southern African case illustrates that while the relationships between various norms may at times be antagonistic, they are also able to coexist, and may even be complementary. In many cases, the precursors of external norms have had their own history of domestic development that predate their arrival at the international level, thus allowing them to be congruent with pre-existing normative frameworks already in place or emerging (Conca, 2006). The ways in which norms and norm sets are institutionalized therefore is also very important. In some settings, such as transboundary river basins and transnational stakeholder collaboration, the presence of transnational agents and their influences are immediately felt. They are able to push norm-based change through certain state channels.

But in other areas where normative change is orchestrated from within, a predominantly domestic or regional logic of appropriateness prevails. Regionally constructed norm convergence is politically prioritized and actively sought by regional norm entrepreneurs. The agency of state and basin actors is evident in their abilities to construct their own norms and identities such as the creation of river basin commissions as the primary institutional arrangement in transboundary water governance. Indeed, for the Orange-Senqu River basin and ORASECOM, the relationship between norms and identities are mutually reinforcing. As norms are standards of appropriate behaviour held by individuals with a given identity, individuals adhere to norms because by behaving in a certain manner, it defines them as belonging to a certain group. At the same time, identities determine and reinforce conformity to a particular norm. Since ORASECOM and the region itself in the form of SADC, are still defining their group identity, instrumental norm construction is occurring where local actors and external actors use this phase of identity creation to construct norms that reflect a desired identity. Similarly, in an attempt to push an agenda of regionalism, actors have conformed to emerging standards of behaviour because it helps define them as members of the region.

Which norms become dominant and how?

The norms that have become dominant in the SADC region, and in the Orange-Senqu Basin specifically, have been those that have been able to be reframed to smaller or wider audiences, as well as those norms that are congruent with pre-existing norms. Sovereignty and power asymmetries are still key drivers in determining which norms become dominant and how this occurs. However, due to the political emphasis placed on regional integration, regional accords have an increasing importance, as do the external donors that help to fund such initiatives. Normative agendas are therefore materially driven by power and money just as much as by the desire by some local actors to form a regional community. Identities are in turn constructed around the notion of the 'regional team player'.

Why do some win out over others?

When reviewing why some norms win out over others, their legitimating qualities are critical. Conca (2006) argues that in southern Africa, norm dynamism is reflected in the controversies over how water is valued and who may participate in its governance. These have been the primary drivers for creating new water-related practices and relationships. As Jacklyn Cock suggests, a powerful form of social activism in South Africa today is the struggle of the poor majority for 'social citizenship' in terms of clean water, electricity, public health and other survival and livelihood considerations in the face of the state's neo-liberal inclinations and policy orientations (Cock, 2003). Norms and principles that better capture these sentiments are most likely to receive broad-based acceptance in South Africa. The challenge to achieve social citizenship for all played itself out in recent xenophobic and other violent attacks in South African informal settlements particularly towards Zimbabweans and immigrants from other African countries (Jacobs and Turton, 2009). Most of the causes cited for these outbreaks included poor service delivery (particularly of clean water and sanitation), poor governance and a lack of capacity at the local level (Johnston and Bernstein, 2007) which compounded with an influx of foreigners from neighbouring African countries, has resulted in localized hotspots for conflict. This example illustrates how water is valued (as a basic human right for all) and how a critical mass will mobilize to advocate for the socialization of a particular norm at the national level, albeit on the back of other, more politically charged and racially based norms (i.e. the South African government should first prioritize South African citizens in terms of access to water, sanitation and jobs before providing for other nationalities).

In the Orange-Senqu River basin, norms need to have a legitimating characteristic for them to be accepted. There is however a complex and intricate balance that needs to be drawn between achieving national objectives (based on the need for reform and the political consequences of this) and local objectives (based on the need for adequate service delivery).

Whose interests are accepted and whose interests are redefined?

The case of the Orange-Senqu shows that while the global norm set of transboundary cooperation has been diffused in a non-linear fashion, regional and national interests have not had to be redefined. Instead, norm congruence with pre-existing national norms facilitated faster diffusion of these global norms. Similarly, commitment to regional norms by SADC member states helped to legitimize national policies, and a sense of good neighbourliness. It also helped to foster the incremental process towards a common understanding, prioritized in SADC's objective of regional integration.

Resistance to particular national norms may have been experienced at the local level. It is at this level of scale, where interests are mostly redefined, as norms are reframed, repackaged and grafted. Despite having a degree of agency (to mobilize transnational advocacy networks, to push their agendas by reframing norms to appeal to wider audiences), local actors are inherently disempowered, either excluded from organizational platforms where norms and principles are brought to the fore, lack the capacity and awareness of these political processes when they are present to articulate their interests or are used to legitimize governmental decisions in the name of public participation. Until power asymmetries are recognized, and the playing field levelled, local-level interests will always be disadvantaged in multi-level normative frameworks.

Norm convergence in the Nile Equatorial Lakes Sub-Basin (NELSB)

Norm convergence in the NELSB has been equally complex and multi-faceted. Like the Orange-Senqu case, sociopolitical histories of the past shaped the normative landscape of principled cooperation, however, recent political developments illustrate how the 'winds of political change' hold great influence in redirecting norm convergence and facilitating the development of a community of interests in the NELSB.

In the case of top-down global norm diffusion

What factors determine how the global norm set is translated in various ways?

Top-down norm diffusion of the global transboundary norm set has neither been a smooth nor linear process in the NELSB, and some might argue that it has not occurred at all. If one examines the influence that the Nyerere Doctrine has had on contesting pre-existing colonial treaties based on historic rights, and similarly, the unwillingness to sign and ratify the UN Convention, there is a clear distrust of external normative frameworks in this basin. These factors reiterate the assertion that regional identities are created more from within than from without. Global norm diffusion, in the NELSB context is therefore largely dependent on the ability to which global norms can be localized as well as the ability to which perceived contradictions in various external norms can be reconciled. These factors are both social and material.

For example, a normative clash is evident between the principles of equitable utilization, on the one hand, favoured by upstream states; and the principles of no harm and acquired and historic rights, on the other hand, favoured by downstream states. Given the fact that most Nile riparian states in attendance at the adoption of the UN Convention abstained during the voting process, the contested principles in the UN Convention have not been able to be socialized by a critical mass in a direct and linear manner. This is in large part, a function of the wording of the UN Convention and its inability to reconcile the two principles of no harm and historic rights.

How does the global norm set of transboundary cooperation, once constructed internationally, emerge and become socialized in various regional, basin, national and sub-national contexts?

Similar to the SADC example of the incorporation of the global norm set in the Revised SADC Water Protocol and the indirect adoption of these principles by SADC member states, the NBI's organizational frameworks, such as the guidelines for the Nile Basin Strategic Action Programme, also include the principles of 'equitable and reasonable utilization' and 'no harm' in its vision.

Additionally, the process of norm localization has been critically important to institutional development on the Nile and in the NELSB particularly. Subsidiarity is one such externally induced principle brought about by World Bank conditions. In the NELSB, the principle of subsidiarity as an institutionalized norm has been incorporated into basin and sub-basin operational frameworks and instrumental commitment to it has been displayed on the part of local as well as external actors operating in the region. Organizations such as the NBI and EAC have based their organizational structure on this practice in the hope of facilitating buy-in from riparian states. Institutions have therefore attempted to foster institutional credibility within the sub-basin and region. In this regard, it has been incorporated into the guidelines for the NBI's Subsidiary Action Programmes. The subsidiarity principle has been interpreted, reinterpreted and re-represented (Acharya, 2004) in an attempt to make it congruent with a constructed local normative order of sub-basin importance and applicability. Moreover, since norm localization is also a process whereby the agency role of local actors is prioritized, 'global norm transformers' within the NBI operational structure have borrowed the principle of subsidiarity, to gain credibility and prestige, both from local constituencies, idea-recipients and external norm entrepreneurs. The principle of subsidiarity has therefore facilitated the strengthening of the NBI's objectives of bottom-up development, public participation and stakeholder involvement. Secondly, it has strengthened the roles and bargaining power of previously disenfranchised voices in river basin management (such as the riparian states of the NELSB), and local actors have actively used it to do so.

Several criticisms of the way in which subsidiarity has been implemented (predominantly through formalized channels), have argued that traditional, informal institutions and customary law may be a more realistic starting point for implementing this principle, and obtaining public participation in an equitable and efficient manner (Maganga, 2003; Maganga et al., 2004; Sokile and van Koppen, 2004; Sokile et al., 2003). However, these authors also point out the challenges to using informal mechanisms. Sokile and van Koppen (2004) show how formal courts nullify the rulings of traditional, informal mechanisms. Maganga et al. (2004) further elaborate that in Tanzania, local people who know how the new water architecture works, deliberately turn to formal courts when informal decisions have gone against them.

Why is the global norm set incorporated into regional/basin/national policy and/or behaviour?

Instrumental commitment to the global norm set of transboundary cooperation is also evident in the basin, and reflected in regional and sub-basin policy through the NBI frameworks that have used the language of this norm set to orchestrate global credibility. Instrumental commitment to global principles is therefore, encouraged due to the desire of Nile riparians to maintain good relations with their international donors, particularly the World Bank.

For whom and by whom? is the global norm set created?

Additionally, international donors, such as the World Bank, and donor states, such as China have played significant roles in influencing the normative framework in the NELSB. The international norm set dominant in this sub-basin has therefore been created by global frameworks (i.e. UN Convention pushed by European pioneering states), donors and imperatives formulated in the AU, AMCOW and NEPAD. Moreover, the global norm set in the NELSB is not different to that existing in the greater Nile and as such, the recipients of this norm set are not confined to NELSB states.

In the case of lateral norm convergence from state-to-state or state-to-basin-to-region

What factors in the regional/basin/sub-basin configuration account for a powerful norm set at these levels of scale?

Regional norm convergence has been deliberately orchestrated in the Nile Basin, and consequently also, in the NELSB. It is arguably the case that the NBI has orchestrated the socialization of specific norms through its Strategic Action Programme (SAP). This approach can be regarded as an attempt to facilitate trust, create ownership by all riparians and local communities and propel and steer regional norm convergence in a particular direction. Collectively, SVP activities have helped to promote common understanding of the interaction between national policies, regional needs and cooperative development, forming a more effective basis for cooperation at the regional and sub-regional levels (Waako, 2008).

Regional norm convergence has also been facilitated by several drivers such as trust and confidence-building, policy alignment and the progression towards a benefit-sharing paradigm. The NBI has focused on policy harmonization within its institutional frameworks and practices in all riparian states through its institutional strengthening project (ISP). It has also encouraged riparian states to align national policies due to the lack of harmonized institutional and regulatory frameworks to deal with transboundary watersheds. Most riparians have developed new policies for water and environmental management, however, the degree to which they incorporate transboundary concerns or principles vary from country to country. The process of national policy alignment is a long-term one that involves harmonizing water policies with a shared vision of good water management and defined goals for cross-border cooperation through ongoing technical implementation and co-riparian dialogue. This contributes to a gradual progression towards norm convergence.

How do norms converge regionally or within a basin?

The shift in power asymmetries due to increased political and economic stability of NELSB riparians over the past decade has facilitated norm convergence at the sub-basin level. The EAC and NBI have been instrumental in facilitating this power shift, enabling East African countries to better articulate their interests in a collective manner, and in so doing, giving them bargaining power in basin-wide arrangements.

Norm convergence in the NELSB is also evident by the way in which upstream riparians have solidified their longstanding objections to colonial-era water treaties such as the 1929 and 1959 Agreements. They have done this by constructing national norms (embodied, for example, in the Nyerere Doctrine) to legally oppose external norms such as historic rights that favour downstream countries.

Why are regional norms incorporated into regional/basin/state policy and/or behaviour?

Regional norm convergence in the NELSB has therefore occurred almost by way of necessity. Sub-basin cooperation was required for equatorial states to increase their bargaining power in basin-wide fora. Moreover, NELSB countries have done this by advocating strongly for the establishment of a multilateral treaty agreement governing all ten Nile riparian states. Additionally, NELSB countries have also formed sub-basin institutional arrangements that articulate interests specific to the sub-basin such as economic development relating to Lake Victoria, and the impact of future factors on them specifically, such as climate change, changes in the flow of the water itself, infrastructural development and the growing pollution problem.

For whom and by whom? are regional norms created?

Regional norms have in the past been largely created by non-NELSB countries, particularly hegemonic states such as Egypt. However, in the past decade NELSB countries have given greater voice to their interests with the help of institutions such as the LVBC, the LVFO and the NBI. Important donors such as the World Bank as well as China are also influential in this sub-basin and have, to varying degrees, help set the normative framework. They have achieved this by providing financial resources and capacity to enable water infrastructure development projects (China) and facilitate institutional development (World Bank). However, they have also helped to determine what acceptable behaviour is and what it is not.

In the case of bottom-up (local to national) norm convergence

What factors determine the success to which they influence state policy and behaviour or their inability to do so?

The multitude of values and norms at the household and community level in the NELSB does not represent a homogenous national identity. NELSB states consist of a multitude of actors, cultures and different layers of identities. These identities often transcend or divide political and territorial units. However, the multiplicity of actors at the local level does not translate into the inclusion of several local voices or louder civil society voices at the negotiating table where norms are debated. This raises significant questions about who the most important actors are. Indeed, state actors still determine the regional normative agenda, however, this is not to say that local non-state actors are in fact powerless or redundant. Rather, the multiplicity of local actors dilutes efforts to be heard as a single voice. Moreover, the NELSB exists within the greater Nile region, which adds another degree of complexity in terms of the basin's heterogeneity. Due to this diversity, it is difficult to track normative development from the local level to the national level. Research on African languages indicates that there are as many as 400 languages spoken within the Nile River basin (RAK, 2006). Factors that determine the success to which local culturally specific norms are infiltrated into state policy and behaviour therefore include the degree to which institutions are sensitive to cultural diversity by actively exploring ways in which to integrate this into internal and external processes as described above.

How do local (culturally specific) norms affect national-level water governance, if at all possible?

As previously noted, due to the diversity of cultures in the NELSB, it is difficult to track normative development of culturally specific norms from the local level to the national level. However, having said that, the NBI has made provisions within its programmes for stakeholder engagement and public participation. The Nile Basin Discourse (NBD) is the representative umbrella NGO network operating within the basin to facilitate dialogue between the NBI and civil society in order to promote dialogue on poverty eradication, sustainable and equitable development, peace and mutual understanding regarding issues pertaining to the basin (Kameri-Mbote, 2005). In essence, the NBD was created to 'bring the voices of stakeholders other than government to the process of the development of the Nile basin' (ibid.: 7). However, despite the existence of the NBD, the issue of civil society engagement and representation is still contentious. Some scholars have argued that the NBD in indeed not representative enough of civil society (Kameri-Mbote, 2005). As Kameri-Mbote (2005: 8) notes, 'given the open nature of dialogue and the involvement of diverse entities, the challenge of meaningfully putting in place an agenda that is not captured by the interests of powerful groups remains. Moreover, providing adequate resources for the dialogue continues to be a challenge.'

If one takes a historical perspective, several geographical, cultural and historical barriers have separated the Nile's cultures for centuries, and this separation not only magnified their distinctive identities but also impeded cooperation, the exchange of experiences and mutual understanding. According to Erlich and Gershoni (2000), myths, mysteries and misconceptions took over where direct communication lagged behind. An insightful quote from their closing chapter is pertinent: 'Only by recognising diversity and legitimising pluralism can regional cooperation and unity of action be achieved' (Erlich and Gershoni, 2000: 271). This captures the essence of the importance of local norms and values. While they may be underrepresented, their absence in state, sub-basin and basin policy mystifies and estranges them from political processes where regional norm convergence is negotiated. This has contributed to the separation of peoples of the Nile.

Cultural adaptations and the livelihoods they create are therefore linked to the languages, social systems, customs, knowledge systems and local histories of the Nile Basin. They create what is referred to as cultural diversity (RAK, 2006). The question then is: how is cultural diversity incorporated into national-level water governance? Recently, there have been major developments in exploring various policy initiatives to develop an integrated approach to the role played by cultural diversity in sustainable development and the protection of biodiversity (Hazeltine and Bull, 2003; RAK,

2008; Visscher, 2006; Visscher et al., 2006). The process of institutionalizing culturally specific norms is evident in the progression towards Cultural Diversity Mainstreaming, which involves an awareness of cultural diversity and integrating it at all levels of the project management cycle. This ensures that culturally specific issues are identified in the analysis of programmes and projects and are subject to specific interventions whenever appropriate (UNESCO-IHP, 2007, 2009).

Why do external norms face local resistance due to longstanding domestic norms?

Local resistance to external norms in the greater Nile and the NELSB has largely been as a result of the contradictory nature of external norms and incompatibility of interests. Unless external norms are able to be localized, the uptake of these norms will not occur. External norms face local resistance in so far as infrastructural development projects have not taken into consideration the effects these projects have had on local cultural practice and belief systems. Local resistance to external norms also reflects local actor suspicion of particular external actors and their motives in funding development projects.

For whom and by whom? are local norms created?

Due to the heterogeneity of the sub-basin, a wide range of local and context-specific norms exist. While states are still the main proponents and receptors of norms regarding transboundary cooperation, the role and influence of the donor community, particularly the World Bank, in crafting the NBI institutional structure and objectives has been met with concern by many local actors (Kameri-Mbote, 2005). Local actors are therefore less likely to support external (be they global or regional) norms that are perceived to be crafted and pushed by 'distrusting' external actors. It is therefore difficult to distinguish between locally based norms and external norms because oftentimes various actors (external and local) shroud external norms in culturally specific rhetoric to enable easier acceptance of the norm in question.

In the case of norm dynamism or contestation

What are the relationships between various levels of norms? What are the asymmetric power relations at play?

The relationships between particular norms are more contentious in the Nile River basin than in the Orange-Senqu. However, the normative power battle also mirrors the power asymmetries and the change thereof in the past decade.

Which norms become dominant and how?

Sub-basin norms have therefore been most dominant and have had both a regulative and constitutive effect. As constitutive instruments, norms of sub-basin cooperation (through sub-basin organizations such as the LVBC and the LVFO) have legitimized goals of economic development, given greater voice to NELSB riparians and have therefore acted as motives (Klotz, 1995). And as motives, they have also helped to determine the goals towards which NELSB states should strive, that is economic growth through the sustainable utilization of sub-basin resources such as, Lake Victoria.

Why do some win out over others?

The most notable clash of principles: sovereign ownership and exclusive rights over one's resources versus the principle of shared ownership of an international river, plays itself out in the hydropolitics of the Nile. While the principles of equitable utilization and no harm have been codified in basin and sub-basin institutional frameworks, implementation at regional and domestic levels is more challenging. The fact that the 1997 UN Convention is yet to enter into force can largely be explained by the reluctance of certain states to sign away their various hard-line stances. The process of normative reconciliation and convergence, in this regard, will be a long process and involves the complex task of analysing the different needs of the water users in each riparian state and how they can be amicably met. However, while the competition between sovereign ownership and exclusive rights over one's resources versus the principle of shared ownership is ongoing and the winners are still to be determined, the NELSB countries have begun to organize themselves and articulate their interests in a joint manner. Once a common standard of appropriate behaviour is identified, slowly some norms begin to win our over others.

Whose interests are accepted and whose interests are redefined?

The example of the NELSB case study shows that despite norm contestation, norms can coexist. While Waterbury (2002) argues that a community of riparians does not exist in the Nile, and that no accepted norms of group behaviour have been developed that could shame riparians into complying with a particular code of conduct, this study has shown that first an identity of a community of interests/riparians needs to be created. This has been actively and deliberately orchestrated by various local and external actors. Waterbury (2002) also argues that the main frameworks that can promote and sustain cooperation are contract and hierarchy, with the catalysts to cooperation being third-party entrepreneurs located in the donor community. From this point of view, nation states pursuing their strategic and national interests are still the most senior players, and any action between them will be based on contract and hierarchy (ibid.). In contrast, this study highlights the gradual change in the balance of power and the creation of a collective sub-basin identity through the articulation of joint interests in the NELSB. The position of the hegemon in the Nile is now questionable given the 2011 Egyptian Revolution and fall of former President Mubarak. And a new voice, that of South Sudan has to be considered. While power asymmetries still permeate all levels of scale, the burgeoning power in the collective NELSB identity may be the key to levelling the playing field.

Theoretical implications of norm convergence

Based on the analysis of the Orange-Senqu and the NELSB case-study areas, four primary conclusions are therefore drawn as illustrated in Figure 5.1:

1. A norm and/or norm set created at a particular level of scale can interact and diffuse directly to any other level of scale and need not go through a linear top-down or bottom-up process provided that it resonates with context-specific normative understandings. As was the case in the SADC region, global norms were not socialized through the ratification of the UN Convention. Instead, these principles were entrenched in the Revised Water Protocol, thus allowing SADC member states to side-step the deliberate vagueness of the UN Convention. Similarly, local actors, such as NGOs and other interest groups, are now able to further their agendas through transnational networks with other NGOs and INGOs worldwide, made easier as a result of the accessibility of the internet. As a result norms do not need to cascade down from one level to the next lower level of scale, or diffuse up sequentially.

2. A norm/norm set can penetrate several levels of scale simultaneously. The subsidiarity principle is a case in point. In the NELSB, this norm has interacted with regional, basin, sub-basin and national levels, and has been accepted (in various ways) in these configurations. Indeed, the applicability and flexibility of norms at multiple levels and contexts contribute to its strength and legitimacy.

3. Sociopolitical, socioeconomic and socio-cultural contexts will change as a result of norm diffusion. The impact norms have on contexts varies depending on the degree of specificity of the norm, the degree to which it can be localized, the congruence it displays with pre-existing norms, the ability it has to be reframed or grafted. That said however, this study has found that even the most ambiguous norms (such as equitable utilization), or the most contentious (such as water privatization or historic rights), display an agential capability. They are therefore able to not only change actor behaviour, but also, change the environment in which these actors operate.

4. Norms will change as a result of contexts. In parallel to the above-mentioned conclusion, norms are inevitably transformed in the context in which they are internalized.

5. Norms will change as a result of the existence of other norms as well as the interaction between them.

6. This multi-level normative framework reveals that norms existing at different levels of scale are not always antagonistic and can at times be complementary, particularly if they help to further interests at other levels of scale. The pervasiveness of instrumental commitments to norms by actors cannot be overlooked. Norms are therefore used, shaped, framed, grafted, manipulated and packaged in ways that further the interests of those powerful enough to dictate and/or influence behaviour.

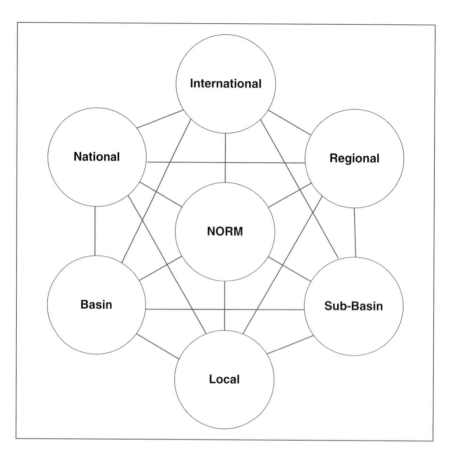

Figure 5.1 Multi-level development of cooperative norms in water governance

Conclusion

This chapter emphasized the importance of holistic and integrated analyses of governance, and the complexities of these systems. A multi-level normative framework was sketched for both case-study areas revealing non-linear diffusion of the global norm set of transboundary cooperation. In the Orange-Senqu, norm congruence with pre-existing national norms facilitated faster diffusion of global norms. Similarly, instrumental commitment to regional norms by SADC member states has helped to legitimize national policies, and create a sense of good neighbourliness thus increasing the costs of norm-breaking behaviour. In the NELSB, context and norm localization as well as internal and external threats to the sovereignty of African states were the key factors in determining the degree to which the global norm set was translated in various ways.

In terms of regional norm convergence in the SADC region, regional norms have promoted the incremental progression towards achieving a common understanding, prioritized in SADC's objective of regional integration. Regional norms have also converged largely a result of the near-simultaneous and transitional nature of national institutional and legal frameworks since the 1990s, as well as social processes such as capacity-building, benefit-sharing, trust-building and technical cooperation between various actors. Resistance to particular national norms may have been experienced at the local level in the Orange-Senqu River basin. Despite having a degree of agency, local actors are generally more disempowered than other actors in policy circles, and are either excluded from organizational platforms where norms and principles are brought to the fore. Additionally, oftentimes (although certainly not always) they lack the necessary capacity and awareness of political processes to and the political skill to articulate their interests in these fora.

In the NELSB, more emphasis was placed on the 'winds of change' and the influence that recent political events have had on norm convergence in the sub-basin. Instrumental commitment to global norms was also found, as a way to ensure global credibility and to maintain relationships with global donors. At the regional level, the NELSB has witnessed a shift in the balance of power and an increase in local actor instrumentality and agency. At the sub-basin level, NELSB states have advocated quite strongly for the establishment of a multilateral treaty agreement governing all Nile riparian states, have taken a largely collective stance on opposing pre-existing colonial treaties, in some instances, citing the Nyerere Doctrine, and forming sub-basin-institutional arrangements that articulate interests specific to these countries such as economic development. In terms of bottom-up norm convergence, the diversity of cultures in the NELSB has resulted in a wide range of culturally specific cooperative norms on water, however, this has also made it difficult to track normative development from the local level to the national level for any one specific locally based norm. What we find in the NELSB is therefore an environment of dynamic relationships between norms operating at different levels of scale. The normative landscape is also more contentious in the NELSB than in the Orange-Senqu largely because of the power asymmetries and the change thereof in the past decade. The process of normative reconciliation and convergence will be a long process and involves the complex task of analysing the different needs of the water users in each riparian state and how they can be amicably met.

This chapter therefore confirmed the non-linear process of norm diffusion from one level of scale to another that does not directly come before or after it. The discovery made is that virtually all interests are redefined, although to varying degrees, when norms are socialized. Power relations are therefore imperative; between actors and also between norms. This chapter also confirmed that governance structures for the environment are found at a multiplicity of levels from the global to the local and that they interact and influence each other in unique, complex and ever-changing ways. Norms and other regulatory mechanisms are therefore closely linked, and make up a complex institutional architecture. An integrated analysis of global, regional, basin-wide and local norms is useful because it illustrates the significance of their interconnectedness in terms of the processes of interaction at play as well as how their content is affected. Theoretically, we find that a more systemic and integrated interpretation of transboundary water governance is needed because each level of scale forms part of a unique governance framework, and various norms interact and function in the context of the system as a whole (De Chazournes, 2009).

Note

1   Similarly, the 1970 Commission of Enquiry into Water Matters, mandated as a result of the droughts in the 1960s, 1970s and 1980s, diagnosed that 'unless effective measures are applied in the planning and development of the Republic's water resources there may be serious shortages of water before the close of the century' (Commission of Enquiry on Water Matters, 1970), paid almost no attention to the international legal context (Conca, 2006). The international dimension is summarized in two sentences: 'Concerning use of waters from rivers in which other riparian countries have interest [referring particularly to the independent TVBC states or black homelands of Transkei, Venda, Bophuthatswana and Ciskei] it seems that international law affecting use of the waters of such rivers is very loose. The use of such waters is generally fixed by agreement' (Commission of Enquiry on Water Matters, 1970: 1.37).

6

Water and Regional Integration in Africa

Understanding the complexity and importance of water cooperative norms and principles not only gives us insight into the multi-levelled nature of institutional and legislative development in particular basins or regions, it also enables us to see how broader policy decisions are made. It provides a useful link to understanding how and why actors behave in a certain way, and how norm development can be used to push political agendas and interests. Most importantly, it emphasizes how truly integrated natural resources are.

This book has argued at length that international river basins are part of an increasingly complex landscape of policies, trading relations and sectoral demands. And this institutional complexity presents challenges but also opportunities for the water sector to increasingly integrate with other sectors in terms of decision-making in agriculture, energy, industry and urban development in particular (Jacobs and Nienaber, 2011). Water in particular can be used to help drive regional integration efforts because of the need to address important resource questions in an integrated manner.

Since the early years of independence, many African leaders have grappled with the challenge of regional integration. This commitment has been articulated in several high-level treaties and declarations as well as in the formation of the Organisation of African Unity (OAU) in 1963 (now the African Union), the African Union Commission (AUC), the United Nations Economic Commission for Africa (UNECA), the African Development Bank (AfDB) and the Regional Economic Communities (RECs). These institutions have been the key players in driving regional integration efforts at the continental level.

Regional integration means a very many things to a very many people and scholars have yet to reach consensus on whether regional integration is a good or bad thing. According to De Lombaerde and Van Langenhove (2007) regional integration is a worldwide phenomenon comprising of territorial systems that increase the interactions between their components and create new forms of organization, coexisting with traditional forms of state-led organization at the national level. Similarly, Ginkel and

Van Langenhove (2003) refer to regional integration as the process by which states in a particular region increase their level of interaction with each other in terms of economic, security, political and also social and cultural issues. In other words, regional integration is a type of cooperation between states usually falling within the same geographic space such that they form a larger entity. It therefore involves the process where states overcome political, physical, economic and social barriers that divide countries from their neighbours and collaborate in the management of shared resources, common regional goods and transnational challenges such as food security, climate change and biodiversity.

The fundamental objectives of regional cooperation and integration in Africa include the promotion of economic development, political stability (a prerequisite for economic development), and poverty-reduction. By achieving this regional integration can arguably transform fragmented small economies, expand markets, widen the region's economic space and improve the economies of scale for production and trade (UNECA, 2010). While policymakers involved in regional integration efforts have traditionally paid more attention to infrastructural developments in the sectors such as transport, information and communication technology (ICT), and energy, there is now a growing awareness of the intrinsic role that water plays in regional development (Grey and Sadoff, 2006; World Water Council, 2011).

Regional integration in Africa

Regional integration in Africa has been a slow process as compared to regional integration in other parts of the world, but has not been without high-level support. The African Union (AU) is the culmination of Africa's regional integration mission, which saw the sprouting up of a number of integration-based institutions in the 1980s through the Lagos Plan of Action for the Economic Development of Africa and the Final Act of Lagos (Granit et al., 2010). This integration agenda was then formalized in the 1990s with the adoption of the Abuja Treaty establishing the RECs, and again in the year 2001, which saw the development of the Constitutive Act establishing the AU (ibid.). Several other initiatives also acknowledge the pivotal role that regional integration plays in African development:

- The African Charter on Human and People's Rights drafted in 1981;
- Africa's Priority Programme for Economic Recovery (APPER) in 1985, to address the emerging crisis of the 1980s;
- The Treaty Establishing the African Economic Community (EAC), known as the Abuja Treaty, in 1991;
- The Sirte Declaration of 1999;
- The 2000 Solemn Declaration on security, stability, development and cooperation of the African continent;
- The AU programme, the New Partnership for Africa's Development (NEPAD) in 2000.

Despite the AU's shortcomings, in terms of implementation and delivery, weak institutional capacity as a result of a shortage of qualified staff, a lack of funding and unresolved tensions with certain RECs; it arguably exerts a degree of influence in shaping the institutional landscape on the continent. The AU's predecessor, the OAU, has been referred to as the 'custodian of the norms of international society that restrictively defined self-determination' and 'whose rigid and inflexible adherence to the principles of international society undermined the maintenance and promotion of peace and security' (Francis, 2006: 122). This refers to the OAU's stance of non-interference regarding intrastate conflicts. In contrast, the AU and its Constitutive Act have created a fundamental shift in the recognition of the deleterious effects on peace and security on underdevelopment, conflict, gross violations of human rights and bad governance (ibid.). In this regard, the AU has attempted to more clearly articulate its role as the presiding supra-national organizational body.

In terms of water governance specifically, the AU has also influenced regional water policy frameworks through its Commissioner for Agriculture and Water, as well as the development agenda of the Water Programme of NEPAD (Granit et al., 2010). Along with the AU and NEPAD, the African Ministerial Council on Water (AMCOW), formed in 2002, also aims to provide supra-regional coordination of water resource management although it still needs to develop into this role institutionally.

More specifically, cooperative water norms have been articulated at the continental level in various water-centric platforms that have argued for a greater focus on how water facilitates regional integration and socioeconomic development. This commitment towards prioritizing water in regional integration has been articulated at the following events and is evident in their resulting declarations:

- Water and Sustainable Development in Africa – Regional Stakeholders' Conference for Priority Setting (Accra Declaration), Accra, 15–17 April 2002 – The primary goals of this conference were to help increase awareness by Africa's political leaders of the central importance of water in sustainable development; to identify African water problems that can constrain the contribution of water resources to the goals of NEPAD; to agree on priorities for water development in Africa; to agree on a concrete Action Programme; as well as to develop a plan for mobilizing financial resources needed to implement the action plans (AU, 2002). The main outcome of the Conference was the Accra Declaration based on identified challenges and issues in the African water sector and recommendations for action plans to address these challenges (ibid.). The Accra Declaration was signed on 17 April 2002.
- The African Ministerial Conference on Water (AMCOW, Abuja), 29–30 April 2002 – This conference followed the Regional Stakeholders Conference, and emphasized the need for African states to assess, and where appropriate, adopt best practices in global and regional programmes dealing with water and sanitation (AMCOW, 2002). This conveys a high-level political commitment to adhering to global norms and principles regarding water governance. At this conference, ministers signed the Abuja Ministerial Declaration on Water.

- The New Partnership for Africa's Development recognizes water's important role in development, endorses the Africa Water Vision and the implementation of IWRM best-practice principles, and supports the promotion of knowledge transfer (SADC, 2003). Additionally, NEPAD's Water Sanitation and Infrastructure Programme aims to develop regional infrastructure, harmonize sectoral procedures, enhance financial flows towards investment in infrastructure and developing skills and knowledge for the installation, operation and maintenance of water and sanitation infrastructure. Both a Short-Term Action Plan (STAP) and a Medium-to Long-Term Strategic Framework (MLTSF) have been drafted.

More recently still, two AU Strategic Plans were drafted, one for the period 2004–7, and the other plan for the period 2009–12. The 2009–12 Plan defines priority areas for this period, such as climate change, the changing realities in the global economy and the challenges of poverty in Africa. Additionally, it identifies the human and financial resources required to manage them, and calls for the development of a common agenda with shared priorities on integration and cooperation (AU, 2009).

These broad-based goals and commitments indicate that (a) there is an awareness of the importance of multi-level normative frameworks, with importance given to both cooperative principles on water and participatory and integrated approaches and (b) that national water sectors throughout Africa are beginning to recognize water's role in regional integration efforts. While these are steps in the right direction, it could also be viewed as attempts to preach to the choir. Dialogue on the role of water in regional integration needs to move beyond the water sector and water-centric platforms.

An important discussion to have in this regard relates to the type of institutions, governmental departments and sectors that are most appropriate to deal with this reality. Are water-centric institutions such as RBOs and shared watercourse institutions (SWIs) in fact the most appropriate vehicles through which to channel development strategies? Are departments of water affairs the only governmental entities that can drive development strategies that include water? While they play an important role in dealing with water governance and development, they need to work with other sectors and multi-level institutions to address the root causes of problems and issues. RECs are key multi-level institutions through which cooperative water governance can take place, particularly as these communities become part of bilateral or multilateral trade agreements with other trading blocs and given their inherent links to RBOs by virtue of country memberships to both entities (Jacobs and Nienaber, 2011).

The role of water in regional integration

This then brings us to the question of the exact role that water can and does play in regional integration – a role that is best understood in two dimensions. First, the need for greater integration of natural resource management and coordination between sectors points out the opportunities and challenges of developing cross-sectoral interventions, and of water's pivotal role in bringing these sectors together. And secondly, the effective management of water plays a key role in sustainable growth and socioeconomic development.

The need for cross-sectoral integration

The integrated and cooperative governance of transboundary waters can act as a tool to facilitate regional and sub-regional cooperation and integration in Africa because of water's linkages to almost all forms of production, in agriculture, industry, energy and transport (Jacobs and Nienaber, 2011). Many of the potential benefits that can be derived from increased cooperation are well documented with frameworks designed to improve decision-making on how to turn cooperation into positive development outcomes (ibid.).

Despite the inherent interlinkages between water resources and other modes of production in a range of sectors, transboundary water management has not formed a significant part of the mainstream regional economic integration discourse to date although this is changing. Traditionally, water, energy and/or food security have been managed in an isolated manner with little consideration of the ways in which they depend on each other. For example, while water is required for power generation, power is also required in the purification, transport and distribution of potable water, and both these resources directly influence food security (ibid.). These synergies are often ignored resulting in partial responses to individual problems (ibid.). As Mohamed Ait Kadi noted in his speech at the 2010 Global Water Partnership's Consulting Partners meeting, any successful policy development and implementation process requires a detailed understanding of complex and interrelated problems (GWP, 2010) (see Figure 6.1).

In addition, complex regional challenges cannot be solved if individual countries act unilaterally (GWP, 2010). In fact, these challenges can actually worsen if states operate in this manner. A country like Malawi, situated on the south-east coast of Africa obtains most of its electricity from hydropower plants on the Shire River, a small

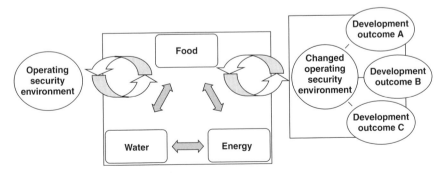

Figure 6.1 Conceptual illustration of the primary processes and causal linkages between water, energy, food security and development (Jacobs and Nienaber, 2011)

outlet of Lake Malawi which flows into the great Zambezi River. Malawi's hydropower supply is vulnerable to the flood season in the Zambezi River because the large volume of flood water flowing eastward from the Zambezi pushes water back up into the smaller Shire River (Jacobs and Nienaber, 2011). This phenomenon retards hydropower generation along the Shire, while further pressure on streamflow may actually bring the entire power-generation process to a halt (ibid.). The problem is exacerbated if floodgates at the Kariba Dam, located far upstream on the Zambezi between Zambia and Zimbabwe, are opened, a process necessary for controlled release and upkeep of the dam (ibid.). Interstate coordination between Malawi, Zimbabwe and Zambia management of water supply and power generation are therefore critically important if the benefits of development options are to be seen. It also alludes to the powerfully negative repercussions of non-cooperation and uncoordinated national processes on several interconnected resources.

The role of water in regional economic growth

The World Bank (2003) outlines four processes through which the effective management of water plays a fundamental role in sustainable growth and regional integration. First, broad-based water resource interventions involving large infrastructural developments such as canal systems, dams and inter-basin transfers, provide national, regional and local benefits from which all people, including the poor can gain (ibid.). This is a highly contentious point that has received wide-spread opposition from advocacy coalitions and communities affected by big hydraulic construction projects. It has also led to the perception that the infrastructural development of water has negative repercussions for the poor and project-affected people and also harms the environment (Grey and Sadoff, 2006). These perceptions have persuaded large amounts of people at all levels of scale of the detrimental impacts of large infrastructural projects, and have ultimately impeded the financing of water development (ibid.). While there is no theoretical limitation to designing water development investments that ensure benefits to local communities and the environment while still having favourable economic results, anti-big dam norms are pervasive in almost all countries undergoing such developments.

Secondly, interventions that aim to reduce poverty are critically important, most notably, investments that improve catchment quality and provide livelihoods for the poor (World Bank, 2003). Thirdly, wide-spread water service interventions, including those that help to improve the performance of water utilities, user associations and irrigation departments, benefit everyone especially the poor and marginalized (ibid.). And fourthly, poverty-reducing water service interventions such as water and sanitation and irrigation services for the unserved poor play a key role in reaching the Millennium Development Goals (MDGs) (ibid.). In most developing countries, growth-oriented, poverty-reducing water resources strategies will therefore involve action in all four of these areas (Grey and Sadoff, 2006).

Viewing water governance in this light, as the starting point to achieving regional integration, as opposed to an outcome of successful integration efforts, encourages a proactive integration agenda in all sectors, fosters a sense of agency in local actors and enables national decision-makers to allocate more funding to water resources and water supply development as this is regarded as investments in broad-based growth and development and not only sectoral growth (Jacobs and Nienaber, 2011).

Grey and Sadoff (2006), in their thematic document of the IV World Water Forum argued that the development of water resources within and between countries can play a key role in Africa's growth and development, but the benefits will be seen so much more if such developments are undertaken as part of, and in concert with, wider regional economic integration efforts. Conceptualizing water's role in regional economic integration was therefore the first step in formulating development agendas. Now, the main challenge is to get water issues prioritized in regional integration agendas in the way that strategic resources such as energy and minerals are given attention.

Prioritizing water in regional integration agendas requires three actions. First, it necessitates the transformation of entrenched perceptions about water as a second-order resource to a first-order strategic resource. Secondly, it requires that water and other resources such as land, oil and human capital are viewed in an integrated and interconnected manner. This also requires a shift in thinking in terms of how water professionals see themselves, from sectorally bound and operating in 'silos' specific to the water sector, to a more holistic awareness of all water-using sectors and the ways in which these sectors are interrelated. Finally, an investment framework for water that applies both to national and to regional-level decision-making is needed to ensure financial viability and sustainability of water development projects. The latter action is critically important given that the capacity for development is predetermined by investment and development policies and is limited by the financing capacity of governments.

The linkages between regional integration and norm convergence

What then is the relationship between regional integration and norm convergence? If one considers norm convergence as the institutional software required to promote and sustain political will to influence water governance, then policy harmonization strategies can be referred to as the institutional hardware that provides an enabling environment for the institutionalization, internationalization and/or socialization of various norms. Regional integration should then be regarded as the resultant process of effective norm convergence and policy harmonization.

Both norm convergence and policy harmonization exist in a symbiotic and mutually reinforcing relationship. Policy harmonization is a primary facilitating tool to foster incremental norm convergence and promote regional integration. Policy harmonization therefore aims to align national policies with joint cooperation goals, and plays a central role in the development of regional water strategies. Policy harmonization also refers to the alignment of national systems for managing and administering the water sector in a way that reduces differences in the operating environment between countries in the region. This entails the establishment of common arrangements, simplification of processes and sharing experiences and facilities for the common good of the region, while maximizing the benefits accruing to each country from its shared water resources (UNECA, 2008).

In essence, policy harmonization does not attempt to make national water policies of member states identical. Rather, harmonization entails improving the compatibility of national policies and strategies with one another (both within and between countries) so that they do not hinder the sharing of international water resources for mutual benefit (SADC, 2003).

Policy harmonization as a cooperation-enabling driver

The rationale for harmonization rests on several characteristics. First, policy harmonization has a cooperation-enabling characteristic, by helping states work together to achieve poverty alleviation using the water sector as a vehicle. A harmonized environment facilitates the creation of a sustainable water sector; helps in the reduction of the costs and risks of doing business across the region; assists in the advancement of transparent, simple and transferable best practice systems; and, helps facilitate economic growth through the reduction of incompatibilities of rules and regulations (UNECA, 2004). Considering that the water sector is one of the region's strategic sectors, in terms of the dependency of other sectors on its successful management and governance, the harmonization of water policies indirectly enables regions to consolidate their positions as global players in the world economy. However, harmonization may be unpopular in some countries, which already enjoy the benefits of water abundance economies and have therefore had no need to develop an outward-looking approach to water security; have recently revised national policies; or who regard it as an added administrative burden requiring time, money and capacity.

Policy harmonization as a strategic imperative

Secondly, the harmonization of policy regimes has been identified as a strategic imperative within SADC, NEPAD and the AU as it helps deepen regional integration. A harmonized policy environment will enhance regional human capital and technological development through the exchange of lessons learned, facilitate regional infrastructure development and enhance the efficient development of natural resources. Regions can, in a timely and adequate manner, respond to environmental and sustainable development challenges in a harmonized environment.

Policy harmonization as a leveraging tool

Thirdly, globalization and the increasing prevalence and popularity of economic blocs in the international political economy, imply that successful policy harmonization practices in regional blocs may increase their negotiating powers in their dealings with other economic groupings. It could also help to reduce prospects for marginalization and encourage funding prospects. Today, open regionalism is considered to be an important step towards globalization and the strengthening of regional activities

(AfDB, 2003). Successful policy harmonization in other African regions would achieve this same objective in the long term (UNECA, 2004).

Policy harmonization as facilitating the evolution of a shared vision

Fourthly, policy harmonization facilitates the evolution of a shared vision on specific issues and development priorities. The evolution of a shared vision is at the centre of norm convergence because it symbolizes the progression towards a common understanding of key issues in transboundary water governance in a basin or region by a collective group of stakeholders. This enables policy harmonization to become the vehicle through which benefits, costs and risks of transboundary river basin cooperation can be quantified and shared. Moreover, it emphasizes that agency rests with all states, and that this is an inclusive process of the identification of joint priorities.

Policy harmonization as a necessity due to the nature of the resource

Fifthly, policy harmonization is essential for all regions in Africa, because of the nature of the resource – strategic and shared, which heightens the need to cooperate and harmonize standards in order to prevent a single party jeopardizing river health. As water stress increases over time, conflicts arising out of policy differences, and more importantly out of differences in the intensity of the implementation of policies, are likely to become both more severe and longer lasting (SADC, 2003).

Policy harmonization at different levels of scale

The need for policy harmonization at different levels of scale is articulated in Table 6.1. This includes harmonization of policies between countries, between sectors, between SWIs and between regional institutions.

Policy Harmonization in the Orange-Senqu River basin and SADC

SADC's commitment to water's role in regional integration and policy harmonization is reflected in the SADC Treaty establishing SADC, signed in Windhoek in August 1992 as well as in the Regional Indicative Strategic Development Plan (RISDP). The SADC Treaty's programme for action includes the commitment to 'promote sustainable and equitable economic growth . . . through regional integration'; to 'harmonise political and socio-economic policies and plans of Member States'; and to 'eliminate obstacles to the free movement of capital and labour, goods and services, and of the people of the Region' (SADC, 1992). Therefore, both norm convergence and policy harmonization exist in a symbiotic and mutually reinforcing relationship.

Table 6.1 Policy harmonization at different levels of scale

According to the *Guidelines for the Development of National Water Policies and Strategies to Support IWRM* (SADC, 2003), the following needs/justification for policy harmonization were crafted:	
Harmonization of policies between countries	Significant policy inconsistencies or interstate policy contradictions are evident in the text of existing water policy statements (SADC, 2003). However, as noted in the Guidelines (ibid.), these conclusions were reached within the time and budget constraints of this project (AAA.9 and AAA.10 Phase 1). The policy review conducted then did not extend to a detailed SADC-wide analysis of all Member States' legislation (ibid.).
Harmonization of policies between sectors	There are likely to be conflicts of interest between significant water-using sectors (e.g. between agriculture and hydropower, between power production and flood control and between a protected environment and other water users) at both the policy and operational levels, nationally and regionally (ibid.).
According to a multi-sectoral study on best practice and lessons learned (Jacobs et al., 2009) the following needs/justification for policy harmonization were crafted:	
Harmonization of policies between regional institutions **Harmonization of policies between SWIs**	The institutional quagmire of states' multiple membership to various regional integration agreements (RIAs) poses challenges but also opportunities for SADC member states in terms of policy harmonization. Within the water sector, this implies the consideration of harmonization of interstate water policy, but also, the harmonization of inter-RIA policy (e.g. SADC and the EAC), as well as policy harmonization between river basin organizations. It is therefore proposed that any policy harmonization implementation in the water sector be multi-level in approach (ibid.).

The starting point for harmonization in the SADC water sector is to ensure full compatibility of national policies and strategies with the objectives of the Revised Protocol (2000). Guideline documents such as the Regional Water Policy (RWP) and the Regional Water Strategy (RWS) reiterate this commitment and encourage member states to promote harmonization of their water policies and legislation with the RWP. In order to assist member states to achieve harmonization of their national policies, the Regional Strategic Action Plan (RSAP 2) spells out concrete regional projects. Under the project WG 1: Implementation programme for SADC Protocol on Shared Watercourses, the completion of a study on harmonization of legislation, policies and strategies is proposed. These documents make up the policy harmonization framework for the SADC water sector as conceptualized in Figure 6.2.

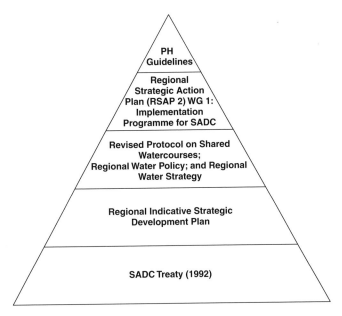

Figure 6.2 SADC Water Sector's Policy Harmonisation (PH) Imperatives

Policy harmonization in the NELSB

Policy harmonization processes in the NELSB are not formalized in a regional policy framework as is the case in SADC. However, through the NBI's shared vision adopted in 1999, NELSB states are encouraged to align national policies with each other and in accordance with national and basin initiatives. The Nile Basin Initiative is guided by the shared vision which was adopted in 1999. The shared vision is 'to achieve sustainable socio-economic development through the equitable utilisation of, and benefit from, the common Nile Basin water resources' (NBI, 2009b). The Nile Council of Ministers also adopted several principles when the Nile River Basin Strategic Action Program was drafted:

1. To develop the water resources of the Nile Basin in a sustainable and equitable way to ensure prosperity, security and peace for all its peoples;
2. To ensure efficient water management and the optimal use of the resources;
3. To ensure cooperation and joint action between riparian countries, seeking win-win gains;
4. To target poverty eradication and promote economic integration; to ensure that the programme results in a move from planning to action.

While member states have formulated new policies or revised old ones in accordance with international best practice principles, greater harmonization has been called for between sectors and of IWRM practices (NBI, 2006). Countries also differ in the intensity and effectiveness of their implementation of national policies, mainly as a result of capacity constraints, available resources and strictness of implementation of written policies as opposed to the policies themselves (ibid.)..

The benefits and challenges of policy harmonization for regions in Africa

While harmonization is a fundamental requirement for regional integration and cooperation, as well as for the creation of a bigger economic space capable of consolidating the regions' positions in the global economy, there are many other benefits expected to accrue to member states (UNECA, 2008). Primary benefits include the promotion of free movement of capital, labour, technology, ideas and norms. These factors are critically important, particularly given that capacities for human and knowledge development, as well as sources of capital, are unevenly distributed across the SADC and NELSB regions.

However, despite this, the successful implementation of policy harmonization is a challenging endeavour and requires concerted political will and effort at multiple levels of scale as explained in Table 6.1. This is compounded by the institutional complexity in which states find themselves as members to several regional integration agreements (RIAs). Despite the clear need for policy harmonization in the water sector in Africa, the lack of capacity to implement policy harmonization processes is a primary constraint to effective policy harmonization (SADC, 2003). It should also be noted that policy harmonization, on its own, is not a sufficient condition for better regional integration or norm convergence, but should be implemented as part of a whole basket of mutually reinforcing initiatives contributing to the same objectives (Jacobs et al., 2009). This includes an awareness of the impact that norms have on behaviour and contexts, and in turn, how they can be changed according to context.

It should also be noted that policy harmonization, on its own, is not a sufficient condition for better regional integration or norm convergence. It should be implemented as part of a whole basket of mutually reinforcing initiatives contributing to the same objectives (Jacobs et al., 2009). This includes an awareness of the impact norms have on behaviour and contexts, and in turn, how they can be changed according to context. Understanding the way we do things allows us to change what should be changed, and preserve what should not.

Policy harmonization and institutional complexity

Some scholars and policymakers have regarded Africa's institutional complexity as a chronic disabler to policy harmonization and integration processes. Characteristic to

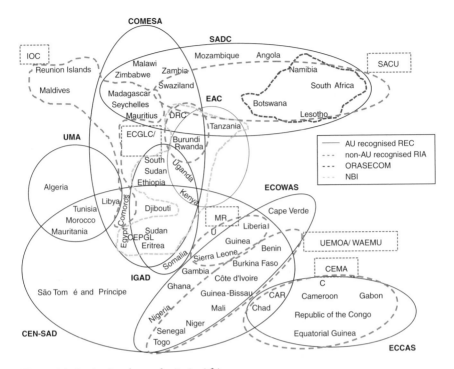

Figure 6.3 Institutional complexity in Africa

both southern and East Africa is the evidently large number of overlapping RIAs (see Figure 6.3). Currently, there are eight RECs recognized by the AU, each established under a separate regional treaty:

1. the Arab Maghreb Union (UMA)
2. the Common Market for Eastern and Southern Africa (COMESA)
3. the Community of Sahel-Saharan States (CEN-SAD)
4. the East African Community (EAC)
5. the Economic Community of Central African States (ECCAS)
6. the Economic Community of West African States (ECOWAS)
7. the Intergovernmental Authority on Development (IGAD)
8. the Southern Africa Development Community (SADC)

All NELSB states are party to more than one of the above-mentioned RECs, which has resulted in a highly complex institutional landscape of overlapping memberships. This formed the theme of the 2006 Banjul summit, and at the July 2007 Accra summit the AU Assembly finally decided to adopt a protocol on relations between the AU and the RECs with the objective of facilitating the harmonization of policies and ensure compliance with the Abuja Treaty and Lagos Plan of Action time frames.[1]

Additionally, there are other RIAs not officially recognized by the AU including:

1. Economic and Monetary Community of Central Africa (CEMAC)
2. West African Economic and Monetary Union (UEMOA/WAEMU)
3. Economic Community of the Great Lakes Countries (ECGLC/ CEPGL)
4. Indian Ocean Commission (IOC)
5. Mano River Union (MRU)
6. Southern African Customs Union (SACU)

With the exception of Mozambique, all other SADC countries belong to at least two of these regional groups (Kritzinger-van Niekerk and Moreira, 2002). Botswana and South Africa, for example, are members of both SADC and SACU. Namibia and Swaziland are both members of SACU, SADC and COMESA (ibid.).

Additionally, the on-going negotiations with the EU on the EPAs (Economic Partnership Agreements) have been challenging for the same reason. The EU EPA negotiations were launched in July 2004 in Windhoek, Namibia. Since the EU prefers to negotiate EPAs with regional groupings, this requires various regional groupings to make significant progress in their internal regional integration projects (Hurt, 2003, 2004). There are currently five EPA groupings into which African states fall including:

1. The SADC EPA (comprising of Angola, Botswana, Lesotho, Namibia, Mozambique, Swaziland and South Africa);
2. The Eastern and Southern Africa (ESA) (comprising of Comoros, Djibouti, Eritrea, Ethiopia, Madagascar, Malawi, Mauritius, Seychelles, Sudan, Zambia and Zimbabwe);
3. The EAC EPA (comprising of Burundi, Kenya, Rwanda, Uganda and Tanzania);
4. The West Africa EPA (comprising of all 15 members of ECOWAS and Mauritania); and
5. The Central Africa EPA (comprising of all six members of the Economic Community of Central African States (CEMAC), plus the Democratic Republic of Congo and São Tomé and Príncipe).

The SADC member states are therefore party to four of the five EPA configurations, with each configuration negotiating separately with the EU. According to Hurt, 'These are externally imposed and do not in most cases correspond to existing regional organisations' (Hurt, 2003: 173). The implication of having four free trade agreements (FTAs) established with the EU within a single REC, will have serious implications for SADC's own integration agenda (Tralac, 2008). Trade policy experts have pointed out technical challenges with respect to overlapping membership and the costs related to the implementation of these various EPAS (ibid.). Within the water sector, this implies the consideration of harmonization of interstate water policy, but also, the harmonization of inter-RIA policy (e.g. SADC and the EAC), as well as policy harmonization between river basin organizations. It is therefore proposed that any policy harmonization implementation on water be multi-levelled (Jacobs et al., 2009).

Regional integration opportunities in institutional complexity: the EAC-COMESA-SADC Tripartite Task Force

Despite its challenges, a growing school of thought views regional integration not only as attractive but as a prerequisite to deal with institutional complexity (Granit et al., 2010). Recent developments in SADC, COMESA and the EAC prove that institutional complexity can indeed be leveraged through regional integration and harmonization efforts.

The EAC, already a Common Market, is party to four member states in COMESA (Burundi, Kenya, Rwanda and Uganda) and one member state in SADC (Tanzania). In addition, five SADC member states are also members of SACU (Botswana, Lesotho, Namibia, South Africa and Swaziland).

This results in a total of ten countries in the region that are already members to existing customs unions (Granit et al., 2010). However, these ten member states (as well as the other non-Members to existing customs unions) have also been involved in negotiations to establish alternative customs unions to the ones they currently belong (Mwapachu, 2010). For instance, COMESA and SADC share seven member states that are not part of any customs union but are involved in customs unions preparatory negotiations (ibid.). Therefore, of the 26 countries that constitute the total membership of COMESA, EAC and SADC, 17 (or almost two-thirds of the total membership) are already either in an existing customs union, or participating in negotiating an alternative customs union to the one they already belong to, or are in the process of negotiating two separate customs unions which would be contrary to WTO rules (ibid.). In order to resolve these challenges, the three Regional Economic Communities (SADC, EAC and COMESA) formed a Tripartite Taskforce with a view to harmonize their trade-related programmes, and to eliminate duplication of efforts.

With this mission in mind, the COMESA, EAC and SADC Heads of State met in Kampala on 22 October 2008 and decided to establish a single FTA covering the 26 countries of the three RECs. In 2009, a draft Tripartite FTA was prepared, with a revised (due to several delays) roadmap that projects the establishment of the Tripartite FTA in 2012. The objective of the Tripartite FTA is to leverage the existing FTAs of SADC, EAC and COMESA, and build infrastructure programmes designed to propel the regional market through interconnectivity (facilitated for instance by different modes of transport, telecommunications and energy interconnections) as well as promote competitiveness (for instance through adequate supplies of energy) (ibid.).

The benefits of the Tripartite FTA include a larger market to its member states as well as the creation of a single economic space more conducive to investment and large-scale production (Granit et al., 2010). Together, the EAC, COMESA and SADC currently have a combined population of 527 million and combined GDP of US$625 billion (African Executive, 2010).

The Tripartite FTA could very well alleviate institutional complexity challenges by advancing harmonization, integration and coordination initiatives (Granit et al., 2010). If successful, the Tripartite will greatly contribute to Africa's economic integration through which a framework for water investments could be designed and implemented. However, it remains to be seen how the three RECs, each with its own unique historical trajectory, each member state with its own political membership agenda, will develop into a community of interests.

Conclusion

Water resources in Africa are part of an open and complex system (Allan, 2001) extending into global trade and movement of people, finance as well as the normative dimensions of sociopolitical contexts. This transcends a single hydrological boundary and ensures that the resource is subject to economic and social forces beyond the capacity of individual states. The effective management of river basins therefore needs to be combined with broader regional-level decision-making within river basin organizations but also a wide range of non-water-specific institutions such as economic communities.

Cooperative water norms help define the nature of these open and complex systems by fostering the development of communities of interest around cooperative governance over shared water resources. Communities of interest need not necessarily be perfectly aligned with geographically or economically defined regions. Subsidiarity norms contributed to the delinking of the White and Blue Nile branches to create a sub-basin community of interest that did not neatly fit with REC identities or even hydrological delineations (because Egypt and Sudan hold observer status in the NELSB grouping and also form part of ENSAP).

Transboundary water resources, cooperative water norms and regional integration are therefore mutually re-enforcing. Norms influence the way in which water is managed and shapes institutional and legislative development, while water resources can help drive regional integration efforts. Similarly regional integration may encourage spill-over effects from integration in trade and other issues (Strand, 2002) and facilitate cooperative governance of transboundary rivers.

Additionally, some scholars have advocated for the development of regional environmental organizations (REOs) arguing that environmental governance can mirror regional trade integration (ibid.). Strand (2002) suggests that REOs could operate in the same manner as regional development banks cater to concerns of regional members but focused on environmental concerns. Analyses such as these that argue for the appropriateness of a singular level of scale have led to the examination of the advantages and disadvantages of an increasing decentralization or fragmentation of governance structures (Biermann and Bauer, 2005; Vogel, 1997). More particularly, the role of regions in vertically and horizontally linking different governance systems operating at various levels of scale has also been assessed with greater frequency.

The practical justification for the need to explore alternative models of environmental governance (regional approaches, multi-level approaches) stems from the concern with increasing transaction costs of global regimes and the resultant 'global convention fatigue'. These concerns are producing a shift in the locus, impetus, implementation and innovation to regional levels. Additionally, the theoretical applicability of alternative approaches relates to the observation that studies of regional politics now require an expansion beyond traditional preoccupations with economic integration and security, to areas of environmental security and sustainable development.

The applicability of multi-level governance is also relevant if one considers discussions about security and economic integration at the regional level, where regions have been perceived as either 'stumbling blocks' or 'building blocks' to free trade and socioeconomic development. Now, a third actor (environmental security) enters this discussion, and questions whether the regional level is the most appropriate level to address water security concerns.

Note

1 Decision on the Protocol on Relations between the African Union and the Regional Economic Communities (RECs), Assembly/AU/Dec.166 (IX).

Conclusion: Scaling Out to Environmental Politics

Cooperation in transboundary river basins has received much attention in academic as well as policy circles over the past years (Bruch, 2005; Earle, Jägerskog and Öjendal, 2010; Nakayama, 2003). This is attributable to the relevance and uniqueness of water as a resource indispensable to human activity, potential rivalry and complexities (Kranz and Jacobs, in press; Wolf, 1998; Wolf et al., 2005). Given this unique position, what lessons can we learn from transboundary water and the multi-levelled manner in which cooperative management norms develop that are relevant to other forms of environmental management?

In answering this question we start with the issue of scale. Water management is a field that is particularly sensitive to issues of scale because its primary unit of analysis, the biophysical hydrological system, comprises of different levels from small catchments to large river basins, and also includes multiple users that form complex linkages with levels of scale and actors not immediately part of the system (Dore and Lebel, 2010; Falkner, 2007; Moss and Newig, 2010). In this regard, the multi-level transboundary water governance framework provides a starting point for understanding how central governments and other public and private actors interact with each other in the formulation and implementation of policies from international to national and local levels of action (Corfee-Morlot et al., 2009; Hooghe and Marks, 2003). The field of transboundary water management therefore offers useful lessons for the broader area of environmental governance and management in terms of spatial scale and multiple levels of governance (Moss and Newig, 2010).

The utility of multi-level normative frameworks

Norms as connectors of levels of scale

First, an analysis of global, regional, basin-wide and local norms is useful and has implications for multiple contexts in the management of natural resources, because of the way in which norms act as *connectors* of levels of scale. Each level of scale forms part of a complex system of cooperative norms influencing the governance of transboundary water, and various norms interact and function in the context of the system as a whole. Each level therefore gives meaning to how norms are translated and socialized. In this regard De Chazournes (2009) describes the phenomenon of a double process of nurture, which occurs at the global level. While international agreements such as the 1997 UN Convention, act as guiding instruments for the establishment of treaties at the regional and basin levels, providing comprehensive codifications of global norms, they also offer a frame of reference or a basis for the development of more specific legal instruments that can address particular characteristics of individual watercourses (ibid.). Global agreements therefore facilitate the harmonization and integration of norms and practices relating to the management and protection of freshwater resources at other levels. In this regard, global norms have helped to shape the content of instruments adopted at the regional and basin levels (ibid.).

Regional and basin-specific agreements give better effect to the geographical and sociological particularities of a specific watercourse because these agreements take into consideration the norms, interests and concerns of riparian states. As such, regional and basin-specific norms define the content of the 'rules of the game' more precisely and allow for the adjustment of the general framework to the specificities of a watercourse (ibid.).

In terms of the interaction between these various levels of scale, the governance and law applicable to transboundary freshwater resources include the problematique of the articulation between general (global) norms, and context-specific rules (ibid.). Norms established at the global, regional, basin and local levels therefore have to be read together in an integrated manner.

Internationally, there has been an increased realization in recent years of the importance of multi-actor, multi-sectoral and multi-level approaches to norm convergence. This realization has been directly and indirectly captured in various international and regional fora including: *the Global Consultation on Safe Water and Sanitation for the 1990s,* held in 1990 in New Delhi that resulted in the New Delhi Principles, which is based on the premise of 'some for all rather than more for some' and community management (UNDP, 1990); the *International Conference on Water and the Environment, held in 1992 in Dublin,* that resulted in the Dublin Principles, which emphasizes the economic value of water, gender, participation and the need for the integrated management of water (ICWE, 1992); the *International Conference on Environment and Development (Earth Summit), also held in 1992 in Rio de Janeiro,* that highlighted the economic value of water as a social good as well as an economic good and also resulted in several significant documents such as the Rio Declaration on Environment and Development, and Agenda 21, to mention a few (UNEP, 1992a, 1992b). Similarly, the *Earth Summit + 5 programme of action,* taking place five years after the Earth Summit, stressed the role of technical transfer and financial support from developed countries to assist with the development of IWRM. Additionally, it stressed the important role of greater cost recovery in developing countries with respect to water and sanitation services (SADC, 2003).

The *second World Water Forum (WWF) and Ministerial Conference,* held in The Hague in 2000 resulted in the Ministerial Declaration of The Hague on *Water Security in the 21st Century*, and was signed by Ministers and Heads of State on 22 March 2000. It called for full cost recovery, massive increases in investments and a much greater role for the private sector as key stakeholders (though this was heavily contested at the conference) (ibid.). Additionally, it recognized water as a basic need and proposed targeted subsidies for the poor. It also challenged governments to act as enablers and regulators rather than merely players (ibid.).

The **Millennium Summit and the Millennium Development Goals (MDGs)**, held in September 2000 stressed the importance of reducing poverty and improving conditions in urban slums and resulted in the MDG targets. This was a critically important international development that elevated water to a resource of global importance. Next came the **International Conference on Fresh Water**, held in Bonn in December 2001 that saw the signing of the Bonn Ministerial Declaration. This declaration re-emphasized many themes articulated in the earlier fora, but focused particularly on the important role of good governance and the responsibility of governments to promote and ensure IWRM, improved transboundary management of water and access to basic services (Bonn, 2001). The need for capacity-building and technology transfer was stressed, along with the role of the international community and the importance of participatory approaches to transboundary water management that includes gender aspects (Bonn, 2001; SADC, 2003). The role of the private sector was again heavily contested at the Bonn conference.

At the World Summit of Sustainable Development (WSSD), Johannesburg, September 2002 – a significant commitment was made that by 2015, the number of people in the world without adequate sanitation would have reduced by half. It was also stressed that sanitation needed to be integrated into IWRM strategies. Two key documents were drafted: a Political Declaration that expressed commitments and direction for implementing sustainable development (WSSD, 2002a); and a negotiated programme of action (referred to as the Johannesburg Plan of Implementation) to guide government activities. The Johannesburg Plan of Implementation aimed to develop IWRM and water efficiency plans by 2005 (WSSD, 2002b). Several actions to be taken are listed in this Plan, prioritizing satisfying basic needs and protecting fragile environments (ibid.).

These and other international events, along with legal instruments such as the 1997 UN Convention, have set the international agenda and normative framework for transboundary water governance. This international agenda has also slowly changed over time to include participatory and integrated approaches to managing transboundary rivers. Global normative frameworks therefore are flexible, and international norm convergence is an incremental and often slow process that evolves over time.

The perspectives of many developing countries (including that of African countries) have also been included in these international and regional events (SADC, 2003). These events and resulting plans and declarations, have to a large extent, influenced the agenda for national policies and strategies, especially within developing countries. Indeed, the New Delhi and Dublin Principles have become socialized at various levels of scale and codified into global, regional and national agreements and treaties. When aware of the multi-level interactions between normative frameworks, policymakers are better able to understand sociopolitical and socioeconomic influences as well as the power asymmetries at play.

Scale matters

Water management is a field particularly sensitive to issues of scale, because the hydrological scale with its different levels from small catchments to large river basins, dictates where interventions can and should be made. Yet many of the scalar issues touched on here are also relevant to other fields of environmental management including air pollution control, ecosystem management and biodiversity governance (Young et al., 2006). These areas are all potentially subject to socially constructed and contested scaling and rescaling of their units of governance (Moss and Newig, 2010). The challenge of managing any environmental issue area that fluctuates in time and space is that more often than not the biophysical delineations of the units of analysis (i.e. the river, the air) do not correspond with political or jurisdictional boundaries. This reality challenges the conventionally accepted state-centric, fixed-rule regulatory approach for governing environmental resources (Holling and Meffe, 1995). But it also allows managers of environmental resources to free themselves from the bounded logic of the biophysical scale.

Several other scalar mismatches arise as a result of incompatible spatial relations among biophysical processes, administrative structures and procedures or individual preference (Moss and Newig, 2010; Young, 2002). These include for instance:

- **Problems of misfit between different scalar dimensions (problems of scalar fit).** Scalar misfits occur whenever conventional political jurisdictions, that is sovereign states and their standard political sub-divisions, are not aligned with the boundaries of the natural resource to be managed. This not only holds true for large basins, but also for sub- and even smaller units, which respond to different legislative, political and also cultural contexts (Young, 2002).
- **Problems to identify the 'optimal' scalar level in order to address collective problems (optimal scalar level).** Indeed as Young (2002) argues, developing and implementing policy at the wrong level of scale undermines the effectiveness of environmental management planning and ultimately results in misinformed interventions.
- **Issues of interplay between different levels on one scalar dimension (problems of vertical interplay).** Cross-border issues such as inter-basin diversions and transfers, groundwater extraction, tidal barriers and virtual water in trade make it difficult to manage water solely at the level of the basin (IWRM) discourse (Dore and Lebel, 2010). As a way to overcome this challenge, the EU's Water Framework Directive has institutionalized river basin management. In so doing it has strengthened the need for inclusive and deliberative modes of governance suited to horizontal interplay between hydrological and political or administrative scales and to vertical interplay within each of these levels of scale (Moss and Newig, 2010).

Finally two scalar mismatches that are directly applicable to norm convergence processes, particularly in the way that actors such as norm entrepreneurs orchestrate such processes and (re-)construct scales include: **problems emerging from a reconfiguration of scalar levels (problems of rescaling); and efforts to generalize from insights that are valid on a particular scalar level to other scalar levels (problems of upscaling and downscaling).** These instances challenge the static assumptions of finding *optimal* scales inherent to economic and political science approaches (Dore and Lebel, 2010). The normative claims for new forms of good governance and de-centralization are also questioned by the evidence put forward by Thiel (2010), who highlights the importance of power-play in rescaling water management with the example of the Portuguese government creating a 'hydraulic state' (Wittfogel, 1957) in the Algarve (Moss and Newig, 2010). Certainly the materially driven thesis is still applicable in multi-level norm convergence.

Multi-level norm convergence and its application to climate change and forestry

The benefits of multi-level approaches have also been well documented in other environmental issue areas such as forestry, energy and climate change, where actors interact across horizontal and vertical levels of social organization and jurisdictional authority (Andonova et al., 2007; Corfee-Morlot et al., 2009; Falkner, 2007; Moss and Newig, 2010; Setzer, 2009). Governance structures for the environment are therefore found on a multiplicity of scales, from spatial to temporal; and are also found on a range of levels within each scale, from the global to the local. As Liliana Andonova and Ronald Mitchell (2010: 256) explain, 'Environmental problems previously seen as independent of each other are increasingly seen by practitioners and scholars alike as having multiple interdependent causes of social organisation and institutions for effective resolution.' Norms and other regulatory/constitutive mechanisms are therefore closely linked, and make up a complex institutional architecture.

Climate change

Climate change is an area of increasingly complex multi-level governance (Andonova et al., 2007; Corfee-Morlot et al., 2009; Falkner, 2007; Setzer, 2009; Van Deveer and Selin, 2008). Traditionally, scholars of international relations regarded collective concerns such as climate change to be a global problem requiring a global response (Andonova et al., 2007). And multilateral agreements negotiated by national governments were regarded as the central and ideal mechanism through which interventions needed to be targeted (ibid.). With the benefit of hindsight, we are now able to see the truly complex nature of environmental governance, with governance mechanisms taking on a wide range of forms beyond multilateral agreements, and where authority is diffused across multiple levels of scale, social organization and myriad actors.

The United Nations Framework Convention on Climate Change and its Kyoto Protocol promote issue-based intergovernmental dialogue and provide the global normative framework meant to guide state behaviour. But since it is not yet in force, and several states have since withdrawn from it (e.g. United States and later Canada), a policy vacuum exists at the global level resulting from the absence of international obligations (Setzer, 2009).

At the national level, some states formulate and implement climate policies within a context of national politics and institutions, sometimes under the umbrella of the international climate change regime (e.g. in the case of the EU) but not always (e.g. the United States) (Andonova et al., 2007). Economic regions such as the EU also operate within an environment of regional, supranational cooperation that covers climate along with many other forms of environmental politics (ibid.).

But the greatest degree of mobilization can be seen at the sub-national and transnational levels where patterns of organization are beginning to emerge involving many more actors (Corfee-Morlot et al., 2009; Falkner, 2007; Setzer, 2009; Van Deveer and Selin, 2008). In the private sphere, both non-governmental organizations (NGOs) and corporations have initiated programmes to shape public understandings of climate change and to develop innovative policies and technologies for controlling greenhouse gas emissions.

Additionally, there is now a growing trend of transnational climate cooperation involving cities, states, regions, NGOs, corporations and government agencies (Andonova et al., 2007). Often times these organizations oscillate between the global and local levels. The International Council for Local Environmental Initiatives' (ICLEI) Cities for Climate Protection (CCP) Programme, for example is a network that is simultaneously global and local, state and non-state. Other examples include the Climate Alliance, the C-40 Large Cities Climate Leadership Group, as well as the U.S. Mayors Climate Protection Agreement (Corfee-Morlot et al., 2009).

Cities have similarly been proactive in developing climate change responses to reducing their CO_2 emissions, and have therefore been identified within the multilevel governance literature as a critical arena where climate governance is taking place (Betsill and Bulkeley, 2007; Corfee-Morlot et al., 2009). Many cities have set targets for greenhouse gas (GHG) reductions that even exceed national commitments if national action has been articulated at all (Corfee-Morlot et al., 2009). For example, London, in its Climate Change Action Plan, established in March 2007, calls for a 60% reduction from 1990 to 2025; New York's A Greener, Greater New York campaign, set up in April 2007, sets a 30% reduction from 2005 to 2030, and Tokyo's Climate Change Strategy, established in June 2007, calls for a 25% reduction from 2000 to 2020 (ibid.).

These processes have also been influenced by an individual (norm entrepreneur) dimension, as seen in the gradual involvement of urban political leaders in climate change policymaking, with the former US Vice-President, Al Gore being a case in point (Corfee-Morlot et al., 2009).

Corfee-Morlot et al. (2009) suggest further enabling factors that multi-level governance brings to climate change debates. First, the attention placed on the sub-national or horizontal governance promotes different forms of coordination among local jurisdictions that belong to the same urban metropolitan area or the same rural area or between urban and rural areas. This promotes synergistic interventions at the sub-national level and allows interactions to be organically borne from the bottom-up (ibid.).

Secondly, multi-level governance also facilitates the development of issue-based governance where overlapping jurisdictions address key issues independently but in parallel with decisions on other areas relating to climate change (Hooghe and Marks, 2003). These may include a range of older and more historically embedded policy issues than climate change, for example, energy efficiency, air pollution or water management, where there may be separate instruments or mechanisms already in existence (Corfee-Morlot et al., 2009). Horizontal governance activities also give 'voice' to non-state actors such as business, research and environmental non-governmental organizations in the policy dialogue process (ibid.). A good example of this can be seen in the myriad activities and programmes that non-governmental actors are involved in that are related to climate policy, ranging from the generation of ideas to the formulation of policy, to acting as a 'watchdog' to assess how well policies are performing with respect to the stated goals of policy (Corfee-Morlot et al., 2009; Gough and Shackley, 2001; Levy and Newell, 2005; Setzer, 2009).

Finally, local-scale action encourages dialogue and interaction between experts and local stakeholders to develop a shared understanding about how climate change may affect local development choices and how those choices will impact on the future climate (Corfee-Morlot et al., 2009). This type of local deliberative exchange also facilitates the development and evolution of social norms, for example about how climate protection fits with visions of future development, a normative link that is beneficial to garnering bipartisan political support for policy reforms and action (ibid.).

Traditional approaches to international relations such as regime theory and even transnational networks are therefore limited in their utility to analyse the complexity of multi-level climate change governance. According to Betsill and Bulkeley (2006), traditional approaches obscure the way in which the governance of global climate change is conducted through processes and institutions operating at and between a variety of scales and involving a range of actors with different levels and forms of authority (ibid.). They contend that it is only by taking a multilevel perspective that we can fully capture the social, political and economic processes that shape global environmental governance (ibid.).

Forestry

Forestry is another environmental sector whose governance can benefit from a multi-level lens (Doherty and Schroeder, 2011; Skutch and Van Laake, 2009). In the battle against climate change, the forestry sector has come under intense scrutiny. Forests store more carbon than the global atmosphere and are therefore powerful carbon sinks, however their global cover is decreasing rapidly (Doherty and Schroeder, 2011). A global policy framework for Reducing Emissions from Deforestation and Forest Degradation (REDD+) is being negotiated as part of a new agreement under the United Nations Framework Convention on Climate Change (UNFCCC). It was initially intended to be a scheme focusing only on deforestation, however this framework has evolved over the past five years to include forest degradation. The aim of this agreement is to establish incentives for developing countries to protect and better manage their forest resources by being financially compensated by industrialized countries for halting or reducing domestic deforestation activities (Corbera and Schroeder, 2010; Doherty and Schroeder, 2011).

In terms of the multi-level nature of its governance system, Skutch and Van Laake (2009) explain that reducing emissions from deforestation is an intrinsically multi-level and multi-actor issue involving a wide range of different stakeholders, from national governments to local timber producers, to forest-dwelling indigenous tribes (Doherty and Schroeder, 2011).

Despite the close connections between all stakeholders, the global forest sector still has major gaps between national-level and international-level forest policies and their actual implementation on the ground (Doherty and Schroeder, 2011; Rametsteiner, 2009). A multi-level governance perspective helps to identify such policy gaps at all levels of scale and furthermore, provides a legitimate way to connect these levels via the REDD+ mechanism. Not only that, multi-level governance perspectives also help us understand, 'how best to meet the forest needs of different stakeholders from global to local; (Doherty and Schroeder, 2011: 69)

Beyond Africa

The utility of multi-level approaches also transcends a context-specific focus on Africa, and is applicable in a wide range of regions. The constant challenge for multi-level governance strategies however, is avoiding the dilution of effort and efficacy. Policymaking at multiple North American governance levels is becoming more ambitious in terms of scope and mitigation goals, but in the issue area of climate change, many green house gas emissions trends are still rising (Van Deveer and Selin, 2008).

Multi-level governance frameworks may therefore not necessarily solve the problem, but they do provide a more holistic picture of the problem and the level of scale at which the most appropriate interventions should be targeted. In East Asia, for example, relatively limited attention has been given to the role of urban and regional governments in combating global climate change, with more focus being placed on the international and national activities in the region (Schreurs, 2010). However, East Asian cities and provinces in China and Japan have now begun to develop their own climate action plans, positioning themselves as environmental model cities, and have also started to join local, national and international networks for climate change (ibid.). Coordinated through the Prime Minister's office, Japanese cities can now apply for model city status. Cities such as Kitakyushu, Yokohama and Minamata, previously regarded as severely polluted centres of industrial development have now become urban leaders of environmental industry and emission reductions, and pioneers in eco-friendly urban planning (ibid.). The multi-level governance approach helps us understand the role of cities and municipalities in driving context-specific climate change interventions in East Asia that are based on particular economic, social, cultural and geographic conditions, but are also critical to the implementation of national and international policies and goals (ibid.).

Adding to the complexity

This book, and this chapter in particular, has reflected on important research questions for multi-level governance research related to the emergence and manifestation of regions from the environmental perspective; the evolution, desirability, effectiveness and efficiency of regional water governance; the applicability and role of existing regional institutions in addressing water sector challenges in addition to economic and sociopolitical realities; and relationships within, among, and beyond regions in multi-level arrangements.

We live in an era of global change that necessitates the exploration of new and alternative approaches to the way we govern natural resources. The water cycle is inherently complex and becoming more so, generating important externalities in many domains that are critical for development such as health, poverty alleviation, agriculture and energy (OECD, 2011). Similarly, the policy interventions we develop induce a high degree of complexity, given the multiplicity of actors, norms, interests and scales. This raises crucial considerations for effective governance, and requires us to look at issues of environmental governance from a multi-level lens, one which emphasizes the multiplicity of actors, scale, power, knowledge and agency.

In developed and developing countries alike, and whether water is scarce or abundant, water governance continues to operate in a state of confusion (OECD, 2011). Across a diversity of contexts and boundaries, common challenges occur that include fragmented and even vacuous institutional structures, uncoordinated policy interventions at different levels of scale, limited capacity at the local level, lack of trust, unclear allocation of roles and responsibilities and questionable resource allocation. These challenges arise largely because of the inability to include multiple actors appropriately, and to acknowledge the multiplicity of norms, interests, knowledge forms and power asymmetries in any given challenge related to water.

As we try to align water governance – the practice, and water governance – the field of study, inclusivity needs to be operationalized in both settings. For practice, it means improved management of interactions between stakeholders. For the field of study it means embracing transdisciplinarity as an appropriate research channel through which integrated levels of ingenuity and expertise from a diverse set of disciplines can be achieved. This is the start of a new kind of norm convergence – one that links study to practice and policy to implementation.

Glossary

Basin closure: defined as the situation where all available and utilizable waters in a river basin have already been allocated to some productive activity and therefore insufficient water is available for allocation to new water developments (Seckler, 1996; Svendsen, Murray-Rust, Harmancioglu and Alpaslan, 2001: 184). This definition of basin closure differs from standard hydrological definitions of 'closed river basins' pertaining to an endorheic basin that does not flow into an ocean but instead terminates in an inland sea, lake or other sink (Wester, Burton and Mestre-Rodriquez, 2001: 161).

Benefit-sharing Paradigm: In the transboundary water resources sense, benefit-sharing refers to a paradigm or policy tool that identifies the gains of interstate cooperation beyond merely the sharing of water, but incorporates the sharing of opportunities that water brings to a country, a basin and a region.

Community of Interest: defined as a group of people that shares a common bond or interest. Its members take part in the community to exchange information, to improve their understanding of a subject, to share common passions or to play. In contrast to a spatial community, a community of interest is defined not by space, but by some common bond (e.g. feeling of attachment) or entity (e.g. farming, church group). As such, the definition is broad, leaving communities a lot of discretion in determining which issues are important to them.

Desecuritization: defined as the deliberate or gradual shifting of specific (strategically important) issues out of emergency mode and into the formal bargaining processes of the political sphere (Buzan, Waever and de Wilde, 1998: 4).

Endogenous Water: refers to the portion of the total water resources of a country or region, consisting of precipitation that falls within the geographic area of that country or region, which does not evaporate, and which feeds aquifers and surface water drainage basins (Falkenmark and Lindh, 1993: 82; Turton, 2003d: 9).

Endoreic: An endoreic river system is one that terminates inland, rather than into the sea (exoreic) due to several changes that could occur over time be they geological, or climatic (Seely, et al., 2003).

Hydropolitical Complex (HPC): As defined by Turton, a hydropolitical complex is a derivative of Buzan's regional security complex. It is a conceptual lens that shows the linkages between riparian states by a series of hydropolitical interstate arrangements at a level other than the river basin, showing the extent that water issues have become drivers of cooperative international relations in their own right (Turton, 2003d, 2005, 2008a, 2008b; Turton and Ashton, 2008). The Southern African Hydropolitical Complex (SAHPC) is one such HPC.

Hydropolitical Security Complex (HSC): A hydropolitical security complex, as defined by Schulz (Schulz, 1995: 97) is a particular rendition of a regional security complex that exists when states that are both 'owners' and 'users' of shared rivers begin to view the shared water resources as an issue of national security, and where water becomes securitized, for example, the MENA Hydropolitical Security Complex. The HSC is a derivative of security complexes which is defined as a set of units whose major processes of securitization, desecuritization or both are so interlinked that their security problems cannot reasonably be separated from one another (Buzan, et al., 1998: 201; Turton, 2003d: 17).

Integrated Water Resources Management (IWRM): defined as a process that promotes the coordinated development and management of water, land and related resources, in order to maximize the resultant economic and social welfare in an equitable manner without compromising the sustainability of vital ecosystems (GWP, 2000). Operationally, IWRM approaches apply knowledge from several disciplines and multiple stakeholders to devise and implement efficient, equitable and sustainable solutions to water and development problems. As such, IWRM is a comprehensive, participatory planning tool that involves the coordinated planning and management of land, water and other environmental resources for their equitable, efficient and sustainable use (Calder, 1999).

No Harm Doctrine: refers to the principle that there may be no harm done to a state's watercourse that might affect its natural flow, thus implying that an upstream state such as Ethiopia may do nothing that might affect the natural flow (quantity and quality) of the water into downstream Egypt.

Norm Aggregation: refers to cumulative and lateral norm diffusion (state to state and state to basin) as defined by Conca, reflected in a notable increase of new international basins subscribing to normative elements present in other international basins (Conca, Wu and Mei, 2006). Conca et al. argue that if this process was occurring, one would see a marked increase in basin-specific agreements. In other words, norm aggregation would take place horizontally from basin to basin, and thereby form a unified global normative approach/framework (Conca, 2006; Conca, et al., 2006).

Norm Diffusion: refers to the process where norms cascade/filter up or down and get integrated into other levels of scale or contexts.

Norm Emergence: The first step in Finnemore and Sikkink's norm life cycle is norm emergence, where norm entrepreneurs present new ideas as potential norms. They do this by persuading a critical mass of the moral appropriateness of this potential norm (Finnemore and Sikkink, 1998: 895–6). They oftentimes compete with existing constellations of norms in order for the norms which they advocate to gain acceptance (ibid.: 897).

Norm Internalization: the third and final stage of Finnemore and Sikkink's (1998) norm life cycle model. When a new norm becomes socialized to such an extent that it is taken for granted, and conformance with its dictates no longer (or at least rarely) questioned. If socialization is successful, the actor internalizes the expectations of behaviour, that is beliefs and practices, imparted to him by its social environment, and the norm is viewed as a constitutive element in the identities and interests of socialized norm recipients (Finnemore and Sikkink, 1998: 904–5; Schimmelfennig, 2000).

Norm Socialization: refers to the two-way process where an actor being socialized accepts beliefs and practices from the world and adopts them as its own. Simultaneously, the actor being socialized may well reflect on what it internalizes during the socialization process and even alter its content (Schimmelfennig, 1994: 339 cited in Boekle, et al., 1999: 9). Two types of socialization are identified in this study and elaborated upon in Chapter 3: transnational socialization and domestic socialization.

Norm Convergence: defined as the process whereby riparian interests are transformed from unilateral agendas to multilateral cooperative agendas and as such, converge on a normative trajectory that moves towards amity.

Norms: are 'collective expectations for the proper behaviour of actors with a given identity' (Katzenstein, 1996: 5). They provide standards of appropriate conduct and prescribe social practices (Dimitrov, 2005: 3).

Problemshed: As defined by Allan (2001: 337), the term encapsulates the operational context and the problems that exist within it. The term watershed defines a tract with limited and variable water resources. When the water resources of a particularly watershed become insufficient to meet the demand for water, a management system has to look beyond the watershed for solutions. According to Allan (2001) it is within the 'problemshed' that these solutions can be identified, for example virtual water and other benefit-sharing opportunities.

Protonorm: defined as a norm that has become sufficiently recognizable and well established, so as to become available for application to watershed governance in basins and watersheds that are beyond the direct reach of the agreement concerned (Conca, 2006).

Riparian: defined as a sub-national entity or a nation state which is directly adjacent to a river and has a river bank on a flowing river, and also refers to groundwater bodies (Allan, 2001: 337).

Scale: defined as the spatial, temporal, quantitative or analytical dimensions used to measure, or rank and study any phenomenon (Gibson et al., 2000). In this regard, levels of scale are referred to as the units of analysis that are located at different positions on a scale

Securitization: According to Buzan, securitization is constituted by the inter-subjective establishment of an existential threat with a saliency sufficient to have a substantial political effect (Buzan, et al., 1998: 16). In this study, securitization also refers to the deliberate elevation of an issue into a national security concern through framing.

Transboundary river (used interchangeably with international river or shared river): refers to a river which crosses or flows along international state (and therefore political) boundaries. The term international river is also used in this book and refers to a freshwater source (surface and groundwater) whose basin is situated within the borders of more than one sovereign state as well as the lakes and wetlands through which some of these flows may pass (Turton, 2003d; Wolf et al., 1999). International rivers can therefore be either successive (crossing) or contiguous (flowing along the boundary, which is then normally the 'Thalweg' or deepest part of the watercourse) rivers. ('Thalweg' is the German word for the 'deepest valley' under the water.)

Watercourse: a 'system of surface waters and groundwaters constituting by virtue of their physical relationship a unitary whole and normally flowing into a common terminus' (UN, 1997a: Article 2). The UN Convention also recognizes that as an international watercourse, parts of it are situated in different states (ibid.).

Watershed: refers to the edge of a natural river basin. Sometimes means the same as the river basin being the area drained by a river system as defined by Allan (2001: 339).

Bibliography

Abraham, K. (2003) *Nile Opportunities: Avenues towards a Win-Win Deal*. Addis Ababa: The Ethiopian International Institution for Peace and Development and the Horn of Africa Democracy and Development International Lobby.

— (2004) *Nile Dilemmas: Hydropolitics and Potential Conflict Flashpoints*. Addis Ababa: The Ethiopian International Institution for Peace and Development and the Horn of Africa Democracy and Development International Lobby.

Acharya, A. (2004) 'How Ideas Spread: Whose Norms Matter? Norm Localization and Institutional Change in Asian Regionalism'. *International Organization*, 58(2): 239–75.

— (2007) 'The Emerging Regional Architecture of World Politics'. *World Politics*, 59(4): 629–52.

Adler, E. (2005) 'Barry Buzan's Use of Constructivism to Reconstruct the English School: "Not All the Way Down"'. *Millennium: Journal of International Studies*, 34: 171–82.

Adler, E. and Bernstein, S. (2005) 'Knowledge in Power: The Epistemic Construction of Global Governance'. In Barnett, M. and Duvall, R. (eds) *Power in Global Governance*. Cambridge: Cambridge University Press.

Adler, E. and Haas, P. (1992) 'Conclusion: Epistemic Communities, World Order and the Creation of a Reflective Research Program'. *International Organization*, 46(1): 367–90.

AfDB (2003) 'African Development Report: Globalization and Africa's Development'. African Development Bank. Oxford: Oxford University Press.

The African Executive (2010) 'Historic First EAC-SADC-COMESA Tripartite Summit', 29 November 2008, <www.africanexecutive.com/modules/magazine/articles.php?article=3725> Access date 4 January 2012.

Agnew, J. (1994) 'The Territorial Trap: The Geographical Assumptions of International Relations Theory'. *Review of International Political Economy*, 1(1): 53–80.

Ahmad, S. (1994) 'Principles and Precedents in International Law Governing the Sharing of Nile Waters'. In Howell, P. and Allan, J. (eds) *The Nile, Sharing a Scarce Resource: A Historical and Technical Review of Water Management and of Economic and Legal Issues*. Cambridge: Cambridge University Press.

Alcamo, J. (2000) 'The GLASS Model: Assessing Environmental Threats to Food and Water Security in Russia'. *Environmental Change and Security Project Report*. Washington, DC: The Woodrow Wilson Centre.

Allan, J. (1999a) 'The Nile Basin: Evolving Approaches to Nile Waters Management'. *Occasional Paper No.20*. SOAS Water Issues Group. London, UK: University of London.

— (1999b) 'Water in International Systems: A Risk Society Analysis of Regional Problemsheds and Global Hydrologies'. *Sustainability, Risk and Nature: The Political-Ecology of Water in Advanced Societies*, 15–17 April 1999. Oxford: Oxford University.

— (2001) *The Middle East Water Question: Hydropolitics and the Global Economy.* London: IB Tauris.

AMCOW (2002) 'The Abuja Ministerial Declaration on Water – A Key to Sustainable Development in Africa'. *African Ministerial Conference on Water.* Abuja: AMCOW.

Amnesty International (2010) Pre-election Attacks on Rwandan Politicians and Journalists Condemned, 5 August 2010, <www.amnesty.org/en/news-and-updates/pre-election-attacks-rwandan-politicians-and-journalists-condemned-2010-08-05> Access date 29 December 2011.

Andonova, L. and Mitchell, B. (2010) 'The Rescaling of Global Environmental Politics'. *Annual Review of Environment and Resources,* 35: 255–82.

Andonova, L., Betsill, M. and Bulkeley, H. (2007) 'Transnational Climate Change Governance'. Paper prepared for the Amsterdam Conference on the Human Dimensions of Global Environmental Change, 24–26 May 2007.

Arab Water Council (2009) Arab Countries Regional Report, 24 February 2009, <http://docs.google.com/viewer?a=v&q=cache:ZaRmu-1-aAsJ:www.idrc.ca/uploads/user-S/12392600251MENA_Arab_Regional_Report_2009.pdf+league+of+arab+states+and+egypt+and+nile+and+equatorial+lakes&hl=en&gl=za&pid=bl&srcid=ADGEESjP7JD39UzUNpRl0rImNfhDgFVTfvCH8TGsOV8a_CM269tXJ0DkRIG3k9OjvEfSyUQEkDlB_OP2bP_iKk8V4yi5r0WsAztdKscRpM63Ef25_IokKv3YzFx23xYLy7C5X61ayd6q&sig=AHIEtbTN4f8gH99tIODzZMCuqKzBPgcf7g> Access date: 29 December 2011.

Arsano, Y. and Tamrat, I. (2005) 'Ethiopia and the Eastern Nile Basin'. *Aquatic Sciences,* 67: 15–27.

Ashton, P. (2000a) 'Southern African Water Conflicts: Are They Inevitable or Preventable?' In Solomon, H. and Turton, A. (eds) *Water Wars: Enduring Myth of Impending Reality.* African Dialogue Lecture Series: Monograph Series No. 2. Durban: Accord.

— (2000b) 'Southern African Water Conflicts: Are They Inevitable or Preventable?' *Water for Peace in the Middle East and Southern Africa.* Geneva: Green Cross International.

— (2002) 'Avoiding Conflicts over Africa's Water Resources'. *Ambio,* 31(3): 236–42.

Ashton, P. and Turton, A. (2005) 'Transboundary Water Resource Management in Southern Africa: Opportunities, Challenges and Lessons Learned'. In Wirkus, L. (ed.) *Water, Development and Cooperation – Comparative Perspective: Euphrates-Tigris and Southern Africa, Proceedings of a Workshop Organised by Zentrum 32 für Entwicklungsforschung.* Bonn: Bonn International Center for Conversion.

— (2007) 'Chapter 56: Water and Security in Sub-Saharan Africa: Emerging Concepts and their Implications for Effective Water Resource Management in the Southern African Region'. In Brauch, H., Grin, J., Mesjasz, C., Dunay, P., Chadha Behera, N., Chourou, B., Oswald Spring, U., Liotta, P. and Kameira-Mbote, P. (eds) *Globalisation and Environmental Challenges: Reconceptualising Security in the 21st Century.* Berlin: Springer-Verlag.

— (2009) 'Water and Security in Sub-Saharan Africa: Emerging Concepts and their Implications for Effective Water Resource Management in the Southern African Region. Chapter 50'. In Brauch, H. G., Spring, U. O., Grin, J., Mesjasz, C., Kameri-Mboti, P., Behera, N. C., Chourou, B. and Krummenacher, H. (eds) *Facing Global Environmental Change: Environmental, Human, Energy, Food, Health and Water Security Concepts.* Hexagon Series on Human and Environmental Security and Peace, Volume IV. Berlin: Springer-Verlag.

Ashton, P., Hardwick, D. and Breen, C. (2008) 'Changes in Water Availability and Demand Within South Africa's Shared River Basins as Determinants of Regional Social and Ecological Resilience'. In Burns, M. J. and Weaver, A. v. B. (eds) *Exploring Sustainability Science: A Southern African Perspective*. Stellenbosch: Stellenbosch University Press.

Ashton, P., Earle, A., Malzbender, D., Moloi, B., Patrick, M. J. and Turton, A. (2005) 'Compilation of all the International Freshwater Agreements Entered into by South Africa with Other States'. *Final Water Research Commission Report for Project no K5/1515*. Pretoria: Water Research Commission.

Atkinson, A. (1991) *Principles of Political Ecology*. London: Belhaven Press.

AU (2002) 'Accra Declaration on Water and Sustainable Development'. *Regional Stakeholders' Conference for Priority Setting*. Accra, Ghana: African Union.

— (2009) Strategic Plan 2009–2012. Directorate for Strategic Planning Policy, Monitoring, Evaluation and Resource Mobilisation, 19 May 2009. African Union Commission.

Axelrod, R. (1986) 'An Evolutionary Approach to Norms'. *American Political Science Review*, 80(4): 1095–111.

Basson, M., van Niekerk, P. and van Rooyen, J. (1997) 'Overview of Water Resources Availability and Utilisation in South Africa'. Pretoria: Department of Water Affairs and Forestry – Republic of South Africa.

BBC (2011) 'Profile: Arab League'. BBC News, 9 August 2011. <http://news.bbc.co.uk/2/hi/middle_east/country_profiles/1550797.stm> Access date: 29 December 2011.

Beach, H., Hamner, J., Hewitt, J., Kaufman, E., Kurki, A., Oppenheimer, J. and Wolf, A. (2000) *Transboundary Freshwater Dispute Resolution: Theory, Practice and Annotated References*. Shibuya-ku, Tokyo: United Nations University Press.

Berman, E. and Sams, K. (2000) *Peacekeeping in Africa: Capabilities and Culpabilities*. Geneva: United Nations Institute for Disarmament Research.

Bernauer, T. (1997) 'Managing International Rivers'. In Young, O. (ed.) *Global Governance: Drawing Insights from the Environmental Experience*. Cambridge: MIT Press.

— (2002) 'Explaining Success and Failure in International River Management'. *Aquatic Sciences*, 64: 1–19.

Bernstein, S. (2001) *The Compromise of Liberal Environmentalism*. New York: Columbia University Press.

Betsill, M. and Bulkeley, H. (2006) 'Cities and the Multilevel Governance of Global Climate Change'. *Global Governance: A Review of Multilateralism and International Organizations*, 12(2): 141–59.

Biermann, F. and Bauer, S. (eds) (2005) *A World Environmental Organization: Solution or Threat for Effective International Environmental Governance?* Aldershot: Ashgate.

Biersteker, T. and Weber, C. (1996) 'The Social Construction of State Sovereignty'. In Biersteker, T. and Weber, C. (eds) *State Sovereignty as Social Construct*. Cambridge: Cambridge University Press.

Boekle, H., Rittberger, V. and Wagner, W. (1999) 'Norms and Foreign Policy: Constructivist Foreign Policy Theory'. TAP 34A. Tübingen: *Center for International Relations/Peace and Conflict Studies*, Institute for Political Science, University of Tübingen.

Bohensky, E., Reyers, B., van Jaarsveld, A. S. and Fabricius, C. (eds) (2004) *Ecosystem Services in the Gariep Basin*. Stellenbosch: SUNPRESS.

Bonn (2001) 'Ministerial Declaration: Ministerial Session of the International Conference on Freshwater'. *International Conference on Freshwater*. Bonn.

Brewer, N. (2008) 'The New Great Walls: A Guide to China's Overseas Dam Industry'. *International Rivers*. Berkeley: IRN.

Breytenbach, W. (2003) 'Rulers, Rebels & Mercantilists: Explanation for Resource Wars'. *Africa Insight*, 32(2): 2–8.

Brouma, A. D. (2003) 'Bridging the GAP: Modernity versus Post-modernity', Kokkalis Program Workshop, Harvard, 7 February.

Brown, C. (1997) *Understanding International Relations*. London: Macmillan.

Brown, K. (2007) *Struggling Giant: China in the 21st Century*. London: Anthem Press.

Bruch, C. (2005) Evolution of Public Involvement in International Watercourse Management. In Bruch, C., Jansky, L., Nakayama, M. and Salewicz, K. (eds) *Public Participation in the Governance of International Freshwater Resources: 21–72*. Shibuya-ku, Tokyo: United Nations University Press.

Brunnée, J. and Toope, S. (2002) 'The Changing Nile Basin Regime: Does Law Matter?' *Harvard International Law Journal*, 43: 105–59.

Burchill, S. (1996) 'Introduction'. In Burchill, S. and Linklater, A. (eds) *Theories of International Relations*. London: St. Martin's Press.

Butfoy, A. (1997) *Common Security and Strategic Reform*. Houndmills: Macmillan.

Buzan, B. (1991) *People, States and Fear: An Agenda for International Security Studies in the Post-Cold War Era*. London: Harvester Wheatsheaf.

Buzan, B. and Waever, O. (eds) (2003) *Regions and Powers: The Structure of International Security*. Cambridge: Cambridge University Press.

Buzan, B., Waever, O. and de Wilde, J. (1998) *Security: A New Framework for Analysis*. London: Lynne Rienner.

Calder, I. R. (1999) *The Blue Revolution: Land Use and Integrated Water Resources Management*. London, UK: Earthscan.

Cascao, A. (2009) 'Changing Power Relation in the Nile River Basin: Unilateralism vs. Cooperation?' *Water Alternatives*, 2(2): 245–68.

Cass, L. (2005) 'Measuring the Domestic Salience of International Environmental Norms: Climate Change Norms in German, British, and American Climate Policy Debates'. *International Studies Association*. Honolulu: ISA.

Checkel, J. (1998) 'The Constructivist Turn in International Relations Theory'. *World Politics*, 50(2): 325–6.

— (1999) 'Norms, Institutions and National Identity in Contemporary Europe'. *International Studies Quarterly*, 43: 83–114.

— (2001) 'Why Comply? Social Learning and European Identity Change.' *International Organization*, 55(3): 553–88.

Church, C. (2000) 'Water, a Threat of War or an Opportunity for Peace?' *Conflict Trends*, 2000(2): 18–23.

The Citizen (2010) 'Mwapachu: National Polls Paralyze EAC Operations'. Monday, 25 October 2010, by Zephania Ubwani. <http://thecitizen.co.tz/news/-/5045-mwapachu-national-polls-paralyze-eac-operations> Access date: 29 December 2011.

Cock, J. (2003) 'The World Social Forum and South Africa: The Local and the Global'. *Research Report No. 5*. Durban: Centre for Civil Society.

Collins, R. (1994) 'History, Hydropolitics and the Nile: Myth or Reality'. In Howell, P. and Allan, J. (eds) *The Nile, Sharing a Scarce Resource: A Historical and Technical Review of Water Management and of Economic and Legal Issues*. Cambridge: Cambridge University Press.

Commission of Enquiry on Water Matters (1970) 'Findings and Recommendations of the Commission of Enquiry in Water Matters'. Section 1.3. *Management of the Water Resources of the Republic of South Africa*. Department of Water Affairs. Pretoria: DWAF.

Conca, K. (2002) 'The Case for Environmental Peacemaking'. In Conca, K. and Dabelko, G. (eds) *Environmental Peacemaking*. Washington, DC: Woodrow Wilson Centre Press.

— (2006) *Governing Water: Contentious Transnational Politics and Global Institution Building*. Cambridge, MA: MIT Press.

Conca, K. and Dabelko, G. (2002) 'The Problems and Possibilities of Environmental Peacemaking'. In Conca, K. and Dabelko, G. (eds) *Environmental Peacemaking*. Washington, DC: Woodrow Wilson Center Press.

Conca, K. and Wu, F. (2002) 'Is There a Global Rivers Regime?' *43rd Annual Meeting of the International Studies Association*. 23–27 March 2002. New Orleans: ISA.

Conca, K., Wu, F. and Mei, C. (2006) 'Global Regime Formation or Complex Institution Building? The Principled Content of International River Agreements'. *International Studies Quarterly*, 50: 263–85.

Conca, K., Wu, F. and Neukirchen, J. (2003) 'Is there a Global Rivers Regime? Trends in the Principled Content of International River Agreements'. *Harrison Program on the Future Global Agenda*. Maryland: University of Maryland.

Conley, A. and Van Niekerk, P. (2000) 'Sustainable Management of International Waters: The Orange River Case'. *Water Policy*, 2: 131–49.

Corbera, E. and Schroeder, H. (2010) 'Governing and Implementing REDD+'. *Environmental Science and Policy* (2010): doi: 10.1016/j.envsci.2010.11.002.

Cordesman, A. (2004) *The Military Balance in the Middle East*. Westport, US: Praeger Publishers.

Corfee-Morlot, J., Kamal-Chaoui, L., Donovan, M. G., Cochran, I., Robert, A. and Teasdale, P. (2009), 'Cities, Climate Change and Multilevel Governance'. OECD Environmental Working Papers No. 14, 2009, Paris: OECD Publishing.

Cortell, A. and Davis, J. (1996) 'How Do International Institutions Matter? The Domestic Impact of International Rules and Norms'. *International Studies Quarterly*, 40(4): 451–78.

— (2000) 'Understanding the Domestic Impact of International Norms: A Research Agenda'. *International Studies Quarterly*, 2(1): 65–87.

— (2005) 'When Norms Clash: International Norms, Domestic Practices, and Japan's Internationalisation of the GATT'. *Review of International Studies*, 31(1): 3–25.

Cox, C. and Sjolander, C. (1994) 'Critical Reflections on International Relations'. In Sjolander, C. and Cox, C. (eds) *Beyond Positivism: Critical Reflections on International Relations*. Boulder: Lynne Rienner Publishers.

Cox, R. and Sinclair, T. (1996) *Approaches to World Order*. Cambridge: Cambridge University Press.

Dagne, T. (2010) Tanzania: Background and Current Conditions. CRS Report for Congress. Congressional Research Service, Washington, DC.

Dalby, S. (1998) 'Introduction'. In Tuathail, G. O., Dalby, S. and Routledge, P. (eds) *The Geopolitics Reader*. London: Routledge.

Daoudy, M. (2010) 'Getting Beyond the Environment-Conflict Trap: Benefit Sharing in International River Basins'. In Earle, A., Jagerskog, A. and Ojendal, J. (eds) *Transboundary Water Management: Principles and Practice*. London: Earthscan.

DEA (2006) Policy Brief on Botswana's Water Management. Department of Environmental Affairs (DEA) Gaborone: Department of Environmental Affairs, Ministry of Environment, Wildlife & Tourism.

De Burca, G. (1998) 'The Principle of Subsidiarity and the Court of Justice as an Institutional Actor'. *Journal of Common Market Studies*, 36: 217–35.

De Chazournes, L. B. (2009) 'Freshwater and International Law: The Interplay between Universal, Regional and Basin Perspectives'. *The United Nations World Water Development Report 3: Water in a Changing World*. Paris: United Nations Education, Scientific and Cultural Organization (UNESCO).

Degefu, G. (2003) *The Nile: Historical, Legal and Developmental Perspectives*. Victoria: Trafford.

de Jonge Schuermans, A. M., Helbing, J. and Fedosseev, R. (2004) 'Evaluation of Success and Failure in International Water Management: Orange River Basin, South Africa'. Zurich: ETH.

De Lombaerde, P. and Van Langenhove, L. (2007) 'Regional Integration, Poverty and Social Policy'. *Global Social Policy* 7(3): 377–83.

Dimitrov, R. (2005) 'Hostage to Norms: States, Institutions and Global Forest Politics'. *Global Environmental Politics*, 5(4): 1–24.

Doherty, E. and Shroeder (2011) 'Forest Tenure and Multi-level Governance in Avoiding Deforestation under REDD'. *Global Environmental Politics*, 11(4): 66–88.

Dore, J. and Lebel, L. (2010) 'Deliberation and Scale in Mekong Region Water Governance'. *Environmental Management*, 46: 60–80.

Dougherty, J. and Pfaltzgraff, R. (1990) *Contending Theories of International Relations: A Comprehensive Survey*. New York: Harper and Row Publishers.

Dungumaro, E. and Madulu, N. (2003) 'Public Participation in Integrated Water Resources Management: The Case of Tanzania'. *Physics and Chemistry of the Earth*, 28: 1009–014.

Dunne, T. (1997a) 'Liberalism'. In Baylis, J. and Smith, S. (eds) *The Globalization of World Politics: An Introduction to International Relations*. Oxford: Oxford University Press.

— (1997b) 'Realism'. In Baylis, J. and Smith, S. (eds) *The Globalization of World Politics: An Introduction to International Relations*. Oxford: Oxford University Press.

Du Plessis, A. (2000) 'Charting the Course of the Water Discourse through the Fog of International Relations Theory'. In Solomon, H. and Turton, A. (eds) *Water Wars: Enduring Myth of Impending Reality*. African Dialogue Lecture Series: Monograph Series No. 2. Durban: Accord.

Durth, R. (1996) 'Grenzuberschreitende Umweltprobleme und regionale Integration: Zur Politischen Oekonomie von Oberlauf-Unterlauf-Problemen an internationalen Flussen'. Baden-Baden: Nomos Verlag. *As Cited in Bernauer, Thomas (2002), 'Explaining Success and Failure in International River Management.' Aquatic Sciences*, 64: 1–19.

DWA (2011) 'Water Requirements in the Orange River Basin'. *Orange River Project*. Pretoria: Department of Water Affairs. <www.dwaf.gov.za/orange/waterreq.aspx> Access date: 28 December 2011.

DWAF (1997) 'White Paper on a National Water Policy for South Africa'. Department of Water Affairs and Forestry. Pretoria: Government of the Republic of South Africa.

EAC (2007) 'Treaty for the Establishment of the East African Community'. Republic of Uganda, Republic of Kenya and the United Republic of Tanzania.

— (2011a) 'History: From Cooperation to Community'. Arusha: East African Community. <www.eac.int/about-eac.html> Access date: 28 December 2011.

— (2011b) 'Lake Victoria Basin Commission (LVBC)'. Arusha: East African Community. <www.eac.int/about-eac.html> Access date: 28 December 2011.

Earle, A., Jägerskog, A. and Öjendal, J. (2010) *Transboundary Water Management – Principles and Practice*. London, Washington, DC: Earthscan.

Earle, A., Malzbender, D., Turton, A. and Manzungu, E. (2005) 'A Preliminary Basin Profile of the Orange-Senqu River'. *Integrated Water Resources Management in Shared River Basin in the SADC Region*. Pretoria: AWIRU, University of Pretoria.

East African Business Week (EABW) (2010) 'Burundi Speaks Out on Benefits of Joining Common Market'. 25 October 2010. <www.busiweek.com/10/page.php?aid=1494#> Access date: 25 October 2011.

Eckstein, G. (2002) 'Development of International Water Law and the UN Watercourse Convention'. In Turton, A. and Henwood, R. (eds) *Hydropolitics in the Developing World: A Southern African Perspective*. Pretoria: African Water Issues Research Unit.

Egypt News (2010) 'Quotes about Nile Basin Initiative', 1 July 2010. <http://news.egypt.com/en/quotes-about-nile-basin-initiative.html> Access date: 29 December 2011.

El-Fadel, M., El-Sayegh, Y., El-Fadl, K. and Khorbotly, D. (2003) 'The Nile River Basin: A Case Study in Surface Water Conflict Resolution'. *Journal of Natural Resources and Life Sciences Education*, 32: 107–17.

Elgstrom, O. (2000) 'Norm Negotiations. The Construction of New Norms Regarding Gender and Development in EU Foreign Aid Policy'. *Journal of European Public Policy*, 7(3): 457–76.

Erdogan, I. (2009) 'Fancy Words but No Significant Step over the Nile River Negotiations'. *The Journal of Turkish Weekly*. Ankara: International Strategic Research Organisation (USAK).

Erlich, H. and Gershoni, I. (2000) *The Nile: Histories, Cultures, Myths*. Boulder, CO: Lynne Rienner.

EU (1992) 'Maastricht Treaty'. European Union.

Eyckmans, J. and Finus, M. (2007) 'Measures to Enhance the Success of Global Climate Treaties'. *International Environmental Agreements: Politics, Law and Economics*, 7(1): 73–97.

Falkenmark, M. (1989) 'The Massive Water Scarcity Now Threatening Africa: Why Isn't it Being Addressed?' *Ambio*, 18(2): 112–18.

Falkenmark, M. and Lindh, G. (1993) 'Water and Economic Development'. In Gleick, P. (ed.) *Water in Crisis: A Guide to the World's Water Resources*. New York: Oxford University Press.

Falkenmark, M. and Widstrand, C. (1992) 'Population and Water Resources: A Delicate Balance'. *Population Bulletin*. Washington, DC: Population Reference Bureau.

Falkner, R. (2007) *Business Power and Conflict in International Environmental Politics*. Basingstoke: Palgrave Macmillan.

FAO (1978) 'Systematic Index of International Water Resources Treaties, Declarations, Acts and Cases by Basin. Legislative Study No. 15', 14 March 2009. Food and Agriculture Organisation. http://faolex.fao.org/faolex/index.html.

Farrell, T. (2001) 'Transnational Norms and Military Development: Constructing Ireland's Professional Army'. *European Journal of International Relations*, 7(1): 63–102.

Femia, F. and Werrell, C. (2011) Watch This Space: Nile Basin – Preventing Water Conflict. Centre for Climate and Security, 20 July 2011. < http://climateandsecurity.org/2011/07/20/watch-this-space-nile-basin/> Access date: 30 December 2011.

Finnemore, M. (1996) *National Interests in International Society.* Ithaca: Cornell University Press.

Finnemore, M. and Sikkink, K. (1998) 'International Norm Dynamics and Political Change'. *International Organization,* 52(4): 887–917.

— (2001) 'Taking Stock: The Constructivist Research Program in International Relations and Comparative Politics'. *Annual Review of Political Science,* 4: 391–416.

Flavier, J., Jesus, A. and Navarro, C. (1995) 'The Regional Program for the Promotion of Indigenous Knowledge in Asia'. In Warren, D. M., Slikkerveer, L. J. and Brokensha, D. (eds) *The Cultural Dimension of Development: Indigenous Knowledge Systems.* London: Intermediate Technology Publications.

Flockhart, T. (2004) 'Masters and Novices' Socialization and Social Learning in NATO-Parliamentary Assembly. *International Relations,* 18(3): 361–80.

— (2006) 'Complex Socialisation: A Framework for the Study of State Socialisation'. *European Journal of International Relations,* 12(1): 89–118.

Florini, A. (1996) 'The Evolution of International Norms'. *International Studies Quarterly,* 40(3): 363–89.

Francis, D. (2006) *Uniting Africa: Building Regional Peace and Security System.* Aldershot: Ashgate.

The Free Library (2010) 'Analysis: Will Political Activity in Nile Basin Countries Affect the Water Feud?' 18 August 2010. <www.thefreelibrary.com/Analysis: Will political activity in Nile Basin countries affect the . . . -a0234878436> Access date: 29 December 2011.

Frey, F. (1993) 'The Political Context of Conflict and Cooperation Over International River Basins'. *Water International,* 18: 54–68.

Funke, N. and Turton, A. (2008) 'Hydro-hegemony in the Context of the Orange River Basin'. *Water Policy,* 10(2): 51–69.

Furlong, K. (2006) 'Hidden Theories, Troubled Waters: International Relations, the "territorial trap," and the Southern African Development Community's Transboundary Waters'. *Political Geography,* 25: 438–58.

— (2008) 'Hidden Theories, Troubled Waters: Response to Critics'. *Political Geography,* 27: 811–14.

GEF (2005) 'Development and Implementation of the Strategic Action Programme for the Orange-Senqu Basin, Project Development Facility, Request for Pipeline Entry and PDF Block B Approval'. *OP 9: Integrated Land and Water Management.* UNOPS.

Gibson, C., Ostrom, E. and Ahn, T. K. (2000) 'The Concept of Scale and the Human Dimensions of Global Change: A Survey'. *Ecological Economics,* 32: 217–39.

Giordano, M. and Wolf, A. (2002) 'The World's Freshwater Agreements: Historical Developments and Future Opportunities'. *Atlas of International Freshwater Agreements.* Nairobi: United Nations Environment Programme.

— (2003) 'Sharing Waters: Post-Rio International Water Management'. *Natural Resources Forum,* 27: 163–71.

Gleditsch, N. and Hamner, J. (2001) 'Shared Rivers, Conflict and Cooperation'. *42nd Annual Convention of the International Studies Association.* Chicago, IL: ISA.

Gleick, P. (1993) 'Water in the 21st Century'. In Gleick, P. (ed.) *Water in Crisis: A Guide to the World's Fresh Water Resources.* New York: Oxford University Press.

Gough, C. and Shackley, S. (2001) 'The Respectable Politics of Climate Change: The Epistemic Communities and NGOS'. *International Affairs,* 77(2): 329–46.

Government of Uganda (1999) 'A National Water Policy'. Ministry of Water, Uganda, Entebbe: Ministry of Water, Lands and Environment, Article 3.2.

Granit, J. and Claassen, M. (2009) 'A Path towards Realising Tangible Benefits in Transboundary River Basins'. In Jagerskög, A. and Zeitoun, M. (eds) *Getting Transboundary Water Right: Theory and Practice for Effective Cooperation*. Report No. 25, Stockholm: Stockholm International Water Institute.

Granit, J., Cascao, A., Jacobs, I., Leb, C., Lindstrom, A. and Tignino, M. (2010) 'The Nile Basin and the Southern Sudan Referendum'. *Regional Water Intelligence Report*. Paper 18. Stockholm: SIWI, UNDP Water Governance Facility.

Grey, D. and Sadoff, C. (2006) 'Water for Growth and Development'. Thematic Documents of the IV World Water Forum. Comision Nacional del Agua: Mexico City.

The Guardian (2011) The Big Challenge for a New Egypt: Water, 7 December 2011. <www.guardian.co.uk/commentisfree/2011/dec/07/egypt-water-nile> Access date: 30 December 2011.

Gupta, J., Junne, G. and van der Wurff, R. (1993) 'Determinants of Regime Formation'. In International Policies to Address the Greenhouse Effect. Amsterdam: University of Amsterdam, Dept. of International Relations and Public International Law and Vrije Universiteit Amsterdam, Institute of Environmental Studies.

Gutteridge, W. (1983) 'South Africa's National Strategy: Implications for Regional Security'. *Conflict Studies*, 148: 3–9.

Guzzini, S. (2005) 'The Concept of Power: A Constructivist Perspective'. *Millennium: Journal of International Studies*, 33(3): 495–521.

GWP (2000) 'Integrated Water Resources Management'. *TAC Background Paper No.4*. Global Water Partnership, Technical Advisory Committee (TAC). Stockholm: Global Water Partnership.

— (2010) Exploring the Role of Water Security in Regional Economic Development. The 2010 GWP Consulting Partners (CP) Meeting. Presentation by Technical Committee Chair, Mohamed Ait Kadi, at the CP meeting held in Stockholm, Sweden, 3–4 September 2010.

Haas, P. (1994) 'Do Regimes Matter? Epistemic Communities and Mediterranean Pollution Control'. In Kratochwil, F. and Mansfield, E. (eds) *International Organisation: A Reader*. New York: HarperCollins Publishers.

Halliday, F. (1994) *Rethinking International Relations*. London: Macmillan.

Hammerstad, A. (2005) 'Domestic Threats, Regional Solutions? The Challenge of Security Integration in Southern Africa'. *Review of International Studies*, 31(1): 69–87.

Hamner, J. (2002) 'Weapons Won't Get You Water: State Power and Distribution of Benefits'. *43rd Annual Convention of the International Studies Association*. New Orleans: ISA.

Hangula, L. (1993) *The International Boundary of Namibia*. Windhoek: Gamsberg Macmillan (Pty) Ltd.

Hatfield Consultants Africa (2011) Map of the Orange-Senqu River Basin. Data layers: USGS HydroSHEDS, ESRI, FAO Aquastat, WWF, UNEP. Gaborone: Hatfield Consultants.

Hazeltine, B. and Bull, C. (eds) (2003) *Field Guide to Appropriate Technology*. London: Academic Press.

Helly, D. (ed.) (2009) 'Post-2011 Scenarios in Sudan: What Role for the EU?' ISS Report, November 2009, No. 6. European Union Institute for Security Studies.

Hendricks, L. (2008) 'Speech by Mrs LB Hendricks, Minister of Water Affairs and Forestry National Council of Provinces, Parliament, Cape Town, Western Cape'. *Policy Review Debate on Budget Vote 34 of 2008/09.* Cape Town: Government of South Africa.

Hertslet, E. (1967) *The Map of Africa by Treaty: Abyssinia.* England: Frank Cass.

Heyns, P. (1995) 'Existing and Planned Development Projects on International Rivers within the SADC Region'. *Conference of SADC Ministers Responsible for Water Resources Management,* 23–24 November 1995. Pretoria.

— (2002) 'The Interbasin Transfer of Water between Countries within the Southern African Development Community (SADC): A Developmental Challenge of the Future'. In Turton, A. and Henwood, R. (eds) *Hydropolitics in the Developing World: A Southern African Perspective.* Pretoria: African Water Issues Research Unit (AWIRU) and International Water Management Institute (IWMI).

— (2003) 'Water Resources Management in Southern Africa'. In Nakayama, M. (ed.) *International Waters in Southern Africa.* Shibuya-ku, Tokyo: United Nations University Press.

— (2005) 'Water Institutional Reforms in Namibia'. *Water Policy,* 7: 89–106.

Heywood, A. (1997) *Politics.* London: Macmillan.

Hiddema, U. and Erasmus, G. (2007) 'Legislation and Legal Issues Surrounding the Orange River Catchment'. *Orange River Integrated Water Resources Management Plan.* Pretoria: WRP Consulting Engineers.

Hildyard, N. (2002) 'The Lesotho Highlands Water Development Project – What Went Wrong? (Or, rather: What Went Right? For Whom?)'. *Chatham House Conference: Corruption in Southern Africa – Sources and Solutions.* London. <www.thecornerhouse. org.uk/item.shtml?x=52182>

Hira, A. and Parfitt, T. (2004) *Development Projects for a New Millennium.* Wesport, US: Praeger.

Hobbs, J. 2004. 'Do "Water Wars" Still Loom in Africa?' 15 May 2004, Inter Press Service News Agency <www.ipsnews.net/africa/interna.asp?idnews=23759> Access date: 2 January 2012.

Hoffman, M. (1991) 'Restructuring, Reconstruction, Reinscription, Rearticulation: Four Voices in Critical International Theory'. *Millennium: Journal of International Studies,* 20(2): 169–85.

Hogan, K. (2005) 'The Norms of Water-Sharing: Cooperation Along a Continuum'. *Yale Journal of International Affairs,* 1(1): *no page numbers as web article* www.yale.edu/yjia/articles/Vol_1_Iss_1_Summer2005/Hogan.htm

Holling, C. S. and Meffe, G. K. (1995) 'Command and Control and the Pathology of Natural Resource Management'. *Conservation Biology,* 10(328).

Homer-Dixon, T. (1991) 'On the Threshold: Environmental Changes as Causes of Acute Conflict'. *International Security,* 16(2): 76–116.

— (1994) 'Environmental Scarcities and Violent Conflict: Evidence from Cases'. *International Security,* 19(1): 5–40.

Hoogensen, G. (2005) 'Bottoms Up! A Toast to Regional Security?' *International Studies Review,* 7: 269–74.

Hooghe, L. and Marks, G. (2003), 'Unravelling the Central State, but How? Types of Multi-level Governance'. *American Political Science Review,* 97(2): 233–43.

Hurt, S. (2003) 'Co-operation and Coercion? The Cotonou Agreement between the European Union and ACP States and the End of the Lomé Convention'. *Third World Quarterly,* 24(1): 161–76.

— (2004) 'The European Union's External Relations with Africa After the Cold War: Aspects of Continuity and Change'. In Taylor, I. and Williams, P. (eds) *Africa in International Politics: External Involvement on the Continent*. London and New York: Routledge.

ICWE (1992) 'Dublin Principles'. *International Conference on Water and the Environment (ICWE)*, 26–31 January 1992. Dublin.

IGAD (2009) IGAD News, no. 36, April–June 2009, Intergovernmental Authority on Development.

— (2010) 'About Us'. Intergovernmental Authority on Development, 9 January 2010. <http://igad.int/index.php?option=com_content&view=article&id=93&Itemid=124> Access date: 28 December 2011.

International Crisis Group (ICG) (2009) Jonglei's Tribal Conflicts: Countering Insecurity in South Sudan, Crisis Group Africa Program Report No. 154, 23 December 2009.

International Rivers (2005) 'A Brief History of Africa's Largest Water Project'. Berkeley: International Rivers.

— (2011) Chinese Dams in Africa. Berkeley: International Rivers. <www.internationalrivers. org/africa/chinese-dams-africa> Access date: 30 December 2011.

Jacobs, I. (2006) 'Swimming Upstream and Downstream in the Okavango and the Nile River Basins'. Masters Dissertation, *Department of Political Science*. Stellenbosch: University of Stellenbosch.

— (2010a) Norms and Transboundary Co-operation in Africa: The Cases of the Orange-Senqu and Nile Rivers. PhD Dissertation, School of International Relations, St. Andrews University, Scotland.

— (2010b) 'A Fragile Hegemon, a Fragile Hegemonic Discourse: A Critical Engagement with the Hydropolitical Complex and Implications of South Africa's Hydropolitical Environment for Southern Africa'. *African Security*, 3(1): 21–45.

Jacobs, I. and Nienaber, S. (2011) Waters without Borders: Transboundary Water Governance and the Role of the 'transdisciplinary individual' in Southern Africa, *Water SA*, 37(5) WRC 40-Year Celebration Special Edition: 665– 78.

Jacobs, I. and Turton, A. (2009) 'Chapter 17: South Africa'. In Brandes, O., Brooks, D. and Gurman, S. (eds) *Making the Most of the Water You Have: The Soft Path Approach to Water Management*. London: Earthscan.

Jacobs, I., Chikozho, C. and Funke, N. (2009) 'Summary Report on Best Practices Associated with Policy Harmonisation in the Agriculture, Health and Trade Sectors in SADC'. *GTZ Project on Policy Harmonisation in the SADC Water Sector*. Pretoria: CSIR.

Johnston, S. and Bernstein, A. (2007) 'Voices of Anger: Protest and Conflict in Two Municipalities'. Johannesburg: Centre for Development and Enterprise.

Jordan, A. and Jeppesen, T. (2000) 'EU Environmental Policy: Adapting to the Principle of Subsidiarity'. *European Environment*, 10: 64–74.

Kagwanja, P. (2007) 'Calming the Waters: The East African Community and Conflict Over the Nile Resources'. *Journal of Eastern African Studies*, 1(3): 321–37.

Kalpakian, J. (2004) *Identity, Conflict and Cooperation in International River Systems*. Aldershot: Ashgate Publishing.

Kameri-Mbote, P. (2005) 'From Conflict to Cooperation in the Management of Transboundary Waters: The Nile Experience'. *Linking Environment and Security – Conflict Prevention and Peace Making in East and Horn of Africa*. Washington, DC: Heinrich Boell Foundation.

Karyabwite, D. (2000) 'Water Sharing in the Nile Valley'. *Project GNV011: Using GIS/Remote Sensing for the Sustainable Use of Natural Resources*. Geneva: UNDP/DEWA/GRID.

Katzenstein, P. (ed.) (1996) *The Culture of National Security: Norms and Identity in World Politics*. New York: Columbia University Press.

Keck, M. and Sikkink, K. (1998) *Activists beyond Borders: Advocacy Networks in International Politics*. Ithaca and London: Cornell University Press.

Keefer, E. (1981) 'Great Britain, France, and the Ethiopian Tripartite Treaty of 1906'. *Albion: A Quarterly Journal Concerned with British Studies*, 13(4): 364–80.

Kingdom of Lesotho (2004) 'The Lowlands Water Supply Scheme'. Maseru: Government of Lesotho.

— (2007) 'Lesotho Water and Sanitation Policy'. Ministry of Natural Resources. Maseru: Government of Lesotho.

Kistin, E. and Ashton, P. (2008) 'Adapting to Change in Transboundary Rivers: An Analysis of Treaty Flexibility on the Orange-Senqu River Basin'. *International Journal of Water Resources Development*, 24(3): 15.

Kistin, E., Ashton, P., Earle, A., Malzbender, D., Patrick, M. J. and Turton, A. (2009) 'An Overview of the Content and Historical Context of the International Freshwater Agreements that South Africa Has Entered into with Neighbouring Countries'. *International Environmental Agreements: Politics, Law and Economics*, 9(1): 1–21.

Klotz, A. (1995) *Norms in International Relations: The Struggle against Apartheid*. Ithaca: Cornell University Press.

Koh, H. (1998) 'The 1998 Frankel Lecture: Bringing International Law Home'. *Houston Law Review*, 35(1998): 623–35.

Kranz, N. and Jacobs, I. (in press) 'Leadership Capacity in Transboundary Basins: Institutions and Individuals'. In Gallagher, D., Christensen, N. and Andrews, P. (eds) *Environmental Leadership: A Reference Handbook*. Thousand Oaks, CA: Sage Publications.

Kranz, N. and Vidaurre, R. (2008) 'D 1.3.6a: Institution-Based Water Regime Analysis Orange-Senqu Basin. Emerging River Basin Organisation for Adaptive Water Management'. *Report of the NeWater Project – New Approaches to Adaptive Water Management under Uncertainty*. Berlin: Ecologic – Institute for International and European Environmental Policy.

Kranz, N., Interwies, E. and Vidaurre, R. (2005a) 'Transboundary Regimes in the Orange-Senqu Basin'. *New Approaches to Adaptive Water Management under Uncertainty*. Berlin: NeWater.

Kranz, N., Interwies, E., Vorwerk, A. and von Raggamby, A. (2005b) 'Governance Institutions and Participation in the Orange-Senqu Basin'. *Report to the NeWater Project*. Berlin: NeWater.

Krasner, S. (1983) 'Structural Causes and Regime Consequences: Regimes as Intervening Variables'. In Krasner, S. (ed.) *International Regimes*. London: Cornell University Press.

— (1993) 'Sovereignty, Regimes, and Human Rights'. In Rittberger, V. (ed.) *Regime Theory and International Relations*. Oxford: Clarendon Press.

Kratochwil, F. (2000) 'Constructing a New Orthodoxy? Wendt's "Social Theory of International Politics" and the Constructivist Challenge'. *Millennium: Journal of International Studies*, 29(1): 73–101.

Kritzinger-van Niekerk, L. and Moreira, E. (2002) 'Regional Integration in Southern Africa: Overview of Recent Developments'. Discussion Paper. Africa Region Human Development Department, the International Bank for Reconstruction and Development. Washington, DC: World Bank.

Kubálková, V., Onuf, N. and Kowert, P. (1998) 'Constructing Constructivism'. In Kubálková, V., Onuf, N. and Kowert, P. (eds) *International Relations in a Constructed World*. Armonk: M.E. Sharpe.

Lach, D., Ingram, H. and Rayner, S. (2005) 'Maintaining the Status Quo: How Institutional Norms and Practices Create Conservative Water Organizations'. *Texas Law Review*, 83: 2027–53.

Lange, G., Mungatana, E. and Hassan, R. (2007) 'Water Accounting for the Orange River Basin: An Economic Perspective on Managing a Transboundary Resource'. Pretoria: University of Pretoria.

Lawrence, P. (1998) 'Pretoria Has its Way in Lesotho'. *African Report*, March–April: 50–1.

Lawrence, R. Z. (1991) 'Emerging Regional Arrangements: Building Blocs or Stumbling Blocs?' In O'Brien, R. (ed.) *Finance and the International Economy 5*. The AMEX Bank Review Prize Essays. New York: Oxford University Press.

Legro, J. (1997) 'Which Norms Matter? Revisiting the "Failure" of Internationalism'. *International Organization*, 51(1): 31–63.

Lesotho Review (2011) 'An Overview of the Kingdom of Lesotho's Economy'. 2011 Edition. Wade Publications. <www.lesothoreview.com/construction.htm> Access date: 28 December 2011.

Levy, D. L. and Newell, P. J. (eds) (2005) *The Business of Global Environmental Governance*. Cambridge, MA and London: MIT Press.

LHWC (1986) Treaty on the Lesotho Highlands Water Project. Kingdom of Lesotho and the Republic of South Africa.

LHWP (2011) Overview of the Lesotho Highlands Water Project. Lesotho Highlands Water Project (LHWP) website. <www.lhwp.org.ls/overview/Default.htm> Access date: 28 December 2011.

Linklater, A. (2000) 'General Introduction'. In Linklater, A. (ed.) *International Relations: Critical Concepts in Political Science*. London: Routledge.

Lowi, M. (1993) *Water and Power: The Politics of a Scarce Resource in the Jordan River Basin*. Cambridge: Cambridge University Press.

Lukes, S. (1974) *Power: A Radical View*. New York: Palgrave Macmillan.

Lynn-Jones, S. (1999) 'Realism and Security Studies'. In Snyder, C. (ed.) *Contemporary Security and Strategy*. 2nd edn. Houndmills: Macmillan.

Maganga, F. (2003) 'Incorporating Customary Laws in Implementation of IWRM: Some Insights from the Rufiji River Basin, Tanzania'. *Physics and Chemistry of the Earth*, 28: 995–1000.

Maganga, F., Kiwasila, H., Juma, I. and Butterworth, J. (2004) 'Implications of Customary Norms and Laws for Implementing IWRM: Findings from Pangani and Rufiji Basins, Tanzania'. *Physics and Chemistry of the Earth*, 29: 1335–42.

Makonnen, Y. (1984) *The Nyerere Doctrine of State Succession: Dar es Salaam to Vienna*. Arusha and New York: Eastern Africa Publications.

Maletsky, C. (1999) 'Orange River Dispute Rambles On'. *The Namibian*. Windhoek.

Mallat, C. (1994) 'Law and the River Nile: Emerging International Rules and the Sharia'h'. In Howell, P. and Allan, J. (eds) *The Nile, Sharing a Scarce Resource: A Historical and Technical Review of Water Management and of Economic and Legal Issues*. Cambridge: Cambridge University Press.

Malzbender, D. and Earle, A. (2008) 'The Impact and Implications of the Adoptions of the 1997 UN Watercourse Convention for Countries in Southern Africa'. Cape Town: African Centre for Water Research.

— (2009) 'Water Resources of SADC: Demands, Dependencies, and Governance Responses'. In Pressend, M. and Othieno, T. (eds) *Rethinking Natural Resources in Southern Africa*. Midrand: Institute for Global Dialogue.

March, J. and Olsen, J. (1989) *Rediscovering Institutions. The Organizational Basis of Politics*. New York: Free Press.

Marcussen, M. (2000) *Ideas and Elites: The Social Construction of Economic and Monetary Union*. Aalborg: Aalborg University Press.

Mare, H. G. (2007) 'Summary of Water Requirements from the Orange River'. *Orange River Integrated Water Resources Management Plan*. Pretoria: WRP Consulting Engineers.

Mattern, J. (2005) 'Why "Soft Power" Isn't So Soft: Representational Force and the Sociolinguistic Construction of Attraction in World Politics'. *Millennium: Journal of International Studies*, 33(3): 583–612.

Mbaziira, R., Senfuma, N. and McDonnell, R. (nd.) 'Institutional Development in the Nile Equatorial Lakes Sub-basin: Learning from the Experience of the Kagera Basin Organisation'. IWMI. <www.iwmi.cgiar.org/research_impacts/Research_Themes/BasinWaterManagement/RIPARWIN/PDFs/11%20Mbaziira%20SS%20FINAL%20EDIT.pdf> Access date: 30 December 2011.

McCaffrey, S. (2001a) 'The Contribution of the UN Convention on the Law of Non-navigational Uses of International Watercourses'. *International Journal of Global Environmental Issues*, 1(3/4): 250–63.

— (2001b) *The Law of International Watercourses*. Oxford: Oxford University Press.

McCaffrey, S. and Sinjela, M. (1998) 'Current Developments: The 1997 United Nations Convention on International Watercourses'. *American Journal of International Law*, 92: 97–107.

McIntyre, O. (2007) International Water Law: Factors Relating to the Equitable Utilisation of Shared Freshwater Resources. Paper 1.2 Prepared for the SIDA International Training Programme in Transboundary Water Resources Management.

Meissner, R. (2000a) 'The Case of the Orange River'. *Conflict Trends*, 2000(2): 24–7.

— (2000b) The Involvement of Interest Groups in the Lesotho Highlands Water Project. www.up.ac.za/academic/polsci/awiru 17 July 2002.

— (2000c) 'In the Spotlight: Interest Groups as a Role Player in Large Water Projects'. *SA Bulletin*, 26(2), 24–6.

— (2001) 'Drawing the Line: A Look at the Water Related Border Disagreement between South Africa and Namibia'. *Conflict Trends*, 2: 34–7.

— (2004) 'The Transnational Role of and Involvement of Interest Groups in Water Politics: A Comparative Analysis of Selected Southern African Case Studies'. PhD Dissertation, Department of Political Science. Pretoria: University of Pretoria.

— (2005) 'Interest Groups and the Proposed Epupa Dam: Towards a Theory of Water Politics'. *Politeia*, 24(3), 354.

Meissner, R. and Jacobs, I. (in press) 'Complex Water Governance in Africa: Transboundary River Basins as Complex Adaptive Systems'. *Water Policy*.

Meissner, R. and Turton, A. (2003) 'The Hydrosocial Contract Theory and the Lesotho Highlands Water Project'. *Water Policy*, 5(2): 115–26.

Menya, W. (2010) 'Kenya Signs Nile Basin Pact', *Saturday Nation*, 19 May 2010. <www.nation. co.ke/NewsKenya%20signs%20Nile%20Basin%20pact/-/1056/921332/-/8bccxi/-/ index.html> Access date: 13 November 2011.

Meyer, J., Frank, D., Hironaka, A., Schofer, E. and Tuma, N. (1997) 'The Structuring of a World Environmental Regime, 1870–1990'. *International Organization*, 51(4): 623–51.

Mills, G. (1998) 'Is Lesotho Foray a Lesson Learned?' *Business Day,* 28 October 1998.

Mirumachi, N. (2004) 'Incentives for Cooperative Water Management in International Rivers: The Case of the Lesotho Highlands Water Project'. *The 2nd Asian Pacific Association of Hydrology and Water Resources (APHW) Proceedings.* Kyoto: APHW.

Mohammed-Katerere (2001) 'Review of the Legal and Policy Framework for Transboundary Natural Resources Management Initiatives in Southern Africa'. Paper No. 3. IUCN-ROSA Series on Transboundary Natural Resources Management. Harare: IUCN-ROSA.

Mohamoda, D. (2003) *Nile Basin Cooperation: A Review of the Literature.* Uppsala: Nordic African Institute.

Mopheme (1998) 'Lesotho: Can the Scars Turn to Stars?' *The Survivor.* Maseru, 20 October 1998.

Morgenthau, H. (1974) *Politics Among Nations: The Struggle for Power and Peace.* New York: Alfred Knopf.

Moriarty, P., Butterworth, J. and Batchelor, C. (2004) 'Integrated Water Resources Management: And the Domestic Water and Sanitation Sub-sector'. In IRC (ed.) *Thematic Overview Paper (TOP).* International Water and Sanitation Centre (IRC).

Moss, T. and Newig, J. (2010) 'Multilevel Water Governance and Problems of Scale: Setting the Stage for a Broader Debate'. *Environmental Management,* 46: 1–6.

Mutayoba, W. (2008) 'Tanzania: Water Resources Management Structure'. *Symposium on Science and Policy Linkages,* 24–26 September 2008. Entebbe: United Nations University.

Mwapachu, J. V. (2010) COMESA-EAC-SADC Tripartitie Framework: State of Play, Report by the Chair of the Tripartite Task Force July, 2010. <www.eac.int/tripartite-summit. html> Access date: 4 January 2011.

Mwendera, E., Hazelton, D., Nkhuwa, D., Robinson, P., Tjijenda, K. and Chavula, G. (2003) 'Overcoming Constraints to the Implementation of Water Demand Management in Southern Africa'. *Physics and Chemistry of the Earth,* 28: 761–78.

Nadelmann, E. (1990) 'Global Prohibition Regimes: The Evolution of Norms in International Society'. *International Organization,* 44(4): 479–526.

Nakayama, M. (2003) 'Institutional Aspects of International Water-System Management'. In Nakayama, M. (ed.) *International Waters in Southern Africa.* Tokyo, New York, Paris: United Nations University Press.

NBCBN-RE (2011) 'Nile Basin'. Nile Basin Capacity Building Network for River Engineering. <www.nbcbn.com> Access date: 28 December 2011.

NBI (2000) 'The Nile Basin Cooperative Framework: Draft'. Entebbe: Nile Basin Initiative.

— (2001) *Nile River Basin: Transboundary Environmental Analysis.* Entebbe: Nile Basin Initiative.

— (2006) 'Water Policy Guidelines and Compendium of Good Practice, Shared Vision Program, Water Resources Planning and Management Project'. Entebbe: Nile Basin Initiative.

— (2007) 'NBI Factsheet'. Entebbe: Nile Basin Initiative. <www.nilebasin.org> Access date: August 2011.

— (2008) 'Strategy for Addressing Environmental and Social Safeguards under the Proposed NBI Institutional Strengthening Project'. Entebbe: Nile Basin Initiative.

— (2009a) 'Nile Cooperative Framework Agreement to be Discussed at Extraordinary Nile-COM Meeting in Kinshasa'. Entebbe: Nile Basin Initiative, 22 May 2009. <www.nilebasin. org> Access date: October 2009.

— (2009b) 'Policy Guidelines for the Nile Basin Strategic Action Program'. Council of Ministers of Water Affairs of the Nile Basin States, Entebbe.

— (2010) 'Agreement on the Nile River Basin Cooperative Framework Opened for Signature', <www.nilebasin.org/index.php?option=com_content&task=view&id=165&Itemid=1> Access date: 13 November 2011.

— (2012a) 'Kenya' NBI Country Profiles. Nile Basin Initiative Website. <www.nilebasin.org/ newsite/index.php?option=com_content&view=category&layout=blog&id=35&Itemid =67&lang=en> Access date: 22 January 2012.

— (2012b) 'Uganda' NBI Country Profiles. Nile Basin Initiative Website. <www.nilebasin. org/newsite/index.php?option=com_content&view=category&layout=blog&id=35&Ite mid=67&lang=en> Access date: 22 January 2012.

— (2012c) 'Burundi' NBI Country Profiles. Nile Basin Initiative Website. <www.nilebasin. org/newsite/index.php?option=com_content&view=category&layout=blog&id=35&Ite mid=67&lang=en> Access date: 22 January 2012.

— (2012d) 'DR Congo' NBI Country Profiles. Nile Basin Initiative Website. <www.nilebasin. org/newsite/index.php?option=com_content&view=category&layout=blog&id=35&Ite mid=67&lang=en> Access date: 22 January 2012.

Ngana, J., Mwalyosi, R., Madulu, N. and Yanda, P. (2003) 'Development of an Integrated Water Resources Management Plan for the Lake Manyara Sub-Basin, Northern Tanzania'. *Physics and Chemistry of the Earth,* 28: 1033–8.

Nicol, A. (2003a) 'The Dynamics of River Basin Cooperation: The Nile and Okavango Basins'. In Turton, A., Ashton, P. and Cloete, E. (eds) *Transboundary Rivers, Sovereignty and Development: Hydropolitical Drivers in the Okavango River Basin.* Pretoria: African Water Issues Research Unit.

— (2003b) *The Nile: Moving beyond Cooperation.* UNESCO-IHP.

Nkhoma, B. and Mulwafu, W. (2004) 'The Experience of Irrigation Management Transfer in Two Irrigation Schemes in Malawi, 1960s–2002'. *Physics and Chemistry of the Earth,* 29: 1327–33.

Nye, J. (1993) *Understanding International Conflicts: An Introduction to Theory and History.* New York: HarperCollins College Publishers.

Nyeko, D. (2008) 'Lake Victoria Fisheries Organisation: Governance Issues – Past, Present and Future Roles'. *Symposium on Science and Policy Linkages,* 24–26 September 2008. Entebbe: United Nations University.

OECD (2011) *Water Governance in OECD Countries: A Multi-level Approach.* Paris: Organisation for Economic Co-operation and Development (OECD).

Ohlsson, L. (1995) *Water and Security in Southern Africa.* Stockholm: Swedish International Development Agency.

Ohlsson, L. and Turton, A. R. (1999) 'The Turning of the Screw: Social Resource Scarcity as a Bottleneck in Adaptation to Water Scarcity'. Proceedings of the Stockholm Water Symposium, Stockholm, Sweden, 9–12 August 1999.

Okidi, C. (1990) 'A Review of Treaties on Conceptive Utilisation of Waters of Lake Victoria and Nile Drainage Basins'. In Howell, J. and Allan, J. (eds) *The Nile: Resource Evaluation, Resource Management, Hydropolitics and Legal Issues.* London: School of Oriental and African Studies (SOAS).

— (1994) 'History of the Nile Basin and Lake Victoria Basins through Treaties'. In Howell, P. and Allan, J. (eds) *The Nile, Sharing a Scarce Resource: A Historical and Technical Review of Water Management and of Economic and Legal Issues.* Cambridge: Cambridge University Press.

Onuf, N. (1989) *World of Our Making: Rules and Rule in Social Theory and International Relations.* Columbia, SC: University of South Carolina Press.

ORASECOM (2000) *Agreement between the Governments of the Republic of Botswana, the Kingdom of Lesotho, the Republic of Namibia and the Republic of South Africa on the Establishment of the Orange-Senqu River Commission.* Windhoek.

— (2012) 'Overview of the Orange-Senqu River Basin'. Orange-Senqur River Commission Website. Pretoria: Orange-Senqu River Commission (ORASECOM). <www.orasecom. org/about/orangesenqu+basin.aspx> Access date: 10 January 2012.

Ostrom, E. (1991) *Governing the Commons: The Evolution of Institutions for Collective Action.* Cambridge: Cambridge University Press.

Othieno, T. and Zondi, S. (2006) 'Co-operative Management of Africa's Water Resources: A Basis for Resolving Conflicts on the Nile River Basin'. *Institute for Global Dialogue,* May: 1–4.

Parsons, T. (1951) *The Social System.* London: Routledge & Kegan Paul.

Paterson, M. (2001) 'Green Politics'. In Burchill, S., Devetak, R., Linklater, A., Paterson, M., Reus-Smit, C. and True, J. (eds) *Theories on International Relations.* 3rd edn. New York: Palgrave.

Payne, R. (1996) 'Non-profit Environmental Organisations in World Politics: Domestic Structure and Transnational Relations'. *Policy Studies Review,* 14 (Spring/Summer 1995): 171–82.

— (2001) 'Persuasion, Frames and Norm Construction'. *European Journal of International Relations,* 7(1): 37–62.

Pegram, G., Mazibuko, G., Hollingworth, B. and Anderson, E. (2006) 'Strategic Review of Current and Emerging Governance Systems Related to Water in the Environment in South Africa'. Report No. 1514/1/06. Pretoria: Water Research Commission.

Phillips, D. J. H., Daoudy, M., McCaffrey, S., Öjendal, J. and Turton, A. (2006) *Transboundary Water Cooperation as a Tool for Conflict Prevention and for Broader Benefit-sharing.* Windhoek: Phillips Robinson and Associates.

Porter, T. (1998) 'Environmental Security as a National Security Issue'. In Tuathail, G., Dalby, S. and Routledge, P. (eds) *The Geopolitics Reader.* London: Routledge.

Postel, S. (1999) *Pillars of Sand: Can the Irrigation Miracle Last?* New York: W.W. Norton and Company.

Postel, S. and Richter, B. (2003) *Rivers for Life: Managing Water for People and Nature.* Washington, DC: Island Press.

Postel, S. and Wolf, A. (2001) 'Dehydrating Conflict'. *Foreign Policy,* 126: 60–7.

Pottinger, L. (2004) 'Can the Nile States Dam their Way to Cooperation?' Berkeley: International Rivers.

RAK (2006) 'Nile River Awareness Kit (Nile RAK)'. *River Awareness Kit Project.* Vancouver: Hatfield Consultants.

— (2008) 'The Orange-Senqu River Awareness Kit: A Tool for Capacity Building in Transboundary River Basin Organisations (OS-RAK)'. *River Awareness Kit Project.* Vancouver: Hatfield Consultants.

Rametsteiner, E. (2009) 'Governance Concepts and their Application in Forest Policy Initiatives from Global to Local Levels'. *Small-scale Forestry,* 8(2): 143–58.

Ramoeli, R. (2002) 'SADC Protocol on Shared Watercourses: Its History and Current Status'. In Turton, A. and Henwood, R. (eds) *Hydropolitics in the Developing World: A Southern African Perspective.* Pretoria: African Water Issues Research Unit (AWIRU).

Republic of Kenya (2010) Constitution of Kenya. Dated the 28 August 2010. Published by the National Council for Law Reporting with the Authority of the Attorney General, S. A. WAKO, Attorney-General.

Republic of Namibia (2004) *Water Resources Management Act No.24.* Windhoek: Government of Namibia, Ministry of Agriculture, Water and Forestry, Private Bag 13193, Namibia.

— (2008) *Water Supply and Sanitation Policy.* Windhoek: Government of Namibia, Ministry of Agriculture, Water and Forestry, Private Bag 13193, Namibia.

Republic of South Africa (1998) *National Water Act.* Pretoria: Government of the Republic of South Africa, Department of Water Affairs and Forestry.

Republic of Uganda (1999) *A National Water Policy.* Entebbe: Republic of Uganda, Ministry of Water, Lands and Environment, Uganda.

Risse-Kappen, T. (1994) 'Ideas Do Not Float Freely: Transnational Coalitions, Domestic Structures and the End of the Cold War'. *International Organization,* 48(2): 185–214.

Rubin, B. (1998) 'The Geopolitics of Middle East Conflict and Crisis'. *MERIA Journal,* No. 3.

SADC (1992) *SADC Treaty.* Southern African Development Community (SADC). Windhoek, Namibia.

— (1995) *Protocol on Shared Watercourses.* Southern African Development Community (SADC). Windhoek, Namibia.

— (2000) *Revised Protocol on Shared Watercourses.* Southern African Development Community (SADC).

— (2003) 'Guidelines for the Development of National Water Policies and Strategies to Support IWRM'. *SADC Water Sector, RSAP Projects 9 and 10,* 30 June 2003. Gaborone: Southern African Development Community (SADC).

Sadoff, C. and Grey, D. (2002) 'Beyond the River: The Benefits of Cooperation on International Rivers'. *Water Policy,* 4 (2002): 389–403.

— (2005) 'Cooperation on International Rivers: A Continuum for Securing and Sharing Benefits'. *Water International,* 30(4): 1–8.

Santho, S. (2000) 'Chapter 8: Lesotho: Lessons and Challenges after a SADC Intervention, 1998'. In Philander, D. (ed.) *Monograph No 50, Franco-South African Dialogue.* Pretoria: Institute for Global Dialogue (IGD), the Institut Français d'Afrique du Sud (IFAS) and the Institute for Security Studies (ISS).

Schimmelfennig, F. (2000) 'International Socialization in the New Europe: Rational Action in an Institutional Environment'. *European Journal of International Relations,* 6(1): 109–39.

Schreurs, M. (2010) 'Multi-level Governance and Global Climate Change in East Asia'. *Asian Economic Policy Review,* 5: 88–105.

Schulz, M. (1995) 'Turkey, Syria and Iraq: A Hydropolitical Security Complex'. In Ohlsson, L. (ed.) *Hydropolitics: Conflicts Over Water as a Development Constraint.* London: Zed Books.

Seckler, D. (1996) 'The New Era of Water Resources Management: From "Dry" to "Wet" Water Savings'. *IIMI Research Report No.1.* Colombo, Sri Lanka: International Irrigation Management Institute (IIMI).

Seely, M., Henderson, J., Heyns, P., Jacobsen, P., Nkale, T., Nantanga, K. and Schaschtschneider, K. (2003) 'Ephemeral and Endoreic River Systems: Relevance and Management Challenges'. In Turton, A., Ashton, P. and Cloete, E. (eds) *Transboundary Rivers, Sovereignty and Development: Hydropolitical Drivers in the Okavango River Basin.* Pretoria and Geneva: African Water Issues Research Unit (AWIRU) and Green Cross International (GCI).

Setzer, J. (2009) 'Subnational and Transnational Climate Change Governance: Evidence from the State and City of São Paulo, Brazil'. Fifth Urban Research Symposium 2009.

Skutch, M. and Van Laake, P. E. (2009) 'REDD as Multi-Level Governance in the Making'. *Energy and* Environment, 19(6): 831–44.

Smith, S. (1997) 'New Approaches to International Theory'. In Baylis, J. and Smith, S. (eds) *The Globalisation of World Politics: An Introduction to International Relations Theory Today.* Oxford: Oxford University Press, pp. 165–90.

— (1999) 'Social Constructivism and European Studies: A Reflectivist Critique'. *Journal of European Public Policy,* 6(4): 682–91.

Sokile, C. and van Koppen, B. (2004) 'Local Water Rights and Local Water Use Entities: The Unsung Heroines of Water Resource Management in Tanzania'. *Physics and Chemistry of the Earth,* 29: 1349–56.

Sokile, C., Kashaigili, R. and Kadigi, R. (2003) 'Towards an Integrated Water Resources Management in Tanzania: The Role of Appropriate Institutional Framework in Rufiji Basin'. *Physics and Chemistry of the Earth,* 28: 1015–24.

Spiegel, C. (2005) 'International Water Law: The Contributions of Western United States Water Law to the United Nations Convention on the Law of the Non-Navigable Uses of International Watercourses'. *Duke Journal of Comparative and International Law,* 15: 333–61.

Stone, A. (1994) 'What is a Supranational Constitution? An Essay in International Relations Theory'. *The Review of Politics,* 56(3): 441–74.

Strand, J. R. (2003) 'The Case for Region Environmental Organisations: Regional Integration and Multilateral Environmental Governance'. *International Environmental Governance: Gaps and Weaknesses.* Shibuya-ku, Tokyo: United Nations University Press.

Strydom, W., Funke, N., Nienaber, S., Nortje, K. and Steyn, M. (2010) 'Evidence-based Policy-making: A Review'. *South African Journal of Science,* 106(5/6): 16–23.

Sugiyama, T. and Sinton, J. (2005) 'Orchestra of Treaties: A Future Climate Regime Scenario with Multiple Treaties among Like-Minded Countries'. *International Environmental Agreements: Politics, Law and Economics,* 5(1): 65–88.

Svendsen, M., Murray-Rust, D., Harmancioglu, N. and Alpaslan, N. (2001) 'Governing Closing Basins: The Case of the Gediz River in Turkey'. In Abernethy, C. (ed.) *Intersectoral Management of River Basins.* Colombo, Sri Lanka: International Water Management Institute (IWMI).

Swatuk, L. (2002a) 'Environmental Cooperation for Regional Peace and Security in Southern Africa'. In Conca, K. and Dabelko, G. (eds) *Environmental Peacemaking.* Washington, DC: Woodrow Wilson Centre Press.

— (2002b) 'The New Water Architecture in Southern Africa: Reflections on Current Trends in the Light of Rio +10'. *International Affairs,* 78(3): 507–30.

— (2005a) 'Political Challenges to Implementing IWRM in Southern Africa'. *Physics and Chemistry of the Earth,* 30: 872–80.

— (2005b) 'Political Challenges to Sustainably Managing Intra-Basin Water Resources in Southern Africa: Drawing Lessons from Cases'. In Wirkus, L. (ed.) *Water, Development and Cooperation – Comparative Perspective: Euphrates-Tigris and Southern Africa.* Bonn: Bonn International Centre for Conversion.

Swatuk, L. and Vale, P. (2000) 'Swimming Upstream: Water Discourses of Security'. *Security, Ecology and Community. Working Paper Series.* Cape Town: Centre for Southern African Studies, School of Government, University of the Western Cape.

Tadesse, D. (2008) 'The Nile: Is it a Curse or Blessing?' ISS Paper 174. Pretoria: Institute for Security Studies (ISS).

Tadros, N. (1996–7) 'Shrinking Water Resources: The National Security Issue of this Century'. *Northwestern Journal of International Law & Business,* 17: 1091–103.

Tanzi, A. (2001) 'The United Nations Convention on the Law of International Watercourses: A Framework for Sharing'. *International and National Law and Policy Series,* vol. 5.

Tapela, B. (2002) 'The Challenge of Integration in the Implementation of Zimbabwe's New Water Policy: Case Study of the Catchment Level Institutions Surrounding the Pungwe-Mutare Water Supply Project'. *Physics and Chemistry of the Earth,* 27: 993–1004.

Tenner, E. (1996) *Why Things Bite Back: Technology and the Revenge of Unintended Consequences.* New York: Knopf.

Teti, A. and Hynek, N. (2006) 'Saving Identity from Postmodernism? Disciplining Constructivism and Governing the "International"'. Aberdeen: International Institute of Political Science. Aberdeen: University of Aberdeen.

TFRD (2007) 'The Nile Waters Agreement'. *Transboundary Freshwater Dispute Database.* Oregon: Oregon State University. <www.transboundarywaters.orst.edu/> Access date: 29 December 2011.

Thompson, H. (2006) *Water Law: A Practical Approach to Resource Management and the Provision of Services.* Cape Town: Juta and Co Ltd.

Thomson, J. (1995) 'State Sovereignty and International Relations: Bridging the Gap between Theory and Empirical Research'. *International Studies Quarterly,* 39(2): 213–33.

Thrupp, L. A. (1989) 'Legitimizing Local Knowledge: From Displacement to Empowerment for Third World People'. *Agriculture and Human Values,* Summer Issue: 13–24.

TNV (2008) 'River Nile Talks Hit Deadlock'. *The New Vision.* Uganda.

Toepfer, K. (2005) 'Preface'. *Hydropolitical Vulnerability and Resilience along International Waters: Africa.* Nairobi, Kenya: United Nations Environment Programme.

Toke, D. (2000) *Green Politics and Neo-liberalism.* Houndmills and New York: Macmillan and St Martin's Press.

Tompkins, R. (2007) 'Institutional Structures in the Four Orange Basin States'. *Orange River Integrated Water Resources Management Plan.* Pretoria: WRP Consulting Engineers.

Tralac (2008) 'The Interim SADC EPA Agreement: Legal and Technical Issues and Challenges'. <www.tralac.org/unique/tralac/pdf/20080129_Erasmus_Discussion_InterimSADC_EPA.pdf> Access date: 3 January 2011.

TRC (2006) 'On the Wrong Side of Development: Lessons Learned from the Lesotho Highlands Water Project'. Maseru: Transformation Resource Centre (TRC).

Turton, A. (1999a) 'Precipitation, People, Pipelines and Power: Towards a "Virtual Water" Based on Political Ecology Discourse'. MEWREW Occasional Paper No.11. *Water Issues Study Group, School of Oriental and African Studies (SOAS).* London: University of London.

— (1999b) 'Water and State Sovereignty: The Hydropolitical Challenge for States in Arid Regions'. MEWREW Occasional Paper No. 5. *Water Issues Study Group, School of Oriental and African Studies (SOAS).* London: University of London.

— (2000a) 'Water Wars in Southern Africa: Challenging Conventional Wisdom'. In Solomon, H. and Turton, A. (eds) *Water Wars: Enduring Myth of Impending Reality,* African Dialogue Lecture Series: Monograph Series No. 2. Durban: Accord.

— (2000b) 'Water Wars: Enduring Myth or Impending Reality'. In Solomon, H. and Turton, A. (eds) *Water Wars: Enduring Myth of Impending Reality,* African Dialogue Lecture Series: Monograph Series No. 2. Durban: Accord.

— (2001a) 'Hydropolitics and Security Complex Theory: An African Perspective'. *4th Pan-European International Relations Conference*, 8–10 September 2001. Canterbury: University of Kent, Canterbury (UK).

— (2001b) 'Towards Hydrosolidarity: Moving from Resource Capture to Cooperation and Alliances'. *Water Security for Cities, Food and Environment – Towards Catchment Hydrosolidarity*. Stockholm: Swedish International Water Institute (SIWI).

— (2003a) 'Environmental Security: A Southern Africa Perspective on Transboundary Water Resource Management'. *Environmental Change and Security Project Report*. Document No. 9. Summer 2003. Washington, DC: Woodrow Wilson International Centre.

— (2003b) 'The Hydropolitical Dynamics of Cooperation in Southern Africa: A Strategic Perspective on Institutional Development in International River Basins'. In Turton, A., Ashton, P. and Cloete, T. (eds) *Transboundary Rivers, Sovereignty and Development: Hydropolitical Drivers in the Okavango River Basin*. Pretoria and Geneva: AWIRU and Green Cross International.

— (2003c) 'An Introduction to the Hydropolitical Dynamics of the Orange River Basin'. In Nakayama, M. (ed.) *International Waters in Southern Africa*. Shibuya-ku, Tokyo: United Nations University Press.

— (2003d) 'The Political Aspects of Institutional Developments in the Water Sector: South Africa and its International River Basins'. PhD Dissertation, Department of Political Science. Pretoria: University of Pretoria.

— (2004) 'The Evolution of Water Management Institutions in Select Southern African International River Basins'. In Biswas, A. K., Unver, O. and Tortajada, C. (eds) *Water as a Focus for Regional Development*. London: Oxford University Press.

— (2005a) 'A Critical Assessment of the River Basins at Risk in the Southern African Hydropolitical Complex'. *Workshop on the Management of International Rivers and Lakes*, 17–19 August 2005. Helsinki: Third World Centre for Water Management & Helsinki University of Technology.

— (2005b) 'Hydro Hegemony in the Context of the Orange River Basin'. *Workshop on Hydro Hegemony*. London: Kings College and School of Oriental and African Studies (SOAS).

— (2008a) 'A South African Perspective on a Possible Benefit-Sharing Approach for Transboundary Waters in the SADC Region'. *Water Alternatives*, 1(2): 180–200.

— (2008b) 'The Southern African Hydropolitical Complex'. In Varis, O., Tortajada, C. and Biswas, A. J. (eds) *Management of Transboundary Rivers and Lakes*. Berlin: Springer-Verlag.

Turton, A. and Ashton, P. (2008) 'Basin Closure and Issues of Scale: The Southern African Hydropolitical Complex'. *International Journal of Water Resources Development*, 24(2): 305–18.

Turton, A. and Earle, A. (2005) 'Post-Apartheid Institutional Development in Selected Southern African International River Basins'. In Gopalakrishnan, C., Tortajada, C. and Biswas, A. (eds) *Water Institutions: Policies, Performance and Prospects*. Berlin: Springer-Verlag.

Turton, A., Earle, A., Malzbender, D. and Ashton, P. (2005) 'Hydropolitical Vulnerability and Resilience along Africa's International Waters'. *Hydropolitical Vulnerability and Resilience along International Waters: Africa*. Nairobi: United Nations Environment Programme.

Turton, A., Meissner, R., Mampane, P. and Seremo, O. (2004) 'A Hydropolitical History of South Africa's International River Basins'. *Report to the Water Research Commission*. Pretoria: Water Research Commission.

Turton, A. R. and Hattingh, J. (2007) 'The Trialogue Revisited: Quo Vadis governance?' In Turton, A. R., Hattingh, H. J., Maree, G. A., Roux, D. J., Claassen, M. and Strydom, W. F. (eds) *Governance as a Triologue: Government-society-science in Transition.* Berlin: Springer-Verlag.

UN (1972) 'Stockholm Declaration of the United Nations Conference on the Human Environment'. Doc. A/CONF.48/14 and Corr.1 (1972), reprinted at 11 ILM 1416, United Nations.

— (1977) 'Report of the UN Water Conference'. UN Doc. E/CONF.70/29, 14–25 March 1977. Mar del Plata: United Nations.

— (1997a) 'Convention on the Law of the Non-Navigational Uses of International Watercourses, UN General Assembly Document'. A/51/869, 11 April 1997. United Nations General Assembly, United Nations Publications.

— (1997b) 'General Assembly Adopts Convention on Law of Non-Navigable Uses of International Watercourses'. *Press Release GA/9248,* United Nations General Assembly. Access date: 1 July 2007.

— (2006) *Water a Shared Responsibility. UN World Development Report 2.* France: UNESCO and Berghahn Books.

— (2011) 'Status of Treaties'. United Nations Treaty Collection. <http://treaties. un.org/Pages/ViewDetails.aspx?src=UNTSONLINE&tabid=2&mtdsg_no=XXVII-12&chapter=27&lang=en#Participants > Access date: 4 November 2011.

UNDP (1990) 'The New Delhi Statement: "Some for all rather than more for some"'. *Global Consultation on Safe Water and Sanitation for the 1990s,* 14 September 1990. New Delhi: United Nations Development Programme.

UNECA (2004) 'Harmonization of Mining Policies, Standards, Legislative and Regulatory Frameworks in Southern Africa'. ECA/SA/TPub/Mining/2004/03, SADC.

— (2008) Implementation Plan for Harmonisation of Mining Policies, Standards, Legislative and Regulatory Frameworks in Southern Africa. SADC. ECA/SA/Tpub/2008/01, April 2008.

— (2010) Assessing Regional Integration in Africa IV: Enhancing Intra-African Trade by the Economic Commission for Africa. Addis Ababa, Ethiopia: United Nations Economic Commission for Africa.

UNEP (1992a) 'Agenda 21'.United Nations Program of Action from Rio. *United Nations Conference on Environment and Development.* City: United National Environmental Program.

— (1992b) 'Rio Declaration on Environment and Development'. *United Nations Conference on Environment and Development.* Rio de Janeiro.

— (2002) *Atlas of International Freshwater Agreements.* Nairobi: United Nations Environment Program.

— (2005) 'Hydropolitical Vulnerability and Resilience Along International Waters: Africa'. In Wolf, A. (ed.) *Hydropolitical Vulnerability and Resilience along International Waters.* Nairobi: United National Environment Programme.

UNESCO-IHP (2007) 'Project Concept Paper Meeting of the Expert Advisory Group: UNESCO-IHP Project on Water and Cultural Diversity'. UNESCO-IHP Project on Water and Cultural Diversity. Paris: UNESCO-IHP.

— (2009) 'Mainstreaming Cultural Diversity in Water Resources Management: A Policy Brief'. Paris: UNESCO-IHP.

Van Deveer, S. and Selin, H. (2008) 'Climate Leadership in Northeast North America'. In Cutler, J. (ed.) Encyclopaedia of Earth, Cleveland (Washington, DC:

Environmental Information Coalition, National Council for Science and the Environment). [First published in the Encyclopaedia of Earth 8 December 2006; Last revised 5 August 2008; Retrieved 13 April 2011] <www.eoearth.org/article/ Climate_leadership_in_northeast_North_America>

Van Ginkel, H. and Van Langenhove, L. (2003) 'Introduction and Context'. In van Ginkel, H., Court, J. and Van Langenhove, L. (eds), *Integrating Africa: Perspectives on Regional Integration and Development*. Shibuya-ku, Tokyo: United Nations University Press.

Verhoeven, H. (2011) 'Black Gold for Blue Gold? Sudan's Oil, Ethiopia's Water and Regional Integration'. Briefing Paper. London: Royal Institute of International Affairs, Chatham House.

Viotti, P. and Kauppi, M. (1999) *International Relations Theory: Realism, Pluralism, Globalism and Beyond*. Boston: Allyn and Bacon.

Visscher, J. (2006) 'Facilitating Community Water Supply: From Transferring Filtration Technology to Multi-stakeholder Learning'. Delft: IRC International Water and Sanitation Centre.

Visscher, J., Pels, J., Markowski, V. and de Graaf, S. (2006) 'Knowledge and Information Management in the Water and Sanitation Sector: A Hard Nut to Crack'. Delft: IRC International Water and Sanitation Centre.

Vogel, D. (1997) 'Trading Up and Governing Across: Transnational Governance and Environmental Protection'. *Journal of European Public Policy*, 4(4): 556–71.

Waako, T. (2008) 'The Nile Basin Initiative: The Roles, Functions and Governance Structure'. *Symposium on Science and Policy Linkages*, 24–26 September 2008. Entebbe, Uganda: United Nations University.

Waever, O. (1996) 'The Rise and Fall of the Inter-paradigm Debate'. In Smith, S., Booth, K. and Zalewski, M. (eds) *International Theory: Positivism and Beyond*. Cambridge: Cambridge University Press.

— (1997) 'Figures of International Thought: Introducing Persons Instead of Paradigms'. In Neumann, I. and Waever, O. (eds) *The Future of International Relations: Masters in the Making?* London: Routledge.

Waldock, H. (1972) 'Fifth Report on Succession in Respect of Treaties: Succession of States with Respect to Treaties'. *Yearbook of the International Law Commission: 1972 vol. II.* International Law Commission.

Walt, S. (1997) 'The Progressive Power of Realism'. *American Political Science Review*, 91(4): 931–5.

Walwyn, D. and Scholes, R. (2006) 'The Impact of a Mixed Income Model on the South African CSIR: A Recipe for Success or Disaster?' *South African Journal of Science*, 102: 239–43.

Warner, J. (2012) 'Three Lenses on Water War, Peace and Hegemonic Struggle on the Nile'. *International Journal of Sustainable Society*, 4(1/2): 173–93.

Warner, J. and Zeitoun, M. (2008) 'International Relations Theory and Water Do Mix: A Response to Furlong's Troubled Waters, Hydro-hegemony and International Water Relations'. *Political Geography*, 27: 802–10.

Water Emergency Relief (WER) (2010) 'Burundi Election Update'. 21 September 2010. <www.wer-uk.org/latest-news/burundi-election-threatens-stability> Access date: 29 December 2011.

Waterbury, J. (1979) *Hyrdropolitics of the Nile Valley*. Syracuse: Syracuse University Press.

— (2002) *The Nile Basin: National Determinants of Collective Action*. New Haven and London: Yale University Press.

Wendt, A. (1992) 'Anarchy Is What States Make of It'. *International Organization,* 46(2): 391–425.

— (1995) 'Anarchy Is What States Make of it: The Social Construction of Power Politics'. In Derian, J. (ed.) *International Theory: Critical Investigation.* London: Macmillan.

Westcoat, J. J. (1992) 'Beyond the River Basin: The Changing Geography of International Water Problems and International Watercourse Law'. *Colorado Journal of International Environmental Law and Policy,* 3: 310–30.

Wester, P. and Warner, J. (2002) 'River Basin Management Reconsidered'. In Turton, A. and Henwood, R. (eds) *Hydropolitics in the Developing World: A Southern African Perspective.* Pretoria: African Water Issues Research Unit (AWIRU).

Wester, P., Burton, M. and Mestre-Rodriquez, E. (2001) 'Managing Water Transition in the Lerma-Chapala Basin, Mexiso'. In Abernethy, C. (ed.) Intersectoral Management of River Basins. Columbo: International Water Management Institute (IWMI).

Wiebe, K. (2001) 'The Nile River: Potential for Conflict and Cooperation in the Face of Water Degradation'. *Natural Resources Journal,* 41(3): 731–54.

Williams, P. (2009) 'The "Responsibility to Protect", Norm Localisation, and African International Society'. *Global Responsibility to Protect,* 1: 392–416.

Wittfogel, K. A. (1957) *Oriental Despotism: A Comparative Study of Total Power.* New Haven: Yale University Press.

Wolf, A. (1997) 'International Water Conflict Resolution: Lessons from Comparative Analysis'. *International Journal of Water Resources Development,* 13(3): 333–67.

— (1998) 'Conflict and Cooperation along International Waterways'. *Water Policy,* 1: 251–65.

— (1999) 'Water and Human Security'. *Aviso,* 3: 2.

— (2005) 'Hydropolitical Vulnerability and Resilience: Series Introduction'. *Hydropolitical Vulnerability and Resilience along International Waters: Africa.* Nairobi: United Nations Environment Programme.

Wolf, A., Yoffe, S. and Giordano, M. (2003) 'International Waters: Identifying Basins at Risk'. *Water Policy,* 5(1): 29–60.

Wolf, A., Kramer, A., Carius, A. and Dabelko, G. (2005) 'Chapter 5: Managing Water Conflict and Cooperation'. *State of the World 2005: Redefining Global Security.* Washington, DC: The World Watch Institute.

Wolf, A., Natharius, J., Danielson, J., Ward, B. and Pender, J. (1999) 'International River Basins of the World'. *Journal of Water Resources Development,* 15(4): 387–427.

Woodhouse, P. (2008) 'Water Rights in South Africa: Insights from Legislative Reform'. BWPI Working Paper 36, Manchester: Brooks World Poverty Institute.

World Bank (1994) 'World Bank Operational Policies: Projects on International Waterways'. Operational Policy (OP) 7.50, World Bank.

— (2003) *Water Resources Sector Strategy.* Washington, DC: The World Bank.

The World Factbook (2009) Washington, DC: Central Intelligence Agency, 2009. <www.cia.gov/library/publications/the-world-factbook/index.html> Access date: 10 January 2012.

World Water Council W (2011) 'Water for Growth and Development in Africa: A Framework for an Effective Mosaic of Investments'. Thematic Publication, Marseilles: World Water Council and French Ministry of Foreign Affairs.

Wouters, P. (2000) 'The Relevance and Role of Water Law in Sustainable Development of Freshwater: From "Hydrosovereignty" to "Hydrosolidarity"'. *Water International,* 25(2): 202–7.

WSSD (2002a) 'The Johannesburg Declaration on Sustainable Development'. *World Summit of Sustainable Development*. Johannesburg, South Africa.

— (2002b) 'Plan of Implementation of the World Summit on Sustainable Development'. *World Summit of Sustainable Development*. Johannesburg, South Africa.

Yanacopulos, H. (2004) 'The Public Face of Debt'. *Journal of International Development*, 16: 717–27.

Young, O. R. (2002) *The Institutional Dimensions of Environmental Change: Fit, Interplay, and Scale*. Cambridge, MA: MIT Press.

— (2008) 'Building Regimes for Socio-ecological Systems: Institutional Diagnostics'. In Young, O., King, L. and Schroeder, H. (eds) *Institutions and Environmental Change*. Cambridge, MA: MIT Press, pp. 115–44.

Young, O. R., Berkhout, F., Gallopin, G. C., Janssen, M. A., Ostrom, E. and van der Leeuw, S. (2006) 'The Globalization of Socio-ecological Systems: An Agenda for Scientific Research'. *Global Environmental Change*, 16: 304–16.

Zeitoun, M. and Warner, J. (2008) 'Hydro-hegemony: A Framework for Analysis of Transboundary Water Conflicts'. *Water Policy*, 8(5): 435–60.

Zhang-Yongjin (2005) *China Goes Global*. London: Foreign Policy Centre.

Index